UNDER THE
CHINABERRY
TREE

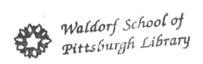

BROADWAY BOOKS

NEW YORK

UNDER THE
CHINABERRY
TREE

Books and Inspirations
for Mindful Parenting

By Ann Ruethling
and Patti Pitcher

PRINTED IN THE UNITED STATES OF AMERICA

BROADWAY BOOKS and its logo, a letter B bisected on the diagonal, are trademarks of Broadway Books, a division of Random House, Inc.

Visit our website at www.broadwaybooks.com

First edition published 2003

Book design by Caroline Cunningham

Illustrations by Louise Popoff

Library of Congress Cataloging-in-Publication Data

Ruethling, Ann.
Under the chinaberry tree: books and inspirations for mindful parenting/Ann Ruethling and Patti Pitcher.—1st ed.
p. cm.
Includes index.
1. Parenting. 2. Child rearing. 3. Best books. I. Pitcher, Patti. II. Title.
HQ755.8.R48 2003
649'.1—dc21   2002074757

ISBN 0-7679-1202-0

1 3 5 7 9 10 8 6 4 2

To our families for the lessons they bring and the love we share.

A.R. and P.P.

In sweet memory of Ben Eder (1980–2001),

the original Chinaberry boy.

A.R.

With thanks to Mary, whose love keeps me going.

P.P.

Contents

Help us to be always hopeful gardeners of the spirit
who know that without darkness, nothing comes to birth,
as without light, nothing flowers.

— MAY SARTON

Introduction

Like clockwork, my baby would awaken just after the most dedicated night owls went to sleep and just before the most fervent early birds awoke. During those hushed moments in between night and day, I was convinced we were the only two humans awake in our time zone. And as I rocked Elizabeth in those almost sacred predawn hours, I came to understand something in a way I've understood few things in my life: that this job of parenting was going to be, by far, the most enormous responsibility I was ever going to have. Along with this awareness, I was overcome with a passionate commitment that nearly every new parent must surely have: to fearlessly stake out a place for myself between my child and any danger, any hurt, that might be headed her way in life. But each night, as I became more firmly grounded in motherhood, I came to know that there would seldom be life-or-death choices I would be called upon to make in order to protect her from all the kinds of pain that visit humans. Instead, there would be a myriad of *small* choices I would need to make day in and day out that would help mold her into the person she would eventually turn out to be. I came to understand that it would be the small choices in parenting that would really and truly matter—the choices that there are hundreds of every single day when you have a child.

On one particular night, I thought back to earlier in the day, when Elizabeth had cuddled on my lap before naptime with a new book open before us. A Mother Goose book. I thought back to how strange it felt to be reading to a one-year-old the ditty about Georgie Porgie, Puddin' and Pie—kissing the girls and making them cry. I remember wondering what could possibly be beneficial about her hearing about an old lady who lived in a shoe with so many children she didn't know what to do, but ended up whipping them all soundly and putting them to bed. And seeing the illustration of Peter Pumpkin Eater smugly standing guard over the pumpkin shell where he'd put his wife (and was keeping her very well), I knew I was at a crossroads. I understood then and there that what I was going to be reading to her before her naptimes, as well as over the upcoming years, was certainly going to be one of those small choices.

Just as surely as I'd come to know in those quiet, predawn hours that parenting was going to turn out to be the biggest responsibility I'd ever have, I knew one more thing, too. I knew that it really and truly matters what we show our babies, and then our children, in books. It matters what stories we tell, for it makes a difference in how they will live their lives if they see from the start people being respectful of one another, people being tolerant, people being honest. It matters that we show them beauty from early on, that they meet in the pages of a book the majestic moon in a breathtaking indigo sky, and the turning of the seasons. That they see people being brave, even if their courage is the quiet kind, the kind about simply being true to what they believe. And so it was from this place that I knew without a shadow of a doubt that the small things do matter. I made a commitment to find books that would help keep the song in her heart alive. For I believed that the more of us here on this earth with each of our own songs still intact, the kinder the world will be for all of us.

Looking for the perfect books to read to Elizabeth became my passion, and before long it grew into a small home business, Chinaberry, through which I shared the jewels I found for my daughter with the world (albeit a small portion of the world). Times have changed: we pack books from a warehouse now instead of at my kitchen table, but my heartfelt intentions have remained the same. No longer am I the only parent choosing and annotating the extraordinary books that are included in the catalog. Indeed, only several years after its humble beginnings, I asked a loyal customer—someone with whom I'd bonded over half a continent and through many of her orders to me—for assistance. It was at that point that Patti Pitcher became a voice in the pages of Chinaberry.

For over twenty years now, Chinaberry has quietly gone about its mission of finding books and other items to enrich families' lives. In the process, our children have grown and taught us much about being fully human. This book is a compilation of what we have learned over the years—what we have learned about books and parenting, and how the two intersect. On these pages you'll find our ruminations about parenting, helpful hints we have found to make it through the days with children and, of course, a multitude of detailed book recommendations to read along the way. You'll meet our children, Elizabeth, Evan, Becca, Laura, Heidi and Aidan, and witness our trials and tribulations as we learn what parenting has to teach us. We don't pretend to have all of the answers. We can only share our own experiences and encourage you to explore yours. The age ranges we offer for the books we describe are merely suggestions; children are all over the map with regard to what book might appeal to whom, and when, and you know your child better than anyone else does. These books represent some of our favorites; you may find that some are out of print, but our hope is that when you explore your library in search of them, you will discover other treasures as well.

We envision you using *Under the Chinaberry Tree* as a reference, as an inspiration for finding the perfect book to give as a gift to a child, as a trusty companion on your trips to the library and perhaps as a book you keep on the bedside table and read alone for a few moments before you call it a day.

If you were to gain two things from reading this book, we wish it would be a profound sense of compassion for how hard it is both to be a parent *and* to be a child; and how, if we approach each day with compassion in our hearts, parenting has the incredible potential to transform us into kinder, gentler people; people guided by love, not fear; people open to the joy inherent in every moment.

Parenting is a journey—an inner journey, an outer journey and a journey of the heart. Parenting brings us to unimagined heights and unpar-
alleled lows. It has the potential to transform our souls, heal our
wounds and lift our hearts. But it also has the power to reduce us to
tears, time and time again. Parenting can bring out the very worst in
our behavior, even when our intentions are stellar. Every wart we
thought we had hidden will somehow be exposed in the process of parenting. No experience has the potency to touch us, challenge us or
transform us like the process of loving a child. Parenting offers us
lessons in how to grow and to strive and to seek. If we choose to open
our hearts to the possibility of transformation inherent in parenting,
our children will teach us how to love, how to forgive and how to be
full expressions of our deepest selves, if only we let them. Their love
has the potential to crack open the hardest parts of our hearts, just as
our love has the potential to carry them through their lives knowing
they are cherished.

UNDER THE
CHINABERRY
TREE

Dailiness

Making It Through the Day

There is no beyond, there is only here,
the infinitely small, infinitely great
and utterly demanding present.
—Iris Murdoch

hen I first became pregnant, I was young and rather naïve. I didn't think at all about the changes a child would bring to my day-to-day life. I only knew deep in my heart that I wanted a child and I wanted her now. I didn't think about never-ending diaper changes or crying babies. I didn't wonder about how I would handle the endless sleepless nights a baby could bring or how expensive raising a child would be. It never even crossed my mind that having a baby would change my level of personal freedom. All I knew was that, without a doubt, I was meant to be a mother, and I suppose I just blindly assumed that all of the details would work themselves out in the end. I was right on both counts: I was meant to be a mother and the details did all work themselves out, but it wasn't as easy as that. I had a lot to learn somewhere in the middle.

During about the fifth month of my pregnancy, a near-paralyzing reality hit home: *I* was going to be a mother. All my pleasant fantasies about the future were replaced by sheer terror. Suddenly, I was no longer so sure this was the right thing for me to be doing, and I was literally left quivering with fear. Was I really up to the challenge of

1

caring for and loving this child?! How did you really love a child, any-way? For a few terrible days I considered the awesome responsibilities of being a mother and I was immobilized. And then, quite suddenly, I realized that worrying about all of this was simply too overwhelming. So I decided to stop fretting and went back to the business of being pregnant. Mercifully, I stopped obsessing about the end product of this pregnancy process (i.e., the baby) and started focusing on things like childbirth classes and labor breathing techniques. (Denial is a wonderful thing sometimes.) Time passed, as time always does, and a few months later, my beautiful, wonderful, incredibly divine baby daughter was born. I knew then that without a doubt, I could love my baby enough and that all we had to do was maintain this amazing bond of ours, and all would indeed be fine.

The intensity of my feelings for my daughter came as quite a shock. (Somebody really should have warned me!) I never knew the power of emotion that a child could evoke in a parent. Whether that feeling be anger, fear, protectiveness, love or joy, the sheer magnitude of emotion can be overwhelming. I was lucky: my first response was pure and simple love, so I could just revel in that warmth. But I knew other new mothers (wonderfully caring women) whose first response was terror. Their passion for their baby incited all of their insecurities. What they had wanted the most for years (their baby) was suddenly this all-consuming, almost immobilizing project that they had no idea how to handle. Faced with a pile of dirty diapers and a crying infant, they were reduced to tears (but when faced with an intense, stressful business meeting, they felt comfortable and in control). What they had imagined to be pure joy was transformed overnight into, quite simply, a lot of work and a feeling of incredible helplessness. Negoti-ating a big contract or planning a conference? A piece of cake. Getting her baby to stop crying? Don't even ask.

How is it that we can love someone so much and have such con-flicted feelings? It must be one of those mysteries of being human. The more we feel toward someone, the more we feel—period—re-gardless of the emotion. Somehow, as parents, we have to learn how to live with all of this contradiction and still let our children know how much we love them. And we have to find a way to accept our children when they are expressing their corresponding mess of emotion toward us, too. "I hate you, Mommy" doesn't mean I hate you forever, but rather "I am angry and want you to know it. If I didn't love you so much

I wouldn't be so angry." Parenting is messy. Our love and concern get in the way of being clear, sometimes. And there we are, filled with love and concern, yet not knowing quite what to do.

Now, after over twenty years of mothering, one truth I have come to know is that parenting always involves accepting dualities and finding a balance that works for my family. Day in and day out, I am juggling two ends of many spectrums, trying to find my equilibrium—a place that invariably lies in the middle of the situation. So every lesson I wish to teach my children has a corresponding opposite lesson that must also be learned if they are all to grow into healthy adults.

It isn't enough to teach my children to respect the needs of others if I don't teach them to respect their own needs, too. It isn't enough for them to learn structure and order if they don't also learn to be flexible enough to flow with the challenges life throws their way. It isn't enough to teach my children to save if I also neglect to teach them to give freely. Both ends of these spectrums have value, and I must find a place of balance in between them. We must give *and* receive. We must have order *and* flexibility. We must work *and* play.

It is not unusual for humans to find that they are much more comfortable with one part of any duality, with one end of every spectrum. For instance, creating rhythm in my child's day is easy for me. When Becca and Laura were little, rhythm played an enormous role in my parenting. It was comforting for all of us to know what to expect. Breakfast after we are dressed and have fed the animals; nap directly after lunch; a walk in the afternoon and two stories before bed. We all did well in our comfortable little routine. But then something would inevitably come along that would disrupt our schedule—a late play date, for instance, and naptime was postponed. Or my husband would come home late from work and innocently want to spend time with the kids, thereby disturbing my already initiated bedtime routine. Suddenly, the kids were cranky and demanding extra attention and I was frustrated because I'd lost control of my day. It took years for me to realize that I needed to embrace flexibility with as much ease as I embraced rhythm if I wanted my days to flow smoothly. While I thought I had found the answer in predictability (one end of the spectrum), I later came to understand that the answer was in welcoming both ends (flexibility and predictability) equally at different times. The trick then becomes to discern which aspect is needed when. Knowing that I am trying to find balance helps me to question if this is a time to compromise. Or is this a moment to stand firm? Is this a time to stick to the schedule? Or to throw my plans away and give in to the needs of the day?

Every one of us is different. Whatever qualities you express naturally (whether it be flexibility or order, softness or firmness, etc.), it is almost guaranteed that your children will offer you opportunities to develop the opposing trait, too. The kindest, softest parent has need for a firm voice some of the time, just like the firmest parent has need for some softness at some point in the day. What has helped me most in trying to incorporate this concept into my life is the simple word "and." I know I can have rhythm *and* flexibility. I can set firm boundaries *and* compromise when necessary. If I pay attention to both sides of the dualities of parenting, I find a comfortable place in the middle, a place where our days flow gracefully (most of the time), and when they don't, we somehow have the perseverance to recover and find our stride the next day (or sometimes maybe not even until the next week).

In the end, the daily tasks of parenting teach us most about ourselves. We will learn some things that come easily to us and some things that we have to work at. If we are open to learning, we will become richer people for our efforts, for the process of parenting will smooth our rough edges and hone our hearts into precise instruments of love that will guide us through our daily lives with grace.

Tips for Having Enough Energy to Survive Daily Life with Small Children

♥ Be sure to get enough rest. It is so easy to stay up late after the children are in bed to have a few precious hours of solitude. But if this time comes at the expense of your sleep, you *and* your family will eventually pay a high price for these few hours.

♥ If mornings are hard for you, make sure you get up before your children. Allow yourself a few minutes to adjust to the day before you are inundated by your children's needs. Have time to take your shower, or drink your morning cup of coffee. Do whatever you need to do to say "Good morning" to yourself. Once you've greeted the day, it is much easier to face the unbounded enthusiasm of a cheery toddler first thing in the morning.

♥ If your children nap, take that time purely for yourself. Parents need downtime, too. Read a book, take a nap, do something creative—anything to nourish yourself. Don't feel as if you have to make that the most productive hour of the day. Think of this time as your time to renew your batteries, not as the hour to get everything done that hasn't been done all day.

♥ Eat regular meals. It is so easy to ignore your own needs. When things get hectic or children become overwrought, it can be a challenge to remember to feed yourself. Even if it is just a five-minute break to eat a peanut butter sandwich and drink a glass of milk, sit down. Show your children how to take care of themselves by taking care of *yourself*.

♥ Remember to drink plenty of water (not Coke, not coffee—but water). It's amazing how much energy proper hydration provides. To figure out how much water you require, divide your weight in pounds by two and drink that number in ounces of water. So if you weigh 140 pounds, you need 70 ounces of water, or just about nine eight-ounce glasses. If that sounds like a lot, you probably aren't drinking enough. Try it for a couple of weeks and see how you feel. You might be surprised.

♥ Plan something fun for yourself every day. This doesn't have to be big or exciting; just a simple act that brings you happiness. For me, it is often a cup of herbal tea on cold afternoons, or a walk outside with the kids—just something for a little break. It doesn't have to take long. Often my walks are only fifteen minutes from start to finish. Choose an activity that is nourishing to you. One of my friends puts her kids in the stroller and walks three blocks every morning for a latté. She's got a houseful (three kids under five), so it is hard for her to find even a moment for herself at home. The children think the walk is a fun outing and don't have a clue that she is doing this for herself. For her, that latté midway through the walk is a precious reminder that caring for herself is also caring for her children.

♥ Create a basic rhythm to your day that is tailored to the specific needs of your family. Look at the basic tendencies or habits of your family and create a pattern that supports these needs. There is a tricky balance to be found in meeting your children where they are and in allowing yourself to be true to yourself, too. Are you a night person with a child who rises with the birds? Then maybe you need to take an afternoon nap right along with your child so you can stay up late and still manage to get up early with your child without over-tiring yourself. Does one parent come home late and you still want to eat together as a family? Then plan a regular five-o'clock snack to ensure that your children can make it to a seven-o'clock dinner with ease. Whatever the specific needs of your family, seek a rhythm that works for you—a rhythm that is flexible enough to allow for change and stable enough to provide a comforting structure.

We all experience a normal variety of ups and downs as we move through our ordinary, day-in, day-out lives with children. Here is a collection of books and practical ideas to get you through the day.

Jesse Bear, What Will You Wear?

by Nancy White Carlstrom
illustrated by Bruce Degen

Jesse Bear, what will you wear?
What will you wear in the morning?
My shirt of red
Pulled over my head
Over my head in the morning.

And so begins Jesse Bear's day. It is one of sunshine, butterflies, sandboxes and family love. The entire story follows Jesse throughout the day, and the lilting verse always asks the same question ("Jesse Bear, what will you wear?"). Whether the answer is "Juice from a pear and rice in my hair, that's what I'll wear at noon!" or "Sleep in my eyes and stars in the skies, moon on my bed and dreams in my head, that's what I'll wear tonight!" there is never a boring moment in Jesse Bear's day.

Children ask for this book again and again. It is a book that families—from child to child, on down the line—read until the book is in shreds. (2–4 yrs.)

Peek-A-Boo!

by Janet and Allan Ahlberg

This is one of those "sleepers" that could sneak by you unless you had a trusted friend to put it in your hand and say it's a book not to be missed. *Peek-A-Boo!* has been the favorite book of many families with very young children. Catchy, inviting and refreshingly attractive, each double-page spread offers a lot to see. In scenes of a wonderfully untidy and lived-in home, a family goes about its day. And as usual, when there is a baby in the house, their lives revolve around the little one. Die-cut pages on every spread showcase this family's precious youngest, inviting us to turn the page to find out just what's going to be happening in the next scene.

Love and warmth are conveyed in the pictures and story, and the amount of detail in the illustrations will keep your babe's eyes busy a long time. If you take the time to look at each spread, pointing to and naming familiar and unfamiliar objects, you'll double your family's pleasure from exploring this wonderful book. And if you haven't had the pleasure of experiencing die-cut holes in a book's pages, you're in for some fun with *Peek-A-Boo!* (1–2½ yrs.)

Provide your child with good quality tools for helping you around the house—a child-size broom, a small wheelbarrow, a small apron. I find it so sad when I run into the attitude that just because something is for a child it doesn't have to be of good quality. If we want our children to grow up to be skilled workers, able to take care of themselves and their environment, we have to teach them. But if we offer them inferior tools, we make their job so much harder. Respect the child by respecting his work and offer him real tools that honestly help with the chore at hand.

Pancakes for Breakfast

by Tomie dePaola

I'm trying to sound as levelheaded as possible, here. That being said, may I suggest that you absolutely, positively, without hesitation, go right out and get this book and read it to your child. It's the story of a woman who awakes with one thought in her head: pancakes for breakfast. This book vividly portrays in wordless form the woman's problems in gathering ingredients to make those pancakes from scratch. (Hint: there is egg gathering, cow milking and batter stirring. A subsequent maple-syrup run leaves the woman's dog and cat at home unattended and that's when the story turns outrageous.) Tomie dePaola's art is uncluttered and colorful, with facial expressions that are half of the fun. *Pancakes for Breakfast* fabulously combines humor and the opportunity to hone prediction skills. And since it is wordless, you can ham it up as much as you want while "reading" it. (1½ –4 yrs.)

When creating a rhythm for your days, think of this rhythm as if it were a rubber band. The rhythm is there as a pattern to hold something in place, to add stability to your day. Yet it's a pattern quite capable of stretching, of being flexible to meet the needs at hand. Like a rubber band, our daily rhythm can only be stretched so far before it loses its structural integrity and everything falls apart. So, nurture a rhythm that allows for both stability and ease. Stability provides the boundaries that small children need to feel safe. Stability creates a comforting sense of predictability, of knowing that naptime always follows lunchtime. A rhythm with general predictability deeply reassures a child's soul that all is well. At the same time, we must avoid the trap of being too rigid by creating a rhythm that allows for ease. A rhythm that is gently flexible makes room for the unpredictable and helps children learn to be adaptable. Flexibility encourages a comfort with life that allows people to flow from one experience to the next, even when things don't go exactly as planned, which, in these radically changing ti a highly useful trait.

Boom, Baby, Boom, Boom!

by Margaret Mahy
illustrated by Patricia MacCarthy

Boom, Baby, Boom, Boom! is the story of a mama who wants to have a little moment of peace for herself in the middle of her day with her baby. So Mama fixes the baby a deluxe lunch, puts the child in the high chair and then sits down at her drums to play while her baby eats. With her back turned away from her child, mama beats away while the baby is supposed to be eating. But you can guess that the baby has other plans! All of her friends are waiting just outside the door for Mama to turn her back so they can slip in one by one and "help" the baby eat her lunch. You can just imagine the fun when a dog, cat, cow, family of chickens and a sheep come to lunch.

Delightfully repetitive language, an absolutely silly plot and scrumptious illustrations make this book a lively hit with little ones. It is particularly wonderful because it is so fun to read aloud. (2–4 yrs.)

Daisy

The Little Duck with the Big Feet
4 First Daisy Books

by Jane Simmons

These hand-size board books are sweeter than apple pie and as cheery as the first birdsong in spring. Daisy is a duckling: on the one hand, always exploring, discovering new things and game for just about any adventure, and on the other hand, sometimes just a little too antsy to go to sleep when it's time to do so at the end of the day.

The simple text comes to life next to the dreamy and colorful illustrations of Daisy romping with her pond pals, or being preoccupied with the sounds of owls *tooh-hooing* and mice *eeek-eeeking* in the moonlight. She's a toddler archetype, if ever there was one. And her bright yellow feathers, her huge webbed feet and her incredibly vivid orange bill make her ever so endearing. (1–3 yrs.)

Power Struggles

If we keep our eyes open, we find inspiration in the small moments of our life with children, even on the worst of days. Sometimes we must slow down, take a few breaths and regroup to find it, but the wisdom is always there, hidden in the shadows of every moment if we take the time to see it. One of my all-time-hardest parenting lessons—and the eventual wisdom that came with it—involved power struggles.

I used to feel so completely helpless in power struggles. How could this small child, whom I loved so dearly, produce such extraordinary levels of frustration and even rage in me? There were such strong feelings over whether or not she could have another cookie. Weren't two cookies enough? Why couldn't she see the reason in the situation? Why couldn't I? The intensity of my feelings (not to mention my child's feelings) astounded me at times. Why won't she bend her will to mine and just make this easier? Doesn't she know I'm the parent!? Does this really have to be so hard? (There is nothing like arguing with a two-year-old in public to humble a person.)

I used to struggle with these questions until one day I had the revelation that the very thing I was battling *against* in my child was a trait that I honor greatly in adults. I *love* adults who persevere against all odds to manifest their dreams. I *love* adults who have the strength of will to stand up and speak their truth. (They know they want that third cookie and aren't going to let anyone stop them from having it!) Nevertheless, here I was arguing with my child when she was directing these identical traits toward me. Like a bolt of lightning, insight dawned in my heart. I realized that I didn't want to squelch these traits in my child, but merely to help her channel them toward more appropriate situations. Suddenly, it became my job to teach when to use willpower and when to be flexible. This enormous will that I had battled so mightily against had many important uses. Why would I ever want to subdue it?

Once I could step aside and see my child's will for the powerful, remarkable trait that it was, it lost its power over me. My anger magically dissipated with this new understanding. Suddenly, it wasn't about winning anymore. It was about honoring this magnificent trait in my child and helping her learn to use her will wisely in the world. In honoring my child's tremendous will, I mustn't let it rule her life and yet, without the strength of her will intact, she might never reach her soul's destination. In the end, it's all about the intention in our heart and the words we choose to use as we reinforce our message. "Yes, sweetie, I know you really hate that you can only have two cookies, but two cookies are a reasonable amount. Asking again isn't going to change my answer. Let's read a story instead."

Respecting the power of our children's will allows us to transform our feelings about it. We no longer have to conquer it. Like a tai chi master, we simply redirect the flow. Respecting the power of my children's will didn't make those times when I knocked heads with my children go away forever, it just transformed how I felt about them and how I responded to them.

Out and About

a Shirley Hughes Nursery Collection

The five books collected in this volume are some of the very favorite books of several families we know. (The individual titles are: *Bathwater's Hot*, *When We Went to the Park*, *Colors*, *All Shapes and Sizes* and *Noisy*.)

Shirley Hughes is one of those rare author/illustrators who can work magic with both words and art. And I do mean magic. Fun-to-read, lilting and rhyming texts combine with detailed, richly colored illustrations of a two-parent, big-sister, little-brother family—and all of the dramas, clutter and necessary cooperation that make a family tick on a down-to-earth, endearing level. Any parent will be struck by the familiar expressions, doings, scenarios, and right-on energy of this book; it is almost impossible to look at the pages without smiling. You will find yourself doing more than simply reading the text; you will be stopping to point out this stuffed animal tucked into somebody's bed, that cat on a wall, this tired-looking mommy, gratefully accepting a snack from her little helper, or that turtle making its way across a patch of ground.

There is something extra special about this collection and it is not just that it covers such concepts as colors and opposites in a subtle, engaging way. It has more to do with the fact that you will end up really enjoying this family and their world—cuddles, clutter and all. (2–4 yrs.)

Children are natural helpers. They love to share our work. But we must slow ourselves down enough to make space for them to work at their own pace and in their own way. They may not do things to our exacting standards the first few years that they are helping us, but with lots of opportunity and encouragement, as well as a healthy dose of acceptance for a job almost done (especially when they are very young), they will grow into capable workers. Teach skills sequentially, gradually adding the more subtle details, and soon you will have children who can see the dirt in a dirty sink and know how to clean!

Once a week, we clean our house as a family. Dividing up the chores, we go through our list and clean everything all at once. Our younger children always have a cleaning partner and are given a small but important job to do. A three-year-old equipped with two paper sacks can quite skillfully be in charge of sorting the trash and the recycling. As long as there is someone in the room with them, my children have always been quite thrilled to have tangible work that is in their care. Each year as we give them more freedoms, we also add to their responsibilities. By the time they are ten, they are capable of doing all the simple chores around the house—dishes, laundry, vacuuming, dusting, cleaning the bathrooms. They still like company when they work, but now their efforts are truly helping. When you clean as a family, no one has to be the "house slave." More important, children learn that work is intrinsically satisfying and that it takes the whole family to make the home run smoothly.

Little Bear books

(Little Bear, Little Bear's Friend, Little Bear's Visit)

by Else Minarik
illustrated by Maurice Sendak

It is our opinion that every child should own at least one Little Bear book.

Author Else Minarik clearly understands the way small children think. Her stories, while deceptively simple, magically and ever so accurately capture the world of young ones. She understands their unique point of view—their need to feel loved and comforted, to know that lunch will be waiting for them when they come home hungry, that someone understands their little joys and their little worries.

Illustrator Maurice Sendak has created a perfect world for Little Bear to inhabit. His drawings evoke the love, comfort and reassuring feeling that the world is a good place in which to be—a feeling that every child should have the opportunity to experience. Quite frankly, these are perfect books for young children!

Each Little Bear book stands well on its own, but don't be surprised if your child falls in love with all three and ultimately loves them till they fall apart. You'll likely have to replace them before your child outgrows them, as they are wonderful for the very young as well as for the new reader. (2½–6 yrs.)

Lunch

by Denise Fleming

It's lunchtime. But more important than that, there is one very enthusiastic mouse all ready to eat. He (she?) pops out of his little mousehole sniffing the air, ready for a good meal. He eats his way through the rainbow, feasting on such delectable items as tasty orange carrots, tart blueberries, shiny red apples and tender green peas. This little mouse has one heck of an appetite. By the end of the book, his belly is absolutely bulging and he is covered from head to toe in food—carrots on his tail, grapes on his foot, watermelon on his belly. He's so full there is simply nothing he can do except take a nap until dinnertime. *Lunch* is toddler heaven. It has everything a toddler loves—humor, peek-a-boo-type suspense, a lovable main character and bold, vibrantly colored art. It is sure to bring more than a few smiles. (1½–3 yrs.)

Remember to keep plenty of healthful snacks on hand. Most children are like little birds. Nibble, nibble, snack, snack. Waiting five hours between meals taxes their physiology. They have tiny tummies and need to eat small amounts often. When handing out snacks, it's easy to think that a cookie here, Popsicle there, doesn't really matter. However, you can soon find that they ate precious little "real" food during the day and are cranky from the lack of protein. A sliced apple can be just as much of a treat as a cookie; offered with a small bowl of peanut butter and a child-size butter knife, it becomes not only a filling, nutritious snack, but an opportunity to gain a new skill! Presentation is often the key to ensuring that small children eat healthfully. A cute plate with a few nourishing foods to choose from makes snacking more fun. I have a variety of tiny bowls and child-size containers that my children love to eat from—twenty-five frozen blueberries in one, a small pile of nuts in another. Soon, the little bowls are empty and the children are asking for more! I find the more real food I keep around (and the fewer junk foods), the fewer battles I have with my kids about what to eat. And as long as I present the nutritious food in an intriguing way, they seem to love it just as much as (or more than) the junky things they crave.

Robert McCloskey

Robert McCloskey is a genius at capturing the joy of life inherent in the toddler/preschool child, and his books have been loved ever since they were released in the 1940s and '50s. Through his ele-

gantly simple but detailed charcoal drawings and straightforward storytelling, his books glorify the specialness of ordinary life. They radiate warmth, comfort, security and love. In other words, they are perfect for a young child.

Make Way for Ducklings

If you didn't encounter this book sometime during your childhood, do yourself *and* your child a favor by reading it now. It's a timeless classic, illustrated in black and white, and is the story of a pair of ducks that settle down in a Boston park to raise a family. Eggs get laid, eggs get hatched and soon it's time to venture out into the world. And it's this part of the story that three generations of children have loved: a policeman stops this hubbub of traffic for a family of nine ducks.

Oh, this is certainly a delightful book! If you happen to have a prejudice against children's books illustrated in black and white, you will find that prejudice dissolving as you watch your child fall in love with this kinder and gentler world where ducks get respect in the middle of a big city! (2½–5 yrs.)

Blueberries for Sal
and One Morning in Maine

Calm and comforting, both of these books give us a look into a small child's life. We first meet this family in *Blueberries for Sal*. Young Sal and her mother go to the blueberry patch to pick berries to can for their winter's food. Sal is old enough to go, but young enough to wander off when Mother is concentrating on her picking. Unbeknownst to Mother, a mama bear and cub are also on the hill eating their fill of berries in preparation for winter. When the two children (human and bear cub) wander off from their respective mothers and find the other mother, excitement ensues (though just for a second, for this book is clearly intended for young children and not meant to frighten). It isn't long before each child is reunited with the appropriate mama and all is well.

The adventures continue in *One Morning in Maine*. This time Sal is older and now a big sister. She's excited to go to town with baby Jane and her dad to gather the weekly groceries. Since they live on an island, going to town means a boat ride. But when Sal wakes up with a loose tooth and worries that she is sick, Mother assures her all is well and explains the difference between baby and grown-up teeth. In a nutshell, the rest of this delightful story involves Sal's losing her tooth while digging clams, and the ensuing developments—which end on a happy note.

Simple and straightforward, both books reflect back to calmer times in a way that modern children can still appreciate. They have much the same comforting, enduring appeal as *Goodnight Moon* and are perfect for bedtime reading. (2½–5 yrs.)

It is important for parents not to focus our complete attention on our children all day. They need to see us doing the important work of living, whether that be cooking or cleaning or paying the bills. But they also need our attention. When we can include our children in our work, by letting them help clean or scrub the dishes, we can do both. Side by side, we can do the work of life. Children are more likely to allow us a moment to do the things they can't help us with when we include them in the things they can. It always amazes me when I see parents expecting their ten-year-olds to help around the house (a natural expectation) when they never spent time teaching them this work when they were younger. Small children love to wash dishes by a parent's side. They love to sweep with child-size brooms. Don't wait until naptime to get all your "work" done; include your child and you'll both be happier for it.

Peter Spier's Rain

by Peter Spier

Who—parent or child—doesn't have a twinge of disappointment when a gloomy, rainy day greets us in the morning? Okay, a rainy day here or there is fine, but, with all due respect to those who thrive on stormy and gloomy days, I still say it is hard to find something good about a string of them.

And then there is this book. *Peter Spier's Rain*, which is scrumptiously wordless and thus allows you to take as much time as you want exploring the illustrations, follows a girl and boy having a ball doing some of the wonderful activities available only on rainy days. Delightfully sloshy, wet scenes show kids splashing in puddles, standing under rain spouts, wading through overflowing gutters, etc. They get hot tea and cookies upon their return home, engage in indoor fun, go to bed and wake up to a sunny day. This book is so inviting it might make you wish for a rainy day to come along. (3–6 yrs.)

I Like to Be Little

by Charlotte Zolotow
illustrated by Erik Blegvad

You don't often run into a book for young children that expresses true wisdom—the kind that you know lives within a little one's heart but that seldom makes its way out because we are simply too busy and preoccupied to create an environment in which such innocent wisdom is acknowledged.

In this story, a little girl discusses with her mother the advantages of being little. What it all boils down to is that the child loves enjoying things that adults just aren't interested in or that they simply don't do. The girl adores how being little allows her to skip when she's glad, sit under the dining room table and trace the flowers in the rug with her fingers, have the ice cream man know her by name, go trick-or-treating, jump in a pile of leaves and eat snow when it first falls. After all of these rather convincing examples of why her child prefers to be little right now, the mother tells the girl that there is something about being grown-up that makes all those neat things happen again: "being the mother of a little girl like you." The book doesn't end here, though. It goes on to get to the heart of why both mother and child believe they are the luckiest people in the world.

This is a loving story that affirms the wonder of childhood. (3½–5½ yrs.)

When you are having a hard time, you're out of patience, your child is cranky and you can't figure it out, just accept it. It's okay. It may not be fun but it *is* okay. Once you accept that you can't control your screaming two-year-old and just allow him to be who he is, you make room for inspiration to guide you. Sometimes inspiration will lead you to change what you are doing, and sometimes it will lead you to change what you are thinking. Often, it will simply reassure you that this too shall pass and encourage you to bring as much love to the moment as you are able. The important thing, though, is to be open for inspiration. It is always there; we just have to be willing to receive it.

Morning Song

by Mary McKenna Siddals
illustrated by Elizabeth Sayles

Singing makes daily transitions so much easier and happier. Often, picking up toys and getting ready for bed can be joyful and fun if you have the right song to sing. I remember finding countless songs for bedtime, but less for greeting the morning. (Not that we usually need to persuade our young ones to rise and shine!)

Morning Song is the perfect book for the child who wakes early in the morning to greet the day. In this book the little boy lovingly says good morning to his blankie, his bear, his book, his chair, until finally he looks up to see his father standing in the door, his best companion of all. This is a cozy, luminous ode to the newborn day, perfect for our little ones. (18 mos.–3 yrs.)

When planning my day, I like to think of how the day will breathe. Breathing in, we do calmer, quieter activities—my children might be playing quietly with their building toys while I am nearby doing a few household chores. Breathing out, we release the tensions we have built from so much concentrated work and allow ourselves to move, have fun, relax. We go outside to run around, or perhaps turn on some music and dance. My best days flow in and out. Not too much of any one pursuit—a little time for chores, a little time for fun, a little time for rest, a little time for rowdy play. If I lean too heavily toward one activity or another, behaviors tend to get out of hand. When I see my children beginning to get frustrated, I try to figure out what might balance the situation. I don't wait for it all to fall apart before I step in. For example, if they have been playing hard (but happily) for an hour and then all of a sudden they start squabbling, it could mean they are hungry. Or perhaps they need to settle down a bit and sit quietly while I read them a story. With a few minutes of settled time to balance all their activity, they very well might be ready for another hour of hard play. On the other hand, if they have been doing a quiet activity for a long time and they suddenly get cranky, they may need to get up and run around. Breathing in, breathing out. Life is a balance.

Owl at Home

by Arnold Lobel

This is the first book we routinely kept out of the library too long and eventually we knew we just had to have a copy of our own. It is a five-chapter Easy Reader that children as young as two and a half can't seem to get enough of. Owl is a lovable, uncomplicated fellow. His innocence and down-to-earthness create stories that youngsters instantly connect with and want to hear over and over and over again. There is something calm and predictable and real about him that makes Owl a friend you want to visit on a regular basis. Owl won't bore you, even after numerous readings, and he will bring chuckles, to boot!

Do invite Owl into your life. He'll make it just that much more enjoyable. A perfect book to span several years. (2½–6 yrs.)

Try to allow for a variety of experiences in the day. Too much of anything makes for cranky children. Rather than doing seven errands one
day and none the next, try doing a few one day with a trip to the park
in the middle and then another few the next day with the library as
your last stop. Pushing your child past her limits (e.g., adding that one
last errand when she is tired or hungry) just encourages her to learn
inappropriate behavior in stores. Help her to learn proper store manners by making sure her needs are met before you go into the store
and then not taxing her patience too much by overstaying your welcome. With a little forethought while they are young, you will soon
have willing helpers who are a joy to take with you into the world.

Tales of Oliver Pig

by Jean Van Leeuwen
illustrated by Arnold Lobel

Oliver is the big brother pig who goes from helping his mom bake
cookies to coping with the antics of a toddler sister to putting up with
the ordeal of piling on layers and layers of clothes for a snowy day outing. Here is a five-chaptered Easy Reader book that so beautifully
communicates the reality—both loving and, of course, frustrating—of
being a family. Maybe that is why toddlers glom right onto it and don't
come up for air, ready to move on to claim another favorite book, until
months later. The good news is that you, as reader to your youngster,
likely won't tire of it because it is just so dear—and hits the mark so
well. Another one of those books that spans a nice length of time, for
it is such a wonderful read-aloud and then read-alone. (2½–6 yrs.)

To Bathe a Boa

by C. Imbior Kudrna

Now, I'm no snake fan. I've passed a lot of time *outside* the reptile
house at the zoo while my children are inside, admiring snakes. But

this book portrays a particular boa so endearingly that I've made some-what of a snake "breakthrough," and I know a number of parents who feel the same way.

This is the story of a little boy who feels responsible for getting his boa into the bath, and a bath is the *last* thing that snake wants!

With soap in hand and water hot,
I called my boa to the spot.
"It's dinnertime," I sweetly lied,
but not a sound did he reply.

This text accompanies full-color illustrations of the boy poised with soap in hand near the bathroom, where the tub has been filled with Boa Bubble Bath, while the boa peeks from around the corner with a *very* concerned, worried look on his face. The rest of this madcap story revolves around the contortions the boy goes through to get the boa in the bath, and how the boa attempts to evade him. (Hint: they both end up in the tub.) This book is funny, crazy and sweet, all at the same time. (2½–5 yrs.)

In these days of Velcro, digital watches and phones with automatic dial-ing features, it's easy to forget to expose our children to basic, often in-trinsically satisfying concepts such as tying a shoe or telling time the old-fashioned way, not to mention what could be a lifesaving capability in an emergency: the habit of memorizing important phone numbers. Of course, when your child is too young to physically master tying a shoe, wearing Velcro actually facilitates her developing self-sufficiency. But later, when she reaches the age of four or five, shoe tying becomes a challenging yet feasible skill to master (especially when taught in in-cremental steps). And what child doesn't feel proud of herself when she knows how to tie her first bow on her shoe or make her first real phone call?

Treasure Hunt

by Allan Ahlberg
illustrated by Gillian Tyler

Have you ever known a child who didn't enjoy a good treasure hunt? It's such a delicious activity. When something you love has been hidden (or is hiding), it instantly becomes *treasure*. And treasure is undoubtedly one of life's most magical offerings.

No one knows this better than little Tilly. And rest assured, Tilly leaves no stone—or laundry basket—unturned as she searches for her treasures throughout the day, beginning with her breakfast banana. Sure, the house may appear a bit tousled, but Tilly's mom and dad continue to enthusiastically hide this and that—here and there. All day. Late in the day, wearing her bathrobe and bunny slippers, she hunts for her stuffed rabbit with her birthday-gift flashlight. Before bedtime, Tilly's parents turn the house inside out looking for their own most cherished treasure. And what—or who—could it be? Youngsters will be comforted by the warm, laughter-filled ending.

The illustrations are probably also best described as being warm and laughter-filled. Poring over them is a treasure hunt in itself. Your own most cherished treasure will enjoy this tender and cheerful story. (18 mos.–3 yrs.)

Good Days Bad Days

by Catherine Anholt

Here is a delightful book that perfectly captures the peaks and valleys of family life. The illustrations exquisitely portray the difference in the feelings that certain kinds of days evoke. For all of us, there are slow days and quick days, home days and away days, sunny days and snowy days. The author's warm and cheery paintings of families together experiencing all these kinds of days portray the contrasts in a delectable way. Lots of detail and down-to-earth attention to the nitty-gritty of real life (like the sink overloaded with dirty dishes on the "home day" page) make this book one that you and your child will likely latch on to right away. The types of contrasts work together to give the reader a sense of how our lives are a real mix of different things. Very brief text leaves open the opportunity to sit and chat about the scenes with your child, and each double-page spread offers several illustrations. This is one of those wise, rare books that speaks to all ages. (2–4 yrs.)

Dear Friends,

The other day a message was left on our answering machine from an old friend. In his early fifties, he's just become a father for the first time and I hadn't talked to him since his wife and baby daughter were just days home from the hospital and everyone was aglow with the high of a brand-new baby in the house. It's now six months into his parenting journey and his voice mail to me went something like this: "Haven't talked to you in a long time, but think about you a lot because you've been through this and what with the baby and the impact she's had on life here, I gotta tell you I'm just blown away, and it'd be great to talk to you and I had no idea it would be like this and I'm not sure I'm up to it but I'm in it, so I have to be up to it and . . . we gotta talk. . . ."

Well, we did talk, and suffice it to say that this man, who is intelligent, has more than his share of life experiences, who has wanted a child for twenty years, is indeed utterly and dramatically overwhelmed at what being a parent is shaping up to be. And his daughter is only six months old . . .

If he had asked me a couple of years ago to tell him what I'd found to be true about parenting, I wouldn't have mentioned the obvious—the wakeful nights, the spit-up or the endless diapers—but rather what a profoundly life-changing experience it is. As I get more and more days of parenting under my belt, though, I realize my advice would come in the form of questions. I would ask . . .

Did you search your soul more deeply than you've ever searched it before deciding to have a baby and do you understand that parenting is forever? Do you understand that no matter how much you prepare or how much you read, you will still find yourself questioning? That the questions get bigger and harder—not smaller and easier—as your child gets older? That there will be times when your child will need you to hold him in his darkest hour—whether he's fifteen months or fifteen years old—even when every bone in your body says you don't have the energy or when your appointment book says you don't have the time? That you will need to take a hard look at what "everybody's doing" and ask for the wisdom to know what is best and the courage to act from your heart? Do you understand, the sooner the better in your parenting journey, that you are not parenting in a vacuum, that your child, raised with the values you have given her, will be impacting the world for better or for worse sooner than you'd ever dreamed? Did you search your soul and even try to understand how our society has reached the point where children kill children?

And I would go on. Are you willing to pray for the guidance to know how to bring some Light into our often dark world, to take steps to soften the hard edges? Do you have the passion to cry with others when there is pain and be full of joy when something of beauty has graced your family's life? Are you willing to slow down; to be sleepless in the middle of the night, wondering if you handled something the best way; to learn more than you thought you ever wanted to learn about things that have nothing to do with advanced degrees or the career track? Can you be vulnerable? Are you willing to be more completely honest than you've ever been? Are you willing to see the places in your life where you stopped growing long ago? Do you understand that to bring a child into the world, as well as to birth yourself as a more compassionate human being in the process of parenting, is not only the hardest thing you'll likely ever do but, just as important, a profound honor?

Yes, I would ask my friend these questions, longing for him to understand in the process of answering them the sacredness of the work at hand. For if his answers are "yes," then I trust that each time he wipes grubby hands, makes yet another peanut butter sandwich and with loving words breaks up a sibling dispute, he knows with each cell of his being that parenting is noble work whose every act is heroic and a task worth doing from the deepest, best place of his soul.

No Matter What

Unconditional Love

*Speak tenderly to them. Let there be kindness in
your face, in your eyes, in your smile, in the
warmth of your greeting. Always have a cheerful
smile, but give your heart as well.*
— MOTHER TERESA

U p until recently in mankind's history, children were brought
into this world mainly because they were considered an
economic plus. The more kids the better—to work the
fields or mines. Yes, there was a need to provide materially for them
and teach them basic morals, but often that was about it. Today,
though, our culture demands much more of us. It demands that we
love our children unconditionally. Many of us, however, have no true
conception of what it feels like to love and be loved unconditionally. In
theory, we know what it is. We've certainly heard the words "unconditional love" bandied about enough, and we know intellectually what it
means to love someone all of the time, no matter what. But how do we
transform this amorphous idea of love into the concrete actions that
make up the everyday moments of parenting? How do we take a concept that we barely understand and that was not routinely modeled for
us and breathe it into our daily lives? It's tough, particularly since
many of us never experienced this type of love as children.

We know we love our children. What parent hasn't felt that profound, remarkable, simply undeniable emotion of love when he gazes upon his sleeping infant or watches his baby take his first steps? The love is there; we just need new skills and especially new understandings if we are to communicate to our children what we feel. For most of us, it is easy to express this love when things are going well, but how do we show our love on hard days when tempers are flaring and behaviors are less than stellar? Perhaps it is by learning how to break our love down into bite-size pieces so our children can be nourished by love's essence, even when we are upset. They need to feel (and so do we) love's essence permeating the very air they breathe. With this potent and ever-present force in their lives, our children will know without a doubt that they are loved.

To begin to express our love unconditionally, we must first understand what these words mean. Does it mean we love our children when they are acting horribly? Yes, it does. But it does *not* mean that we have to love *what our children do* while they are behaving horribly. To convey unconditional love to our children we must become masters at separating the child from her behavior. For example, one day when I was very, very young, my mother was sick in bed. Left to my own devices, I decided to "help" her with her chores since she was unable to do them. I worked hard to drag a twenty-five-pound box of laundry soap out to the front yard. Somehow I managed to dump all of the soap into my wading pool and fill it by running the hose full force. It wasn't long before the entire lawn was covered knee-deep in soap bubbles. By this time, my poor mother (knowing I had been quiet for far too long) came hobbling out from her bedroom to see the entire yard covered in sudsy snow. "Look, Mom, I washed the lawn!" I shouted gleefully as she came to the door. Somehow, she managed to see the humor in it all and congratulate me on my "help" and then proceed to tell me the difference between watering the lawn and washing the clothes. Her response to my innocent mistake graciously applauded the *spirit* behind my action and yet helped me understand why this wasn't such an appropriate choice. As my mother showed in this instance, to unconditionally love our child we must express our love for the soul of the child *and* we must guide him to better behaviors as he learns all of the amazingly detailed specifics of living. We must break our messages of discipline into two pieces—one that affirms our child's basic goodness and another that instructs him in how better to exist in this complicated world of ours. Discipline is both an expression of love and a chance to impart a bit of life wisdom.

For many of us, childhood was filled with words like "No! Bad girl." Or "What a bad boy! How could you . . . ?" Our parents and teachers may have judged us as bad or incomplete when all we really did was make a mistake. Instead of taking this moment to teach us something about how to live better in the world, they managed to damage our sense of self-worth with their personal judgment of our behaviors. I don't believe our parents did this consciously. They certainly loved us with the same depth of passion and complexity that we have for our children; it was just that they didn't have the skills (or perhaps the awareness) to understand the true effect that their words had on our spirits. When we tell our children that they are bad (or good, for that matter) for something they are doing, we subtly communicate to them that their worth depends on their behavior. I find it much more effective to describe to my children what they did, and then describe what I want them to do. When my four-year-old scribbles vivid red markings on the pages of my book, my hackles immediately rise. I'm glad she wants to experiment with drawing, but I certainly don't want her defacing my beloved books. I try to stay calm enough to say, "Books are for reading and sheets of paper are for drawing on. Let me help you find something more appropriate to draw on than our special books." If I am feeling too emotional about my child's behavior to control my tone of voice, I stop and take a breath (or three). Then I preface my words with "I feel very angry (or sad or however it makes me feel) when my books . . ." By owning my own feelings and then describing what it is I expect of my children, I give them information, not judgment. And with information, they are much more likely to make the appropriate choice the next time. Without judgment, their sense of self-worth remains intact.

Unless they are extremely angry (and wanting revenge against some perceived injustice), most children genuinely want to do the right thing. I've noticed that my children generally misbehave for three reasons: they need my attention, they don't understand my expectations of them or they don't know how to get what they desire without misbehaving. It is my intention as a parent to teach them how to behave appropriately. Therefore, when they misbehave, I must look closely at the situation to try to understand the reason they are acting the way they are.

♥ If children are in need of attention, they will find a way to get it, even if it means experiencing negative attention in the form of our displeasure. Anything is better than nothing at this point. When my children start whining or fussing, I ask myself, "Am I too busy or distracted? Have I been too engrossed in my own projects or activities? Is it time to sit down and read a story, sing a song or perhaps even find a way to include my child in my work?" If I give my children the attention they desire, they have little reason to misbehave. With their attention cup full, life invariably proceeds with ease. Some days I find that their attention cups act like sieves. They can't get enough to fill them up. On days like this, if at all possible, I just set aside my plans and spend time simply *being* with my child. And the remarkable thing is, once I have set aside my expectations of how the day *should* be, these especially needy days often transform into some of my favorite times. The serenity we find spending quiet time together dawdling on our little walks outside or reading on the couch nurtures us both. What starts out as giving quickly becomes a gift.

♥ When I realize my children are misbehaving because they do not understand my expectations of them, I find it is easy to set them back on track. A quick, polite lesson in whatever it is they need to learn, followed by a loving hug and we are on our way. "People are not for hitting. I can tell you feel angry about something. Can you use your words to tell me what you need?" If I choose to make the incident bigger than this, we all suffer. If I let *my* feelings about their behavior ignite the situation, or I leave the present and start imagining a future in which this dreaded behavior rules our lives forever, things invariably go sour. It's so easy to extrapolate the future from your child's two-year-old behaviors. "My child hits and therefore he will be the bully everyone hates in school. He'll never have any friends. He'll be lonely and unhappy and end up dying homeless on the street after a lifetime of heroin addiction." (Or fill in your own scenario.) It is important to remember that just because your child hits once (or twice or even two hundred times), it doesn't mean he will hit people when he is grown. Some children learn lessons with one go-round, for others it takes many opportunities. Our job is to give them as many chances as *they* need to learn and to continue to provide gentle teaching for as long as it takes. This is where our ability to separate the child from his behavior comes in handy. If we remember that our child is a beautiful spirit living in a small body that has much to learn, it is easier to let him mature at his own pace. We can graciously remember how very hard it is to be little in a big world.

Part of teaching is exercising the unreserved kindness to allow people to develop at their own rate, even if it takes two hundred mistakes. Unfortunately, it can be frustrating to deal with the consequences of all these mistakes. We must be careful to express our frustration about the *behavior,* not about the child. "Please stop! Whining drives me crazy." Not, "You're such a whiner. Stop being such a baby!" The more you can talk about the behavior and the less you talk about the child, the easier it is for your child to separate himself from his behavior, and learn. If the child feels personally attacked or criticized by your words, it is much harder to learn anything but how to feel bad about himself or to be angry at you (or both).

♥   When my children misbehave to get what they desire, I find the situation more complicated. Occasionally, it's as straightforward as saying, "Grabbing is a mistake. Ask politely and I will hand you the cookie you want." But other times, my children are experimenting with how to use (or abuse) their personal power to get what they want. The lesson here is much more about using power in kind and respectful ways than it is about the specific situation at hand. I need to remind myself during instances like this that it may take years for my children to learn to use their personal power appropriately. It may, in fact, be a lesson we begin in the home and that they take with them out into the world. If this is the case, it is especially important to pace yourself. These are the times when we need to show great levels of compassion both for our children *and* for ourselves. Navigating power struggles and other misuses of personal power requires great clarity on the part of the parent. The calmer and clearer you can be in these situations, the less emotionally loaded it will be for all of you. The *more* emotionally loaded it becomes, the harder it is to express your love. (This is only human.)

As conscientious parents, it behooves us to be aware of the bigger picture so we can act separately from the power of our emotional triggers. For example, if my child has trouble respecting my boundaries (as evidenced by constant pestering or wheedling to get what she wants), I may end up feeling cranky. And yet, I know if I want her to stop this behavior, I must stand firm and kindly show her what boundaries are. Screaming at her or saying "no" five times and then eventually relenting is not going to help. It is only going to make more problems.

My children are quick to show me where my boundaries are weak. They aren't stupid. They naturally head in the direction of least resistance. If I want them to respect my boundaries, I must be firm and consistent in my response when they test these limits. I must also help them to learn about their own boundaries by respecting these boundaries and helping them to realize when they have overstepped their own comfort zone. This situation often comes up for my children in regard to sharing. If they can't share a toy when a friend comes over, our rule is that they must put the toy away until later. Often I find my child trying to control his friend and how he plays with a treasured toy. When this happens, I know my child is feeling, but is unable to articulate, that he can't share that toy right now. It's my job to step in and help by verbalizing his feeling *and* by helping him put the toy away. "It's too hard for you to share that truck today. We are going to put it on the high shelf and you and your friend can choose to play with any of your other toys. Today, the truck is off-limits." It doesn't take too many experiences with this approach before my child begins to anticipate which toys he can comfortably play with that day and then live peacefully within the boundary he has set. What an empowering situation this becomes! Instead of feeling completely out of control and grasping at anything to gain power (and thereby misbehaving), my child has the ultimate power to decide for himself how much he is able to share. And with this kind of power comes grace. His behavior is majestically transformed.

As we move through our days with our children, it is important to remember that each day is only one in a long stream of days in our child's life. If we make a mistake one day, we can apologize the next. Our children can forgive us our imperfections, just as we forgive them theirs. Love is always about give-and-take. Our goal in parenting is to lovingly teach our children the skills they need to be healthy, functioning adults. And the sooner we model and teach our children healthy emotional habits, the sooner they will embody these skills.

Nobody acquires any of these skills in a day, however. We've had our entire lives to learn, while our children are just beginning. We can help them know that learning is a lifelong process if we keep learning, too. We express our love for our children when we expect them to be competent and we teach them how to act in an age-appropriate setting. If we can learn to teach our children these skills without teaching them to excessively judge themselves along the way, we will have shown them unconditional love. They will learn to truly know and love themselves and will be able to truly know and love others in their lives.

It is amazing how many ways there are to say "I love you." What follows is a collection of books and ideas to help us express the all-encompassing love we have for our children.

Baby Angels

by Jane Cowen-Fletcher

When I was young, one of the most reassuring things I was taught was that I had a guardian angel. I still believe I do. And it's clear that many people believe that they, too, have guardian angels. For you who do, this book will nestle its way right into your family's life and be a sweet reminder that we are all protected. A simple text accompanies a troupe of four toddler angels who see to it that their human toddler is never alone—while waking, while bustling around the house and in the yard and even coming in close when there's potential for danger.

Baby angels watch me wake,
follow every move I make.
Baby angels watch me climb,
stop my tumbles every time.

And so on. The colors are soft yet lively. This book is lovely to look at. It is comforting and warm, quietly capturing the aura of blessedness that surrounds the innocent. (1–3 yrs.)

Show your love in little ways. When your child is having a hard time mastering a new skill, sit down beside her and quietly keep her company. Offer your support just by being there. You don't have to offer advice or help. Just be a friendly presence. Our vision of our child offers her just as much as any words ever will. See her as whole and capable, and watch her grow to be just so. Our children know when we believe in them and seek to be worthy of our faith.

A You're Adorable

words and music by Buddy Kaye, Fred Wise and Sidney Lippman illustrated by Martha Alexander

My mother used to sing this song to me. I don't know how far along in life I was before I figured out she hadn't made it up just for me. And I do believe it was my first encounter with the alphabet, too. I never tired of hearing it:

> *A you're adorable;*
> *B you're so beautiful;*
> *C you're a cutie full of charms . . . .*

(Would anyone tire of hearing such a ditty?!)

It went on until "L," which was for the love-light in my eyes, and then worked its way to the end of the alphabet. There was (and is) a set tune to the song, and I think you've probably all heard it at some point in your lives.

This endearing, gentle and unpretentious book adds one more dimension to the sweetness of this old love song: soft and cheery illustrations of children romping through the letters. Your child will love your singing, too. (The melody is included.) My bet is that after a few readings you'll hear your child's voice crooning this tune from somewhere in the house. (10 mos.–3 yrs.)

Owl Babies

by Martin Waddell
illustrated by Patrick Benson

Baby owls may not sound irresistible, but trust me on this one: these owlets will win your heart. Their mother is out finding food. While hunger is definitely an issue, what these little characters want the most is their mommy. Moving closer and closer together on their branch, they face their worry as a threesome, hoping that she'll be back soon. She is, of course, and the reunion is ecstatic. The suspense is delicious (perhaps in part because the story takes place at night), the resolution is heartwarming, and there is just enough repetition in the text to invite your toddler to chime along when the time is right.

The pen-and-ink/watercolor illustrations have a warm and cozy feeling to them, depicting facial expressions and perspectives that will make you and your child smile. (2–4 yrs.)

Runaway Bunny

by Margaret Wise Brown
illustrated by Clement Hurd

Every profession has moments that produce enough stress to make it easy for us to stumble and behave in a less-than-admirable manner. Parenthood is no exception. Even though our intentions are good and our love is whole, we can occasionally catch ourselves acting like creeps. Perhaps it is because the manifestations of unconditional love sometimes seem like such nearly insurmountable challenges that books with this as a theme always appeal to children. What could be more comforting to a child than to know that she (and the Runaway

Bunny, for that matter) will be loved no matter how serious the transgression? This is the story of a bunny who wants to run away but learns that no matter where he goes, no matter what he turns into in order to throw his mother off-course, she will find him and love him anyway. If he becomes a fish in a stream and swims away from her, she will turn into a fisherman and fish for him. If he becomes a sailboat and sails away from her, she tells him she will turn herself into the wind and blow him where she wants him to go. And so on. There is just no getting away from the fact that a mother's love will find you no matter how you test it.

A simple text, vibrant colors and the heartwarming theme of a bunny who will be loved no matter what, all add up to a classic that's been around for fifty years and will doubtless be around for another fifty. (2–4 yrs.)

One day, Elizabeth, Evan and I were picnicking at a park with a group of moms and kids. At one point, we all realized that a couple of the children were missing. We combed the area—rather calmly at first, but the urgency of the moment caused our footsteps to quicken and our calls to become more frantic. They were nowhere in sight, these four-year-old boys! But then, behind a rather dense hedge, they were found playing with their trucks—oblivious to the panic of a second ago and the sheer relief of the present. As has happened before, I was struck with the emotions that such a potential crisis brings out: to have something happen to your child must be the most horrible thing—and in comparison, no other problem, really, is worth getting upset about. It seems that crises are often the catalysts that stir us to hug and appreciate our children. While losing a child, for whatever reason, must be devastating, to allow a child to feel unloved, to allow a child's self-worth to be hacked away or destroyed by our reactions to situations that we perceive as big problems, is a tremendous loss, too—to the child, to you and to humankind. Take your child in your arms right now, when there is no crisis, and let her know how wondrous she is! Live each day as if it were your last with your child, because it really is, you know; she's getting older and changing every single day and will never be exactly the same again.

More More More Said the Baby

3 Love Stories

by Vera Williams

Accompanied by the brightest, happiest watercolor illustrations you'll find anywhere, the three stories in this collection are a bird's-eye view of a few minutes in three babies' lives when loving adults unabashedly demonstrate unmitigated love toward their children. It is amazing how the text can be so incredibly concise, and at the same time portray so exuberantly the joy and abandonment between adult and child.

The artwork is extraordinary: intensely colorful watercolors that result in an extremely visually appealing book, which is also somehow delightfully sensual, because the reader can almost feel the colors and their textures.

If there is any baby or toddler in your life, do *not* miss this book! (1–3 yrs.)

Bunny My Honey

by Anita Jeram

Here is the story of a mother bunny and her baby "who looked just like his mommy, only smaller." Mommy Rabbit likes to call him "Bunny, my Honey" and shows him how to do rabbity things like running and hopping, digging, twitching his nose and thumping his great big feet. He has some pals, too, in the form of a duckling and a mouse, and the three of them play their days away.

One day Bunny ventures out of sight of his friends and finds himself lost in the woods. The more he tries to find his way back, the more lost he gets—until he hears a familiar (motherly) voice calling, "Bunny, my Honey." All ends well with the three young ones and Mommy Bunny safely at home.

Now, this may not sound like much of a plot, but it is in fact a *perfect* first story for a very young child. It shows parental love and devotion, having fun with friends, getting lost (but only momentarily), being found again and then having life return to the safe, loving environment it always has been for him. Just the right amount of suspense and just the right amount of tenderness and all-is-rightness.

Couple this perfect first story with cheery, endearing, cuddly illustrations that just won't quit and you have a wonderful, wonderful book that will hold a treasured spot in your child's library. (1½–3 yrs.)

We constantly influence our children's sense of self by the words we choose when we speak to them. Subtle changes in our phrasing can offer our children a completely different viewpoint of a situation. We can choose words that encourage or words that discourage them. The choice is up to us. Sometimes, depending on how we were spoken to as children, in order to choose encouraging words we have to learn a new vocabulary, and this takes practice. Conscious attention to our wording when we are not upset or overwhelmed will help re-create new speech patterns that affirm our children's essential selves when times are hard. For example, it is easy to discourage a child by saying something like, "You'd better be careful. You know how easy it is to make mistakes." On the other hand, simply stating "You can do it!" and then allowing your child the freedom to try something and yet have the freedom to make a mistake is a very encouraging experience. We parents will never get our wording right all the time, but practice will improve our chances.

Guess How Much I Love You

by Sam McBratney
illustrated by Anita Jeram

Bedtime rituals: the back scratching, the stories, the songs, the innocent and good-natured declarations of "I love you" and "I love you more" in response. There is just something reassuring about how effortless it can be at bedtime to clear up any leftover icky energy that may still be hanging on after a hard day. Unconditional love is alive and well in Little Nutbrown Hare and Big Nutbrown Hare's home.

They have the sweetest mutual admiration society operating at full tilt on this particular night, and we, the readers, can be voyeurs.

The soft pastel watercolors and pen-and-ink drawings make it hard to take our eyes off of this father-son pair. It's Little Nutbrown Hare's bedtime, and he wants to make sure Big knows how much he's loved. And vice versa. Thus begins an arms-stretching-wide, hopping-ever-so-wide, etc., extravaganza demonstrating just how big their love is. And the uncluttered, simple text perfectly conveys in words what the illustrations do visually.

Little's demonstrations are on a smaller scale than Big's simply because of size, but the point is that each loves the other to the max. In a tender moment of calm and quiet, we see the sweetness that invariably comes when a parent finds himself alone with his sleeping child and knows that it just doesn't get any better than this. (2½–5 yrs.)

Have You Seen My Duckling?

by Nancy Tafuri

The dedication page of this big, colorful book depicts a nestful of seven ducklings craning to watch what becomes of the curious and dauntless eighth duckling, who has spotted a butterfly which s/he's following off into the horizon. The dedication reads, "To the little duckling in all of us," an understated reminder of how each of us, in our own way, is a handful.

Thus begins the story of how the mom duck returns to the nest, eyeballs it (we can just *tell* what's going on in her mind: "Oh no! I'm missing a duckling!") and sets out to find her wayward number eight. With her family paddling behind, she queries a bird, beaver, turtle, fish, etc., "Have you seen my duckling?" The most delightful part of the story is how the reader can spot the duckling on each double-page spread, even though the mother duck can't. The little explorer is eventually found, and the last page is an illustration of the family at night, all cozy and complete, sleeping in their nest. This is a wonderful, warm book, with a wonderful, warm feeling. (1½–3 yrs.)

Hug

by Jez Alborough

Heartwarming, undeniably endearing, and nearly wordless, *Hug* is the story of a baby chimp. Passing all of its fellow creatures in the wild, it sees all sorts of parent-child hugs going on. The elephants, hippos, giraffes—they're all happily locked in some sort of embrace. And each time the young chimp sees a hug in progress, it points and exclaims, "Hug!" just as young ones tend to do when they've learned a new word.

But it isn't long before the chimp realizes it is the only one not getting a hug and at that point, with the help of the elephant and its calf, the search begins for the ultimate hug—the hug from Mom. But where *is* she? Not to worry. Eventually the chimp is indeed reunited with his mother.

For the youngster who will be enjoying this lively visual treat of a book, there are pint-size moments of suspense, despair, rejoicing and warmth. Here is a feel-good story if ever there was one. Expressive and colorful illustrations, a theme everyone can relate to and an ending that can't be beat. (1–3½ yrs.)

I Love You, Little One

by Nancy Tafuri

I Love You, Little One is one of those rare books that is contagious: when you finish reading it, you find it impossible not to turn to your child and give him or her a huge hug and kiss. And at that moment you know that love just doesn't get any bigger than it is right then.

This is truly a gem. In it, a handful of baby animals—deer, duck, rabbit, etc.—ask their mothers, "Do you love me, Mama?" In each case, what the mamas say to their babies perfectly communicates how every child wonders about a parent's love, how every child needs to know that love is there and how all-encompassing that love is. At book's end, after the story moves from early morning to nighttime, we see a human mother and child. The same "Do you love me, Mama?"

has been asked. And the mother gives an answer that will ring true to any parent.

The rich, detailed, tender, full-page artwork of some of nature's mother-baby couples makes you want to practically hug the book and not just your child. (2–5 yrs.)

There is something about a cup of warm cocoa that says "I love you." Here is our favorite recipe.

The Ultimate Hot Chocolate Recipe

4 cups milk
1 cup heavy cream
8 oz. good-quality bittersweet chocolate, finely chopped
3 T. sugar

Heat the milk in a large saucepan until almost boiling. Meanwhile whip the cream into soft peaks and set aside. Remove milk from heat and whisk in all but two tsp. of the chocolate. Add the sugar, whisk until foamy. Ladle the hot chocolate into four mugs, top each with a large dollop of whipped cream and sprinkle with remaining chocolate. Serve immediately.

Happy Birth Day!

by Robie H. Harris
illustrated by Michael Emberley

Happy Birth Day! is the first-person account of a mother who has just given birth, and she is telling that day's story to her child.

"I'll never ever forget the moment you were born. Out pushed your head covered with wet and shiny hair. Then the rest of your wet and slippery body slid out and the doctor caught you with both hands. Suddenly, there you were—a whole new person, our baby! We saw all of you from head to toe and we loved you the moment we saw you."

She tells of the first cry that filled her baby's lungs with air, of new skin as soft as wrinkled velvet, of newly opening eyes looking at her face for the first time. She tells of weary but joyful gazes, of tiny fingers grasping big fingers, of parents and newborn finally drifting off to sleep after a very big day.

The graceful, alive illustrations are remarkable. Somehow, their realism makes this baby's birth day and her family's experience of it quite possibly the same as that day in your own life, no matter how different the circumstances and setting. This baby's birth day and welcome is Everybaby's birth day and welcome—or should be, in an ideal world.

Needless to say, this is a fine book for a birth gift or for several birthdays afterward. (2–6 yrs.)

Oh My Baby, Little One

by Kathi Appelt
illustrated by Jane Dyer

You just can't not love this book—its message, its illustrations, everything about it. At first blush it looks to be a beautiful and reassuring picture book about a young child's first days at school. *Oh My Baby, Little One* watches one particular mother and her child as they prepare to part ways for the day. Mother tells her child that the love she has for him is always with him, like the sun is with the sky. Yes, it is always there, nestling in his pocket, even though he won't notice it at all. It's inside his lunch box and under his cap. And so on. The goings-on of a preschool or kindergarten class are chronicled through the day with the reminder of just where her love is at any given moment. But the gears shift, and Mother goes on to tell her child that this love between them is with *her,* too, throughout the day. We watch her at work, and find that the love might hide in her desk drawer or inside her shoe, but that it's always with her, the whole day through.

The text is lyrical, rhyming verse that is both soothing and cheery, perfectly complementing the delightful art. Much more than a book about the first days of school, *Oh My Baby, Little One* creates a sense of the love between mother and child that is always there, perhaps not visible or articulated, but there nevertheless. (3+ yrs.)

Love Is . . .

adapted from the Bible
illustrated by Wendy Anderson Halperin

This intriguing book has so much going for it that it is truly daunting to describe it adequately enough to give you its true feeling and depth. It is exquisitely detailed in its illustrations, refreshingly simple in its text and magnificently deep in its meaning.

Celebrated illustrator Wendy Anderson Halperin has taken the definitions of "love" from 1 Corinthians 13 in the New Testament and has illustrated different scenarios for each of the verses. Across each two-page spread is a single verse such as "Love is patient. Love is kind." On the left-hand page, we see several illustrated examples of what it means *not* to be patient or kind, while the facing right-hand page illustrates the same scenes now reconfigured to demonstrate the alternative. For instance, in one box there's a father mouse looking pretty harried and exasperated standing by his son and his two-wheeler. On the right-hand page, we see patience and kindness in action in the coordinating box with the same father mouse helping his son onto the bicycle. Only this time, they both have smiles on their faces. In addition to the coordinating pictures on each spread, there are also illustrations of ongoing scenarios that evolve over the course of the book. The detail is remarkable—so generous that you will spend quite some time on each spread if you are so inclined.

Love Is . . . is simply one book that must be experienced visually to fully appreciate. And once you do experience it, there's so much to look at and talk about that I'll bet you'll be enjoying it with your child for years and years to come. (3+ yrs.)

An apology is a remarkable thing. It opens the door for forgiveness an builds bridges when feelings have been hurt. When you have made a mistake in dealing with your child, have the courage to say you're sorry. Get down on bended knee, take your child's hand in yours and look him straight in the eye. Tell him exactly what you did that was wrong and apologize. "Honey, when I saw the broken vase and your ball lying right next to it, I assumed you had broken it. I was angry and yelled at you for breaking my special vase. You said you didn't do it, but I didn't believe you. I thought you were lying and sent you to your room. Later Daddy told me he saw the cat break the vase. I had jumped to conclusions and was wrong. I'm really sorry. I'm sorry to have yelled and sent you to your room and I'm especially sorry that I didn't believe you when you were telling the truth. Telling the truth is so important." Having the integrity and courage to be responsible for our mistakes encourages our children to follow our example. The next time they have to own up to one of their mistakes, we will make their job easier for having modeled a gracious apology. And, best of all, apologies make *us* feel so much better. Think how much kinder a place the world would be if we all took responsibility for our actions and apologized when necessary.

Mama, Do You Love Me?

by Barbara M. Joosse
illustrated by Barbara Lavallee

Children love hearing, indeed must hear, that they are loved no matter what. From early on, they must internalize that it is their behavior that sometimes is not lovable, but that they, as persons, will always be appreciated.

This book beautifully conveys the message of unconditional love and in an extraordinary setting, at that. It is a universal story of a child who tests the limits of her independence and learns that a parent's love is always there and everlasting. Set during an interchange between an Inuit mother and daughter, the story is of a child who is re-assured that no matter what behavior prompted her mother to be angry or worried or sorry, she will still love her daughter, no questions asked.

The book has a well-researched glossary that brings meaning to the text, and the illustrations, set in the Arctic, are lovely and rich in color. Its beauty makes its appeal universal. (2–6 yrs.)

Tucking Mommy In

by Morag Loh
illustrated by Donna Rawlins

The hectic pace at which many of us live our lives makes for utter ex-haustion—both physical and emotional—at day's end.

This exhausted mommy tells her bathing daughters that as soon as she tucks them in, she's going to bed herself, because she "can't think straight." (Sound familiar at all?) And sure enough, Mommy passes right out, even before the end of the story that her elder daughter has compassionately offered to tell as her stand-in.

The only problem is that Mommy's still in her clothes, and Jenny and Sue must deal with what is the equivalent of a sack of potatoes in order to get her moved to her own bed and into her nightgown. Mis-sion is accomplished, just in time for them to proudly tell their dad, upon his arrival home from his night-shift job, that *they* have just tucked Mommy in! A gentle "thank you" from him, an extra bed-time story even and then a proper "good night" from Daddy finish this sweet story.

Few things are probably more special to a young child than see-ing her mommy so vulnerable and sleepy that she falls right asleep even before her child. This gentle book captures that rare moment with respect and wonder, allowing all members of the family to rise to the occasion, at their loving best. Subtle yet strong colored pencil illustrations manage to delightfully deepen the book's sweet spirit. (3–6 yrs.)

When Mama Comes Home Tonight

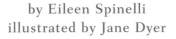

by Eileen Spinelli
illustrated by Jane Dyer

With sentiments from earlier, less complicated times, this quiet, loving book takes the reader and child away to a place that is so easy to forget in today's fast-paced world. It is a late-afternoon and evening place of serenity, simplicity and moments that evolve at a humane momentum, rather than at the crazy speed we have become used to.

When Mama Comes Home Tonight is a gentle and reassuring account of one mama and one child who are reunited when Mama comes home from work. The rhyming, rhythmic story follows the two as soup and applesauce are served, pat-a-cake is played, a few moments are spent looking out the window at the street, counting the cars that go by, wishing upon stars and so forth.

Jane Dyer's illustrations complement this mood seamlessly. Mother and child are not only engaged in quiet, basic goings-on, their appearance is reminiscent of a couple of generations ago. The overall feeling is evocative of comfort, safety and peace—things that every human being longs for. (1–3 yrs.)

The Way Mothers Are

by Miriam Schlein
illustrated by Joe Lasker

The down-to-earth interchanges between Little One, a rambunctious little tomkitten, and his mother makes the concept of unconditional love real both for our children and for us.

Little One asks, "Mother, do you love me?" Mother Cat answers, "Yes, I do." But Little One goes on to ask, "Why do you love me when sometimes I am naughty and run away when you are trying to dress me?" Mother Cat answers in a gentle way, reaffirming her love for Little One. When Little One continues giving example after example of naughty behavior and asking how she can love him when he misbehaves, Mother Cat assures him each time that she loves him regardless of whether he's good or bad. Turning the tables, she asks Little One why *he* thinks she loves him. He answers, but the essence of her response is simply that he is her very own little one and she loved him right from the moment he was born. "That's the way mothers are," she says.

This sweet book explains a confusing concept (unconditional love) in a simple and direct manner. Our children deeply want to feel loved and at the same time they know how hard it is to be good all the time. It is so comforting for them to understand that they do not have to earn our love.

Mother Cat looks happy, exasperated, tired, loving, busy, at the end of her rope and at times flabbergasted—just like real mothers look. Little One exhibits the whole range of behaviors preschoolers are capable of (often in just one afternoon!). In short, Lasker's paintings capture true life with young ones with warmth and vitality. This is a lovely, lovely book with a message that every child needs to hear. (2–5 yrs.)

If you ever forget what unconditional love looks or feels like, look to your child. Our children are amazing models of love for us. No matter what we do, or how far we fall from our ideal as a parent, our child will always love us. Remarkably enough, even severely abused children generally love their parents. If *they* can love and hope and dream that their parents will reciprocate that love someday soon, imagine how strong the love is in children who haven't endured abuse! Children may be angry in the moment, but they know how to forgive, and soon their hearts are radiating their love for us. Their love is like a beacon calling us home.

No Matter What

by Debi Gliori

We parents all know that we'll love our children no matter what. And we do our best to be living examples of that commitment, even when our children aren't acting very lovable. Over the past several years there have been some wonderful books reinforcing the idea that unconditional love does exist and what it looks like in a child's eyes and experience. As parents we really can't be given that image too many times, as we really are learning as we go along.

No Matter What is about Small, who begins the book as a grim and grumpy young—um—fox? who runs the gamut of behavior that tests the limits of his parent's patience. All the while Large, his parent (maybe mother, maybe father—the illustrations are noncommittal), stays calm, shows what better behavior looks like and acts with kindness to eventually assure Small that, no matter what, he (or she, if you wish) will still be loved.

Steering well clear of the saccharine or cloying (not easy to do when you're talking about unconditional love to a child), *No Matter What* has a cheery, offbeat thread running through it that lightens up the whole subject. If you spend a little time taking in the illustrations, you'll find that they are a sweet blend of cheeriness and warmth, with the last pages veritably swelling with shared love between Large and Small as the young one comes to understand that no matter what, he is loved. (3–5 yrs.)

On Mother's Lap

by Ann Herbert Scott
illustrated by Glo Coalson

Put yourself in the shoes of a young child and ponder one of life's biggest and scariest questions: will there always be room on Mother's lap? Little Michael seems to have never had to worry about this.

He, along with his favorite things, Boat, Dolly and Puppy, have always been welcome there—rocking back and forth, back and forth. It is a cold, quiet, shadowy afternoon somewhere in the far North among the Inuit. While Michael's baby sister naps, he has his mother all to himself. Until the infant awakes and wants to be held, that is. Both the reader and Michael wonder how there will be room for everyone and everything on Mother's lap. Somehow we know she'll find a way.

Our confidence in this—even before it happens— says much about the spirit in which this book is written. Mother's love shines through, as does her calming presence and wisdom. Briefly insecure and unhappy about giving up sole possession of his mother and sharing with his little sister, Michael is Everysibling. Yet he sees that there has really been nothing to worry about. There *is* room on Mother's lap.

This lovely book is expressive in both words and illustrations, done in rich, earthy colors. It has a sleepy, lulling feeling to it, comforting and reassuring our children that they can always depend on our love. (2½–5 yrs.)

Dear Friends,

As I write this, nine-year-old Evan's "Family Tree" school project, due today, is sitting on the dining room table. It is supposed to be with him on the school bus right now. I'm wondering if he's realized yet that he's forgotten it. I think I should know in about twenty minutes, when he gets to school. If things unfold as they usually do when Evan forgets to bring some-

thing from home, the telephone will ring at about seven-fifty and he will be on the other end, frantically explaining why he needs me to drive whatever it is to school for him.

I know. This has happened before. Today I've decided that if he calls, I'm going to tell him I won't be delivering it. Why? Because to consistently fix his mistakes for him is doing more harm than good. It's as simple as that. But yuck! Do I feel like an ogre, or what? It's one of those classic cases of "it's going to hurt me more than it's going to hurt you." This whole business of teaching responsibility is probably one of the hardest parts of parenting. But responsibility is so intricately woven into how a person functions in society, his self-respect and the ability to feel capable and in control of his own destiny that I know it is something that needs constant tending to, no matter how distasteful.

When the phone rings, I'll dread picking it up and explaining to Evan that putting his homework in his backpack is his responsibility, not mine, and that I'm not going to bail him out this time. For fleeting moments, I wonder if I'm doing the right thing. (I know in my heart that I am, but I feel like such a meanie!) I even call my husband at work to run it by him and to get moral support. We talk about "natural consequences" and how we've been pretty good about letting Evan experience what happens when he doesn't pay attention. He's seen the consequences of not putting his dirty laundry in the hamper: no clean clothes when he needed them. He's experienced what happened when he left his tools out in the rain: a coating of rust. And he's seen firsthand how overindulging in chocolate chip cookies made him feel really lousy. So many of those lessons were grueling for us to watch him go through, yet it had to be done, we told ourselves. But this was going to be a biggie, because we, his parents, were going to be implicated as part of the natural consequence in our refusal to fix a problem for him.

Parenting doesn't get much harder than when we have to watch our children learn what works and doesn't work in life. We try so fervently to protect them from pain, but in doing so, we're often robbing them of the opportunity to experience it in a small way so that down the road, they may not have to experience it in a big way. For them to know that we're willing to give them more control over their lives with each day they get older—if they show us they can handle it—is one of the very greatest gifts we can give them. It's just that when we're teaching them about this control and responsibility, it often feels more as if we're torturing them than giving them a gift. I tell myself over and over this morning that if I don't come to Evan's rescue when he calls, it will teach him an important lesson about being accountable for his own actions. As the minutes tick by (and in one of those giant steps of logic that parents get so good at taking as they toss things about in their heads and second-guess themselves!), I can even see how I should be "thankful" for these small crises, because they offer opportunities for the lessons of life to at least be routed through his parents, who love him more than anybody does. It is we who can buffer the learning process with empathy and understanding. If our children don't learn to be responsible while we are their teachers, they'll run into much harsher lessons down the road.

So here I sit by the telephone, "Family Tree" project in front of me. My mind is swimming, but my heart knows what I must do when Evan calls. Then, to my surprise, I notice that the morning is half over, and the phone hasn't rung! I wonder if, by any chance, he won't be calling at all. Nope. No way! He spent too much time on that project to just let it slide. But perhaps, just perhaps, I tell myself, the days of expecting Mom to fix everything when he messes up are over. In which case, all this worry and soul-searching has been for naught, and instead, it should be a day for quiet celebration as a parent: one of life's most important lessons, the one about responsibility, seems to be sinking in.

Opening Up the World of Words

Poetry and Imagination

Human beings are born with a great deal of creativity, and by the age of twelve, we've lost most of it. The world just slams it out of us. Our teachers and parents tell us that what comes from our imagination isn't true; it's just "imaginary." I think that what's imaginary is truer than what's "real." Adults prefer facts, because facts are limited. Like truth, imagination is unlimited, so many people are afraid of it.

—Madeleine L'Engle

From those beginning little bubbles and burbles, to the time when you hear your child utter that first "Mama" or "Papa," to that astonishing moment when you hear him express a full idea in words, few experiences in parenting can match the exhilaration of watching a child acquire language. A young one's mastery of the spoken word almost feels like a magical process. One day baby's "pa pa pa" is just a sound and then suddenly the next day Papa walks into the room and baby gleefully coos "pa pa pa" in direct recognition of his father. What a thrill!

As parents, we do so much to encourage our child's language acquisition. Talking to him as we go about our day, pointing out simple concepts as we play with him, or even just smiling at him as he practices making sounds—we have so many opportunities to encourage our child's growth. Our enthusiastic responses to simple verbalizations help him learn. With careful listening, we discern new sounds and help the child associate meaning with his vocalizations by our positive reactions. Our delighted responses illicit more sounds from baby and soon he's learning language at an unbelievable pace. I remember my astonishment as Becca was learning to talk. There didn't appear to be enough words in the world for her to learn. It was all such a marvel to me that I found myself compelled to keep a long list of those words she had newly acquired. Watching the whole process unfold was just so absorbing! And the funny thing is, fourteen years later, when Aidan was learning to talk, my older girls, all of their own accord, posted a list of Aidan's words on the inside of a closet. Each day, they, too, kept close track of his growing vocabulary. Clearly, they were as mesmerized by the process of Aidan's language acquisition as I was by Becca's.

Each child will learn language at his own pace and in his own way. It is quite common, though not a constant, that a first child will learn language much earlier than a second child will. There are many theories as to why this may be, but the important thing is to avoid comparing one child with another. Each one is an individual, and our job as parents is to marvel at and honor their individuality, not judge or compare their differences, however tempting it may be. Looking back at my four children, I can see a direct correlation between each child's language acquisition style and who they are as people today. Becca has always been quick to learn and full of words, and here she is, an English major in college. Laura, who learned verbs first (a highly unusual way to learn speech), has been on the go ever since she was in utero. (I had a bone bruise on one of my ribs for four months due to her wild intrauterine kicking!) "Doing" and "going" are what largely define her day. Nothing could stop her then and nothing does now. It makes perfect sense that she learned verbs first: they helped her get where she wanted to go. Heidi, in keeping with *her* way, learned words in a calm, commonsense fashion. With very little drama, she wisely proceeded to learn the practical words she could use every day. This characterizes much of what she is like today, steadfast and reliable. Aidan enthusiastically chattered as a toddler and he still chatters to this day. He engages the world of language earnestly and energetically. It is too early to tell what he will be like when he is older, but there is no doubt about his enthusiasm. All this is not to say that children don't change as they mature, yet the style they use to learn language, or approach any other new thing in their lives (i.e., crawling, walking, swimming, making friends, etc.), can give you many clues about their innate temperament, clues that can help you better comprehend and parent your child. Does your young one jump right in, happy to make mistakes? Or is he more cautious, checking things out before he tries something new? Are transitions easy for your child or hard? It's amazing what you see when you start to watch for patterns.

Understanding how your child approached learning to speak can assist you when he is learning to read. Laura, for example, is a kinesthetic learner (what a surprise, eh?). At first we didn't worry too much about her late start in reading because it was so obvious she was a bright, curious child, but as the years passed and she still wasn't reading well, we became concerned. Her teacher, one of the wisest women I know, never worried. She knew Laura would learn when she was ready and did her best to accommodate her pupil's special needs. We were fortunate that Laura's teacher was able to adapt her teaching style to address Laura's learning style directly. She had a small class and a great deal of control over her curriculum. Consequently, Laura's learning curve skyrocketed once people stopped expecting her to behave like a more linear, sit-quietly type of child.

Not all children or teachers are so fortunate. Most teachers don't have the opportunity to be so flexible. Schools are crowded and often filled with kids with a wide variety of difficult problems, both at home and in school. It is my experience that the majority of teachers are among the hardest-working, most caring people on the planet. Most of them genuinely love kids or they wouldn't be teaching. The system in which they work makes everything hard. As parents, we have to work as a team with our child's teachers. We need to expect to step in when needed and help. We can start by establishing a working relationship with the teacher, sharing what we know about our child and listening carefully to what insights the teacher has to offer. Together, we can make schools work better for our children.

Parents are in the unique position of being able to know their child almost as intimately as anyone will ever know another person. This unique understanding emerges when we choose to really "see" our child, instead of imposing our own preconceived ideas (or judgments) on him. Our unique knowledge allows us to be better advocates for him as he begins to negotiate the bigger world. A kindergarten or first-grade teacher who understands that moving around may actually help a wiggly child focus will be much more understanding of such a student. This teacher will know that wiggling gives to, rather than takes away from, a kinesthetic learner's ability to concentrate. Some children wiggle because they can't behave. Some children wiggle because they are *trying* to behave. The wise parent and teacher will work together to discern which is the case and take appropriate action. Even highly kinesthetic kids need to learn how to adapt themselves to the classroom. Can they tap their toes instead of wiggling their whole body?

Parents can help their child negotiate both sides of any situation life offers him. How can he fit better into the situation (i.e., wiggling the toes and not the torso) *and* how can we make the world better fit our child? This is a balance that will be harder for some children than others, but by helping our child figure out his own personal balance we empower him, rather than make him feel bad for being who he is. After years of helping Laura do this, I see that she now can do it for herself in high school. (I know it is really hard to imagine your three-year-old as a high school junior, but believe me, the time passes quickly and the skills you model for your small child are the skills she will be using herself later. So bear with me here.) If Laura finds herself in a class with an instructor who teaches in such a way that makes it really hard for her to learn, she goes straight to the counseling office to politely talk the situation over with her guidance counselor. Over time, he has come to trust her judgment and generally moves her to a more appropriate class when he can. She, in turn, does her part by behaving in class and participating to her fullest capacity, even in the classes that can't be switched for one reason or another. Laura and the school are working together to create a win-win situation for themselves. Laura is able to advocate for herself now *because* we started teaching her how to understand her essential nature as a small child and because we continually modeled what we hoped she would learn about herself.

Fortunately, more and more schools (and teachers) are incorporating the relatively new learning style research into their curricula. It takes a while for a teacher to know a child well enough to identify a learning style. As a parent you can help, especially if your child has a style that doesn't fit particularly well in school (such as a child who learns by moving). And if he is the wiggly, kinesthetic type, knowing this will help you find a school more appropriate for your child's essential self. You'll also be able to help him learn to "wiggle appropriately" so he doesn't distract or disturb the other students in class. As your child nears school age, it can be helpful to read some of the books that explain learning styles, such as *In Their Own Way* by Thomas Armstrong, *How Your Child Is Smart* by Dawna Markova or *A Mind at a Time* by Mel Levine.

Parents are remarkably important when it comes to their child's ability to attain literacy. Do you read to her on a regular basis? Is reading done for fun, not dependent on her behavior on a particular day? Does she see you reading regularly? Do you read a variety of things so your child can see how useful reading is? Do you continue to read to her after she learns to read? The desire to read isn't "wired in," as the desire to speak is. We can spark this desire (and thereby greatly increase the likelihood of a child being a good reader) by our behavior. The model of reading we set, as parents, will highly influence our young one's desire to learn to read. Our family has books all over our house. And even Laura, who easily could have been a child who would not have developed into a very good reader, is now a voracious reader. It just took her time to come to it. In the meantime, we read to her as much as we could. We used audiotapes that allowed her to hear those wonderful stories that she couldn't yet read. If reading is hard for you, do you let your child know that and show her how you are working to be a better reader today? Your child may have the exact opposite experience of Laura and be an early reader. If so, you have the added responsibility of finding emotionally appropriate books for highly capable readers. Just because he can read Dickens at age six doesn't mean he should. Wherever your child falls on the reading continuum, it is so important to make emotionally supportive choices.

The best way for him to discover the magic of words is for him to be right by your side. Listening and enjoying books with a parent, day after day, will foster a love of books that no amount of phonics can ever replace. It is the love of books and the love of a good story that keep a child reading, not being the first kid on the block to master the alphabet. Most teachers can tell you that the kids who were early readers in kindergarten aren't necessarily the ones devouring books in sixth grade. Over time, late readers may often emerge into some of the best readers of all (especially if they are allowed to mature at their own pace without feeling bad about themselves). If you want your child to love to read, read to him regularly and show him just how magical the world of books really is. Once it is clear that books are the key to amazing worlds and stores of information, life will never be the same.

The world of poetry, imagination and the playful use of words will inspire your child's lifelong love of language. Here is a collection of books and ideas to help develop the love of language.

 Hand Rhymes

collected and illustrated by Marc Brown

There's just something about this book, and once you sit down with your child and actually do the hand rhymes, you will see why it is "classic" material. From the very youngest child it will evoke those deep-down baby chuckles. From older children it will produce enthusiasm and delight that are impossible to match with just any old book.

Here are fourteen illustrated hand rhymes with clear "prompts" for what to do with your hands and body while reciting the rhyme. And of course, it's that interactive, physical aspect that puts *Hand Rhymes* in a class largely of its own. It is irresistibly illustrated in bright but delicate watercolors and contains the winning combination of engaging critters and happy kids' faces.

Should an older child be happening by when you're reading this to your young one, my bet is that the "big kid" will stick around for a while. The fun is contagious. (6 mos.–5 yrs.)

Some of my favorite times with my children have been times spent with books. The hours we have spent curled up on the couch or tucked in bed reading a good book have enriched our lives beyond measure. Because I was willing to keep reading as my children got older, they were exposed to many stories they never would have read themselves—beautifully written, older "classics" were enjoyed by us all and incorporated into our family's language. When someone had been really naughty, we often jokingly wondered aloud whether she deserved the "black spot," an allusion to Robert Louis Stevenson's *Treasure Island*, a book we greatly enjoyed as a family read-aloud.

As your child grows, stretch his listening abilities by offering him longer, more challenging books. If he has trouble listening to a chapter book, go slowly, but persist. Mix up your reading by alternating between an easy chapter book and favorite picture books. Most five- and six-year-olds (and some four-year-olds) can handle longer, more complicated books if you introduce denser-text books gently. Young children often love funny books about animals and books with short chapters. *Babe, The Gallant Pig* and *Pigs Might Fly* by Dick King-Smith; *Little House in the Big Woods* by Laura Ingalls Wilder; or *Ralph and the Motorcycle* by Beverly Cleary are wonderful first chapter books. If chapter books seem to be too much of a jump for your child, keep reading picture books but gradually increase the amount of text. The pictures will keep him focused and the increased text will stretch his mind. Good listening skills are an important building block for reading.

Each Peach, Pear, Plum

by Janet and Allan Ahlberg

In this singsongy little treasure of a book, the softly colored illustrations exude cheeriness. The idea here is to play an "I Spy" game with your babe. "Each peach, pear, plum . . . I spy Tom Thumb" faces a detailed-packed page wherein Tom can be found if one looks hard enough. Then "Tom Thumb in the cupboard, I spy Mother Hubbard" shows a challengingly hidden Tom along with Mother. And so on.

In the end, everyone gathers together for one last hurrah before you close the book. *Each Peach, Pear, Plum* is especially good for pointing to and naming objects because there is so much detail. The gently colored illustrations are calming to view, page after page. (1–3 yrs.)

Some Things Go Together

by Charlotte Zolotow
illustrated by Ashley Wolff

Some of us grew up with the first incarnation of this book. It's taken on new life with Ashley Wolff's vibrant and lively illustrations, but if you've heard the ditty "Some Things Go Together" even once, I don't think you'll forget it.

> *Peace with dove*
> *Home with love*
> *Gardens with flowers*
> *Clocks with hours*
> *Moths with screen*
> *Grass with green. . . .*

. . . and so on. This is an absolutely enchanting, magical and calming book to read with a young child. Deceptively simple in text, it is everything you could hope for when you consider the lilting rhyme, the concept of things going together, familiar objects, the illustrations that invite pointing to and naming, and the way the whole book ends with a gorgeous spread of a mother and child lying in a field of flowers:

> *Sky with blue*
> *and*
> Me
> *with*
> You!

A memorable classic adorned in perfect attire. (18 mos.–3 yrs.)

Don't forget the magic in a came-from-your-own-heart, straight-out-of-your-imagination, in-your-own-words story. The "Mommy (or Daddy), tell me a story" kind of story. It's a completely different experience from reading a book to your child and I heartily recommend it!

Some of our family's closest times together revolved around that kind of thing. There was a stately old beat-up chair in toddler Elizabeth's room that she named "The Story Chair," for it was where she sat every single night while I told her the animal-filled, gentleness-infused original tale of Whoopie the Whale. (The story was really lame, but she absolutely insisted on it at both naptime and bedtime.) And then there was Evan, whose taste in stories I never quite got a handle on until I learned to routinely ask him to tell me three things he wanted his story to be about that night. (His answer was generally along the lines of "a boy, a policeman and a robot" or "a snake, a bomb and a boy.") Within about ten minutes, I'd told him his made-to-order story, he'd drifted off and I was left in the quiet of the night to caress his back, run my hand through his hair and be full of wonder at the lessons he was teaching me, my heart welling over with love for this tired little boy.

Jamberry

by Bruce Degen

I'm not sure when a book can be officially designated a classic, but surely if *Jamberry* isn't one yet, it will be soon enough. The book pictures a boy and a bear and eventually other animals cavorting in berry country accompanied by a singsongy sort of text:

> *One berry, two berry,*
> *pick me a blueberry.*
> *Hatberry, shoeberry*
> *in my canoeberry.*
> *Three berry, four berry,*
> *hayberry, strawberry.*
> *Finger and pawberry,*
> *my berry, your berry.*

You get the drift. Rollicking, colorful illustrations grace every page. Not too long, the book is perfect for the attention span of the child, who will giggle all the way through this berry nonsense. (1–4 yrs.)

Animal Crackers

A Delectable Collection of Pictures, Poems
and Lullabies for the Very Young

collected and illustrated by Jane Dyer

I love this book. Wish I had had it for my babies years ago. It brings together some of Mother Goose's best, along with other wonderful poems and bedtime nuggets, to make a fine volume that can live in a family for years. (Actually, if I had had *Animal Crackers* for my children, I might never have started Chinaberry. As many of you know, it was in response to a particular Mother Goose book with a questionable [in my mind] selection of nursery rhymes that I set about finding gentler, more nurturing things to read to my babies. Chinaberry was born as a result. If *Animal Crackers* had been our first encounter with Mother Goose, I would have been blissfully satisfied, thinking all children's books were just as wonderful, which, sadly, they aren't.)

This anthology contains the cream of the crop. Both classic, old standbys, as well as contemporary poems, celebrate babies' and toddlers' favorite things, along with significant moments in their lives. ABC's, numbers, colors, shapes, the seasons, food, animals, nursery rhymes, playtime and bedtime are all covered here. And Jane Dyer's detailed, magical, richly colored artwork is unquestionably half of the fun.

Every child should have the opportunity to hear the best of Mother Goose, and this book is just that. A fine birth or soon-thereafter gift, it will be appreciated for years to come. (1–4 yrs.)

Catch Me and Kiss Me and Say It Again

by Clyde and Wendy Watson

With absolutely irresistible rhymes and illustrations of chubby-faced kids, notably a big sister and little brother, this book has amassed quite a following over the years. There's a blurb on the back of the book that says it "has rhymes that turn everything into a game like the touch of gold" and that hits the nail on the head.

Catch Me and Kiss Me and Say It Again is about days in the lives of small children—days that are so much alike, yet so different. Waking up, getting dressed, cuddling, eating, bathing—these things that make up a day are lovingly and cheerily put into rhyme that is contagiously fun to read. A dear illustration of a mommy nibbling on her baby's fist while the baby giggles with delight goes like this:

> *Fee, Fie, Fo, Fum . . .*
> *A gingerbread baby; Come, dearie, come.*
> *First I'll eat the fingers; And then I'll eat the toes*
> *Yes sirree sirrah, sir; And the cherry for a nose.*

You will find remarkable read-aloud fun about the sweetness and, yes, the sometimes topsy-turviness of life with small children. Try not to miss out on this gem, even though you have to search for it because, as of this point in time, it is out of print. (1–5 yrs.)

Ideas for Reading to Very Young Children

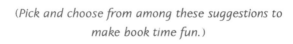

(Pick and choose from among these suggestions to make book time fun.)

The most important thing to remember is that you can customize your book reading to accommodate the needs of your child. You can experiment to find ways to make book time enjoyable for both of you.

♥ If your child tends to be squirmy when you're reading, try *not* reading the text and use your own words instead. Try pointing to the objects on the page while the text "talks" about them. If necessary, disregard the text and talk about the pictures in your own words instead. In many cases, books with singsongy texts will probably be the first ones your child will actually sit through while you read the real text.

♥ Put "life" into the reading with your voice. Be expressive. Give different voices to different characters.

♥ Move your fingers across the page to show that movement is taking place. (As reading adults, we take so much for granted concerning what we "see" in books. Remember that a child has to learn to shift from 2D into the 3D that life really is.)

♥ You might find that your child enjoys book time more if each time you "read" a book, you talk about the same things using the same words. Children love repetition and enjoy it when you say something they expect you to say, and remember, they adore the sound of your voice.

♥ If parts of an illustration aren't familiar to your child's world yet, introduce new objects a few at a time, but be sure that you frequently point to and talk about them (eyes, animals, moon, etc.). Gradually expose your child to more new objects in the illustrations, pointing them out whenever you see them, both in books and in daily life. Anything you do to encourage your child to participate in the story, either while reading or after the fact, by pointing out real-life objects that you've seen illustrated on a page, will enhance enjoyment of the book.

♥ Just talk about the pictures, and don't stay on one page too long. (Four or five seconds is often long enough for the inexperienced listener.) Don't have high expectations of reading all of the book! Soon enough you'll no longer be talking about single objects on the page, but about relationships of characters, for instance, or what caused this or that. You may be pleased to find a little "story" tucked away in a corner, put there by the artist for the observant.

♥ Start with easy-to-read, bright, simple and maybe even aesthetically unappealing (to you, anyway) picture books. Children often need to learn over time to appreciate the classy, beautiful art in so many children's books. Introduce these kinds of books often among your favorites, and when s/he's about twelve to eighteen months old, teach your child to turn pages.

♥ If your child is still at the point of needing you to zip right through page-turning at a pretty good clip (to hold her interest), you might find that you shouldn't bother reading text with a plot. Talk about the pictures instead, and forget the plot for now. Do remember, though, that a book generally recommended for much older children can be used with a toddler if you use the book creatively.

♥ Use the book the way *you* want to use it. For instance: you don't have to teach numbers to a one-year-old with that beautiful

counting book. Just talk about the pictures instead. You don't have to read what the book says. If the story includes a particular event or emotion you'd rather not present, make up your own version. Children over sixteen months particularly enjoy self-concept books emphasizing "me"; at around two years, make-believe is grasped and immensely enjoyed.

 When you don't feel like reading, remember that many requests for book time are merely indications that your child wants to sit and cuddle. Pick a familiar book and let the child take in the illustrations, having *him* indicate when to turn the page. You may find that he simply repeats all you've ever said!

(With gratitude to Anita West for her assistance with these tips.)

 ## 17 Kings and 42 Elephants

by Margaret Mahy
illustrated by Patricia McCarthy

If you read this book aloud once or twice to yourself, you will be richly rewarded when you read it aloud to your child the first time. There is a certain cadence that, when found, makes this the very special book that it is.

It is the story of a handful of kings and—you guessed it—some elephants traipsing through the jungle to who knows where, but who cares? What makes this one of our all-time favorites is the fun of the text, which is rhyming and nonsensical and rhythmic and, well, just *delicious* to read aloud! It's contagious, it's silly and will be well loved. Illustrated with beautiful, richly colored batik paintings on silk. (1½–4 yrs.)

Insectlopedia

poems and paintings by Douglas Florian

This book is nothing short of brilliant! It's as simple as that. And the most wonderful thing about its brilliance is that both children *and* adults can appreciate it equally.

On second thought, perhaps the most wonderful thing about *Insectlopedia* is that it is a scrumptious and lively collection of original poetry (with an insect bent) that might make a lifelong poetry lover of just about anybody. Both old and young alike will be amused and mesmerized by Florian's catchy and artful arrangement of words into poetry, yes, but even sometimes art itself! Take this:

The Army Ants

> *Left*
> > *Right*
> *Left*
> > *Right*
> *We're army ants.*
> *We swarm.*
> > *We fight.*
> *We have no home.*
> *We roam.*
> *We race.*
> *You're lucky if*
> *We miss your place.*

There are twenty-one poems about a variety of common and not-so-common bugs, all of which are quirky and fun. But when the text of the poems starts to take on the shape of the insect, as it does with "The Inchworm" (picture a line of words in the shape of an inchworm as it bends into an upside-down U), then you've got more going on than simple poetry. Couple all of this creativity with lavish and offbeat art, and you've got a book that I don't think you'll ever tire of reading and your child will never tire of hearing. (2 ½ + yrs.)

In these days of educational television, computer games designed for preschoolers and accelerated reading programs, it is easy to feel as if you must expose your child to a hearty dose of media for him to be ready for school. And while educational TV may be quite useful for some families, programmed media is by no stretch of the imagination the only (or best) way to prepare your child for school. Playing with language (what four- or five-year-old doesn't love to come up with silly lists of rhyming words?), getting outside to hop, skip and jump, reading children's poetry to explore the many ways language can be used and reading to your child, period, are all excellent ways to help your child be ready to enter school without the help of television. We can do much at home to encourage the growth of our children's focus and attention span. Reading that extra story your three-year-old requests has hidden benefits that researchers have yet to announce, but we parents know in our hearts. Attention spans grow with practice, especially when practicing the things we are interested in! Letting our child become engrossed in his interests, whether it be building with Legos, watching bugs or playing with dolls, develops focus—focus that can later be translated into the staying power it takes to master a difficult math problem or vocabulary word. The more opportunities our children have to interact with their world, rather than simply watch it passively (as when they sit and watch TV), the more they learn. Each time they build pictures in their minds from the stories we read to them, they stretch their imaginations. And a strong imagination is an essential building block for the critical thinking skills that school (and life) will soon require of them.

Mammalabilia

poems and paintings by Douglas Florian

Take all of my superlatives from *Insectlopedia*, think "mammal" instead of "insect," and plug them in here. Now you have *Mammalabilia*. Here's an example of what can be found here.

The Ibex

The daring ibex risk their necks
On scary, airy mountain treks.
Each one must climb with skill complex,
Or else become an ex ibex.

(Just a bit simpler than its predecessor, this book is appropriate for those aged 2+ yrs.)

Millions of Cats

by Wanda Gag

This book's been going strong for over fifty years, delighting children with the story and line drawings of an incredible number of cats. Plenty of children will relate easily to the man who intends to adopt one kitty, but can't resist taking them all home: "hundreds of cats, thousands of cats, millions and billions and trillions of cats!" You might take one look at this simple book and want to dismiss it because it isn't visually flashy, but refrain from any judgments until you sit down with your child and read it. Honestly, it's a delight!

Those of you who remember *Millions of Cats* from your childhood will probably be happy to know it's still around. (2–5 yrs.)

Tikki Tikki Tembo

by Arlene Mosel
illustrated by Blair Lent

If I had to name the most fun read-alouds to ever hit our home, *Tikki Tikki Tembo* would certainly be among our favorites. It combines deliciously smooth text with a story that contains just enough plot and suspense to enable the book to survive as a favorite long after others may have come and gone from the "read every day" (or more!) list. It is a folktale of how the Chinese came to give all of their children short names. This family's firstborn son is called Tikki tikki tembo-no sa rembo-chari bari ruchi-pip peri pembo. (Go on. Read that aloud and you'll get an idea of the outrageousness that has made this book endure for so many years.) The story concerns how he pays his dues for having a name a mile long.

Illustrated with watercolors that delightfully complement the Asian origins of the folktale, it is a book you just might eventually know by heart. (2–5 yrs.)

A Few Words About Wordless Books

Many adults shy away from owning and "reading" wordless books because they feel they must make up a story to go with the pictures. However, the story is already there (in the pictures) and all they have to do is tell the story in their own words. I find that nothing could be easier! In fact, when one customer asked what our family's all-time favorites are, I heard myself naming books that all turned out to be wordless. Perhaps it's because I don't feel encumbered by someone else's words (and can use the words I feel like using just then) that these books have turned out to be such a joy. Perhaps it's because I know just what words my children can understand or are ready to learn that wordless books are such a hit in our house. Except for the very basic baby board books that have just an illustration of, say, a baby and a sock, there is always a story ready-made for you. (Actually, the baby-and-sock is a story, too: "Baby. Sock." [while pointing your finger] can be upgraded in a few days or weeks to "There's a baby. There's a sock." to "There's a baby and a yellow sock." to "I wonder if the baby's going to put on the yellow sock." Get it?) Wordless books allow you to customize a book exactly for your child and give her an opportunity to interact on a personal level with the book when she decides to tell *you* the story in *her* own words! We think wordless books are wonderful— *and* they tend to span a greater period of a child's life simply because they *are* so versatile.

Chicka Chicka Boom Boom

by Bill Martin and John Archambault
illustrated by Lois Ehlert

This delightful book is a rollicking rhymefest about the alphabet. The basic story is quite simple. The characters (the letters A–Z) are all trying to climb up to the top of a coconut tree; the big question is, will there be enough room? Just when they all squeeze in, the tree leans over from the weight and all of the little letters fall out in a big heap on the ground. Doesn't sound like much, but if you add a little rock and roll to your voice, a simple story becomes great fun. Here's a sample:

> Skit skat skoodle doot.
> Flip flop flee.
> Everybody running to the coconut tree.
> Mamas and papas and uncles and aunts hug their little
>   dears,
> then dust their pants.

The illustrations are done in a brightly colored graphic style that creates a cheery visual feast.

This book has so much personality it is bound to be a hit around your house—especially if you are harboring a secret desire to ham it up with no one but your little one watching! (2–6 yrs.)

 Wynken, Blynken and Nod

by Eugene Field
illustrated by Joanna Westerman

> Wynken, Blynken and Nod one night
> Sailed off in a wooden shoe—
> Sailed on a river of crystal light,
> Into a sea of dew.

This lyrical account of a wee one's dream has softly colored illustrations of sleepy children, a smiling moon and glistening fish—gently evocative of the dreams of those who must not have a care in the world. The moon here feels like both a kind guide, as well as a glowing jewel in the sky; the sea is a friendly place, and the fish are fine companions on this magical journey. Yes, it is a perfect book for the times when sleep is near, but the words create a safe and soothing atmosphere any time of the day.

You may remember this wonderful poem from your own childhood and, if so, you shouldn't be surprised that it is still around. There is a word for such books: timeless. (2½–4 yrs.)

Many young children bring the imagination of a poet to their relationship with language. Driving around town with a toddler in the car is often like being inside a living linguistic laboratory. There is a sense of utter playfulness attached to their experimentations with words and sounds. (Isn't it wonderful how their most serious learning happens through their play?) Personally, I think this is why young children like poetry so much.

Poetry is an adult's version of playing with words. Many adults are afraid to try poetry (and wordless books, for that matter) with their children. I haven't figured out why, but my guess is that there is some leftover resistance to having to *do* poetry in school, where there was a *right* way and a *wrong* way to understand it. If you are one of those people, now is your chance to try it again without your English teacher nearby. Give it a shot: read poetry to your children and watch a whole new world open up for both of you. When gently exposed, without expectation, children are natural lovers of poetry; perhaps because, like children, it distills moments to their very essence and speaks the truth of things.

The Grey Lady and
the Strawberry Snatcher

by Molly Bang

This book is a masterpiece—so unusual and quirky, it is one of those books you either see the magic in—or you don't. It is the wordless story of a woman, cloaked all in grey, who buys strawberries at the fruit market. She is followed home through an eerie swamp by an equally eerie and strange-looking character who has only one thing on his mind: strawberries. The chase goes on for most of the book, but the grey lady eventually gets away. The snatcher, in the meantime, discovers a blackberry patch, and the last we see of him he is there, feasting on some big, ripe, juicy ones.

One of my favorite things about this book is that there is so much to notice despite countless readings. Turning to a new page is like opening a treasure chest. The colors are magnificent; the idea and the execution of the book are one of a kind. Since the book is wordless, you, the "reader," have the power to choose the overall tone of the story. While this weird-looking character chasing a woman who has just bought a box of strawberries can come across as scary if you give your voice ominous tones (which I am fairly sure wasn't the intent of this highly acclaimed author), you will be pleasantly surprised if you simply keep the story exciting and upbeat. Be observant of the absolutely amazing detail in the book and you and your child will enjoy it for years. (2+ yrs.)

A Child's Garden of Verses

by Robert Louis Stevenson
illustrated by Tasha Tudor

If you need an extra nudge to help you decide whether or not to own an edition of *A Child's Garden of Verses*, here it is. As a parent who wants to instill the love of books and literature in your child, you'll run into poetry here and poetry there. But until you allow Stevenson's work into your life, you'll never find verse that so gracefully invites the imagination to roam freely, exploring exotic lands, the magic of day passing into night, the sheer joy of swinging through the sun-filled air and the coziness of dreaming in front of a fire on a winter's night.

This lovingly illustrated volume has oodles of soft, detailed watercolors that evoke a slower, softer world. Tasha Tudor's classic style is a perfect complement to Stevenson's poems. Tender and old-fashioned without being sentimental, the illustrations capture the romance of childhood that Stevenson has captured so beautifully in words. (Whenever you feel your child will enjoy poetry: as young as 2½ but maybe not till 5 and up.)

Cultivating the Imagination

Imagination lies at the heart of being human. Without imagination, life has no meaning and no sparkle, problems remain unsolved and life becomes flat. While giving lip service to the importance of imagination, our culture does much to dampen our children's imaginative abilities. Toys that have only one answer, prepackaged entertainment (i.e., television, videos and many computer games), schooling that involves too much rote memorization, and even the negative, fear-based attitudes that pervade our culture all deaden our children's ability to live in the imaginative world. If ever we have needed imagination, it is now. Imagination is the key to solving our world's problems. As Einstein said, "Imagination is more important than knowledge." All the knowledge in the world won't fix anything unless we have the creativity to imagine new solutions and new ways of living.

As parents, we have so many ways to foster our children's imagination. I guard my children's imaginations like a jealous hound, for I know that the more we encourage our children to exercise their creativity, the stronger learners they will become. Allowing our children the time to experience hours of fantasy play and hours of outdoor play with a minimum of toys, and even giving them plenty of opportunities to be bored without rescuing them, fosters our children's creative abilities. When we fill our house with the materials to make things (and it is remarkable what they will create out of string, sticks and boxes!), and we allow our children the freedom to make messes *and* mistakes with these materials, their imagination will lead them to amazing heights. The more tightly we structure days and close off the opportunities for open-ended play, the harder it is for our children to strengthen their imaginative muscles. When making decisions that affect our children's day, do we keep imagination in mind? If we send our child to day care, how much time does that facility dedicate to open-ended play? If we are home with our children, are we home long enough each day for them to fall into the land of make-believe deeply enough that they almost forget about the real world? When we buy toys, do we look for toys that engage our children's imaginative capacities? The simple choices we make over and over again will facilitate or dampen our children's relationship with the imaginative world.

The Dragons Are Singing Tonight

poems by Jack Prelutsky
illustrated by Peter Sis

Many of us have had a fling with the idea of dragons. It's not too hard to figure out why. They're a mysterious blend of that which is and that which is possible. They live in our imaginations, in legends and in art. We want to believe that they may have existed at one time and yet we are afraid to believe that they really did. It's a delicious fear/fantasy. And to top it all off, there's probably something in our genes that keeps us from dismissing them as make-believe: dragons, through the ages, were recognized by some spiritual traditions as being the ultimate symbol and embodiment of the spirit of transformation and change. They're a mystical and magical bunch.

So this book is right up the alley of anyone who has paused just a little longer than the next person to look a dragon in the eye, whether in a painting or in a dream. There is nothing frightening or ominous about these particular dragon characters, though. Richly colored and whimsically detailed illustrations perfectly accompany Prelutsky's one-of-a-kind poetry to introduce us to dragons in all walks of life—

from those who are someone's giant pet, to those who howl at the moon from mountaintops, to one who is a child's secret friend.

> .... *My dragon's very gentle,*
> *My dragon's very kind.*
> *No matter how I pull its tail,*
> *My dragon doesn't mind.*
> *We splash around together*
> *And play at silly things,*
> *Then when I'm finished bathing,*
> *It dries me with its wings.*

These are the types of poems that are as fun to read aloud as they are to listen to. Combine them with art that does all the humor, tenderness and cantankerousness justice, and you have a wonderful book! (4–7 yrs.)

Child of Faerie, Child of Earth

by Jane Yolen
illustrated by Jane Dyer

There is a message, an intriguing idea, in this story. Could we humans really make lasting friendships with the faerie folk? What would that mean for our earth? I ask this with some trepidation, knowing that few adults really believe in faeries. Yet, just watch your child's face when you read this book to her. I bet you anything a glimmer of hope and excitement shines in her eyes, for deep down she knows such magic is possible. After experiencing Yolen's poetic verse and Dyer's obvious understanding of the ways of earth and faerie, you may believe as well.

It is All Hallows' Eve. The faerie boy asks the girl if she is afraid, and when she says no, he takes her by the hand and leads her to his underground hall, where she dances all night with "the elven crew." When he wants her to stay and be his queen, the girl knows she must remain a "child of the day." But she invites her friend to dance with her in her world—to feed the chickens and milk the cow, to make a bed and eat brown bread. He does so, in great awe, but when the girl longs for him to stay, he finds he must remain a "child of night, of cold, cold stars, of moon and thistledown." I will not tell you how they find a solution to their dilemma, so you and your children can discover it on your own. While you are reading, don't forget to wonder: are such friendships possible? One never knows for sure! (4–8 yrs.)

The simple practice of pointing out objects as we take our babies and toddlers on walks is a potent way to encourage our children's language development. Talking about the blue sky and the gray cloud and the brown bark of the tree may feel funny at first, but as your baby begins to acquire language, his response will soon be your reward. People—both children and adults—learn best in the context of real experience. The more we, as parents, can offer our young children opportunities to touch, taste, feel, see and hear for themselves (and in true interaction with others, as opposed to watching something passively on TV), the richer their lives will be. The words and concepts they learn will have more meaning because they are grounded in real knowledge of the world. Nothing, even books, can ever replace real-life experience.

Talking Like the Rain

A First Book of Poems

selected by X. J. Kennedy and Dorothy M. Kennedy

Talking Like the Rain is a magnificent introduction to wonders of poetry.

Exquisitely illustrated, it is a delightful collection of child-friendly poetry. Reading it makes you want to hop, skip or leap back into the happy land of childhood. Blending the best of today's poets with a sprinkling of the old masters, this collection of poetry could convert just about anyone to a love of words. The poems are about seasons and nature, animals, childhood experiences, magic and fantasy and just plain silliness. Every page is generously illustrated with soft watercolors that capture the spirit of every poem. Simply put, *Talking Like the Rain* is filled with the joy of life! (3–8 yrs., but older people will enjoy it, too.)

Heart to Heart

Dear Friends,

When Elizabeth was about six weeks old, I went to the dentist about a nagging jaw and cheek achiness I'd been experiencing ever since she was born. The pain was on both sides of my face and most noticeable when I smiled.

Ascertaining that cavities were definitely not the problem, the dentist asked me about the nature of the pain, in hopes that he could track down the source. Having had braces as a kid, I compared this feeling to that of sensing that your teeth were slowly and forcefully being moved into another position, only this time, there was no apparatus on my teeth. He asked me to try to remember if I'd been doing anything differently in the past six weeks since my symptoms began, and the obvious thing came to mind: I was the mother of a new baby, a mother who spent nearly every waking minute smiling at this angelic being who had come into my life, a mother whose "smiling muscles" were getting such a workout that I guess they were slightly affecting the structure of my jaw. We decided that that was likely the answer to my dilemma and, delighted that I did not have some rare degenerative jaw disease or need exploratory surgery, I left the dentist's office with a smile on my face. Over time, I experienced less and less pain.

Whether it was because my jawbones just eventually accommodated to that new pressure being exerted on them daily, or because I stopped smiling so much, I'm not sure. But I have a clue.

Those earliest "passages"—Elizabeth's first smile, the day she first rolled over, the look on her face when she ate her first bite of mashed banana— were such big events. I wrote down the dates, we celebrated them, I called my mother long distance. Then the milestones started to come faster: crawling, first tooth, jabbering, waving bye-bye, mimicking animal sounds, first step, etc. Every day seemed to bring something new, and while each milestone was beautiful, it was no longer earth-shattering. Gradually, the behavior signifying normal growth and emotional health began to include a few "Me do it's," the ability to play for four hours at a friend's house without missing me one bit, and a propensity for making a two-block walk to the post office take an hour. By now, a lot of the magic was gone and my "smiling disease" had long since disappeared.

Much water has flowed under my bridge since those days. Concerns have changed from what Elizabeth thought she wanted to take to kindergarten show-and-tell to how late in the evening her end-of-the-year class party can last and how loudly they'll be able to play their music. I see her attitudes being reformulated to include the ever widening sphere of influence, and I sit on the edge of my seat, waiting to see how well the values her father and I have offered her have taken root. Just as when she was a baby, there are milestones aplenty; they're just buried, harder to spot now, and somehow don't automatically strike me as cause for celebration. These milestones speak of her emerging individuality, her growing need for independence and the ways she is blossoming into a person who, each day, finds out a little bit more about who she is. It's a challenge to keep my head in a space where I can appreciate milestones such as her taste in music, her embarrassment when I act too dorky in front of her friends and her diminishing need to have me read aloud to her. Yet, they are as profound as those I wrote about in her baby book because they signify that she is becoming capable and free.

I am fairly certain that from here on out my children's milestones won't be the type to make me float blissfully around the house, smiling from ear to ear (causing a reoccurrence of the "smiling disease"). Yet I believe it is important to keep a couple of things in mind to retain that sense of "magic" for a family at the stage where the camera is no longer poised for cute candid shots, and the baby books have not had an entry made in them in recent memory. One is that parenting is an adventure, and countless discoveries will, of necessity, be made by all involved in it. The other is that the really profound discoveries and growth won't likely come when the road is smooth and straight. They will come when there are bends in the road—bends that are more easily passed if we recognize and lovingly embrace those which, at first glance, might appear to be obstacles.

Near and Far

Reaching Out with Compassion

Look for the beauty, my mama says. Always look
for the beauty. It's in every single body you meet.
—Jacqueline Woodson

'***ve*** always wanted my children to have a deep under-standing and respect for the profound richness and in-credible diversity of people on this planet. I've wanted them to know that every culture has an important lesson to teach us about being human. Unfortunately, translating this desire for under-standing to my children hasn't always been easy, and the reason lies within me. Without holding myself in check, I can be a rather judg-mental person. You could call it "discriminating" on my good days, but on bad days there is no other word for it but "judgmental." It took me many years (and a lot of hard knocks upon the head) to acknowledge this trait in myself. I certainly couldn't see it when Becca was born. I was only twenty-three then—barely an adult. I was still busy figuring out what I thought about the world. I was bound and determined to be the very best parent I could be and I brought every ounce of my inborn enthusiasm and love for my child to the task. I just knew that if I could be the right kind of parent then she could have the right kind of life, a life that would surely be less painful than mine had been. Marvelous intentions, I grant you, but what I did with those intentions was not so great. From the goodness of my heart, I set about deciding exactly what was good and what was bad for my child, and seriously shielding her from anything I deemed bad. I evaluated every aspect of Becca's life, from her toys to her food to her friends. And since we didn't live in a neighborhood full of kids, this was easy for me to do. Now, to give myself a break here, I do tend to have great taste. And I offered Becca all I could in terms of love and experience; but what I didn't offer her was an example of tolerance. Yet, it is tolerance that teaches respect and trust, the two things at the heart of honoring and understanding others.

It almost broke my heart when I realized what I was doing, but luckily, she was only two or three when I started to understand how I was hurting Becca with my desires to create the perfect childhood. Gradually, I began to embrace rather than reject differences, and we both were able to discover new ways. I stopped trying to find the perfect experiences and instead began learning from the experiences at hand. Things became grayer. No more black and white. Instead of seeking new friends for her when kids presented challenging dynamics, I started saying things like: "Yes, Amy has quite a temper, but look at how much fun she is to play fairies with! What can you do when she gets really angry?" We began to look at how we could find the beauty in an experience and gather new understandings from the difficulties in our path.

It's a lofty goal to wish to teach our children to respect others, for it calls upon us to be models of integrity. While I learned the hard way, children can learn more easily because they are natural mimics and the people they imitate most consistently are the ones they love the best. When children are young, they are rather indiscriminate about what they copy and which beliefs they adopt. The basic truth is that to teach our children tolerance, we must exhibit tolerance ourselves. There's a delicate balance between teaching them values and teaching them to be judgmental. The values and/or judgments will speak for themselves, solely by the way we live our lives; as the old adage goes, actions speak louder than words.

If we wish our children to learn to be respectful of others, we must see and openly acknowledge the beauty in others. We must help them find the good in people even if that good is something different from the good we had expected to find. We must help them see that people act from the same basic needs—to feel safe, to feel loved, to have power—and that sometimes people choose to meet these needs in very different ways. That is exactly why I love teaching my children about different cultures. I delight in their learning that while burping at the table is something to apologize for in our family, it is a compliment to the cook in some other cultures. I want my children to open their eyes to the diversity on this planet, not shut their hearts in judgment.

In the process of becoming more tolerant myself (and in hoping to share this trait with my children), I have found the importance of seeing beneath the surface of things. When faced with my own judgment or that of my child, I know now to stop for a moment and just breathe. I let the situation just be, without trying to explain or escape it. I accept that this is the way it is. If I am uncomfortable, my children always know it. I must somehow embrace that feeling of discomfort and discern what is behind it; is it a safety issue or is it an issue of tolerance? So, when confronted with situations that bring up discomfort, I must help my children learn to see beneath the surface. I acknowledge that yes, that homeless person looks a bit scary, but maybe that is because he has no place to take a bath or can't afford to wash his clothes or go to the dentist. When they meet people at school or in the world that have different ways of coping with problems (perhaps a young child hits instead of using words, or another constantly teases), I try to help my children learn that while hitting (or teasing) is a mistake, their friend actually has a reason for acting so. Perhaps he is frustrated when his words don't work immediately, or perhaps he learned at home that hitting equals power and he is feeling powerless at the moment. If my children can't learn to solve the small problems of their lives with tolerance, how can they learn to have tolerance for different cultures and different ways of life? I try to remember to ask my children, "Why do you think Jacob hit?" "What happened before Sarah started to tease you?" Small children are too young to know all of the answers, and we can help them navigate these tricky situations, but they are never too young to begin to be curious about why things happen the way they do. Teaching children to ask questions about troubling situations fosters their developing sense of tolerance. People seldom act cruelly without a reason. Their cruel action might stem from a hurt they experienced perhaps a long time ago, which, rather than an excuse for their behavior now, can be explained to help our children develop compassion—which makes the road to tolerance much less bumpy.

In my opinion, this all comes down to building bridges. How can I help my children see how we are all so alike and yet all so unique? How can I teach them to honor the uniqueness in themselves and in others, while knowing that we all have the same basic needs to survive and feel loved? Honoring diversity is tricky business that demands of parents the utmost respect and integrity and the honest willingness to learn and grow ourselves. Our children are quick to point out when we fall short of our ideals. Are we able to own up to our inadequacies and have the courage to learn new ways? If we can, they are sure to learn from our mistakes and honor us all the more for our efforts to grow. The bottom line is that for better or worse, when our children are young, we are their interpreters of the world. They learn to see the world through our eyes and our filters. And it is up to us to make sure those filters are clean.

Finding ways to share your values and beliefs without being judgmental can be difficult. The books and ideas here celebrate diversity and help us encourage thoughtfulness, compassion and tolerance in our children.

Max

by Bob Graham

Be prepared to have a grin on your face from the moment you open this book to a few moments after you close it. *Max* is not only poignant and true for any of us who have had the frustration of expectations that are slow in being realized, it is also perfectly and subtly humorous. A sheer delight of a book. Max is the superbaby of superheroes Captain Lightning and Madam Thunderbolt. Not only that, his grandma and grandpa have left behind a legacy of superheroism, so there's a bloodline thing going. Bottom line: Max has big shoes to fill.

It's never too early to start priming a superbaby to follow in his parents' footsteps, though, so in the big yellow house that's shaped like a thunderbolt amid the tract houses in suburbia somewhere, a toddler crawls out of his crib to start his day. Now, we all know that you can't be a superhero unless you learn how to fly, but it looks as if Max is going to be a late bloomer in that regard. He loves playing with the dog on the floor while Dad hovers near the ceiling, urging Max to come play with the parakeet. You get the picture. The reality is that Max is just like any other kid as he grows up. Can he fly? Not on your life! Is his family getting just a little concerned about his disinterest and inability to fly? Uh-huh.

Max's turnaround comes the early morning he looks out his upstairs window and spies a baby bird falling from its nest. Before he knows it, he is flying to the rescue and once he gets the taste for flying, he never looks back.

This is a wonderful book! Lively and sweet and packed with offbeat surprises. The bottom line of the story is that *everyone* is different in some way. Its humor is perfectly accessible to children and at the same time sophisticated enough for adults to appreciate even after many, many readings. (3–5 yrs.)

How we feel about our place in the world changes as we grow. To young children, a trip across town might as well be a trip to the other side of the planet! Our neighborhood is our child's first "world" and she becomes more and more familiar with what lies beyond the neighborhood as you venture out on errands or explore new things. When you are out and about, either on foot or in the car, it is fun to ask your young one if she can direct you home from, say, two turns away. "Go that way, Mommy. Now go *that* way," and you are home. (Or not!) Next time, ask when you are a little farther away. Or ask her to direct you to the market or to school. Little by little, over the years, she will become confident as she ventures farther and farther away from home and into the world.

My father played this game with me, and by the time I was eight, I could direct him home from almost anywhere in the Los Angeles area—twenty-five to thirty miles at a shot. He would, of course, take my *wrong* turns, too. I wonder to this day if these adventures have anything to do with my sense of direction, which is amazingly good.

Miss Rumphius

by Barbara Cooney

Would that every child were given such wonderful advice by a loved one: when you grow up, do something to make the world more beautiful.

This is the story of a young girl who vows to travel and see faraway places and to live beside the sea. But that is not all, for she believes what her grandfather has told her about the mark she can make on the world. So, as we watch her live her life and grow older, we all know— the reader and Miss Rumphius herself—that she must figure out, and then do, what it is that will make the world more beautiful.

Does it turn out to be something that makes history? No. Does it turn out to be something that is earthshaking? No. Does it turn out to be something that many, many people can appreciate even though her actions were simple and unassuming and straight from the heart? Yes. And that is what has made *Miss Rumphius* a book that some would say belongs in every family's library. Its message is one of understanding that we all have the power to do good and that good most often comes in small, doable, down-to-earth doses.

The illustrations are colorful and warm, as is the character, Miss Rumphius, and the spirit of this lovely book (3–7 yrs.)

My kids always tease me about where I meet my friends. My innately sociable nature leads me to talk to and sometimes even bring home people from all walks of life. One woman I know I met because of a long conversation in the rain, waiting for the bus. Becca and Laura were quite young when I met this woman, six and three, I believe, and still to this day they tease me about bringing home friends from the bus stop. Though she lived in my neighborhood, Natalie was someone I never would have met in the course of my daily life had I not spoken to her that day in the rain. Thankfully, I did, for I wouldn't have missed her friendship for the world.

Natalie grew up in completely different circumstances from those I experienced. Mentored by her genteel grandmother, Natalie was an amazing painter. She was also influenced by her decidedly eccentric father, who spent his days trapping and fishing from a flatboat in the backwaters of the Louisiana wetlands. Growing up on the remains of an old plantation, she told stories that left my children's eyes wide while they asked questions for days. I think Becca's fascination with history was in part fueled by Natalie's family stories of her great-grandfather's plantation journal, stories of what it was like to own slaves. (The thought just horrified Becca. How could this person standing here before her actually be related to someone who *owned* hundreds of people?) The stories that stuck with me the longest were her tales of sharing her family's pond with the neighborhood alligators. I'm sure my mouth was wide open as she enlightened us on how to tell if an alligator was hungry. She figured that as long as the alligator was full, swimming was safe. Part of me thought she was crazy to *ever* dive in that water, and part of me admired her pluck. Either way, we were all amazed by Natalie's life!

If I hadn't opened my mouth that day at the bus stop to make some silly comment about the rain, Natalie would never have dropped into our lives. But then, I suppose, Natalie could have been a dangerous, crazy person. It's a funny thing about life: I clearly want my kids to be safe and yet I don't want them to be afraid to reach out and meet all kinds of folk. Personally, I like to assume that people are by nature kind, until I sense otherwise. I suppose this idea could get us into trouble someday, but in my experience most people *are* rather kind. And if they aren't, they make their unkindness readily apparent. This doesn't mean I encourage my children to talk openly to strangers when they are alone, but I also don't want them to miss out on life's variety simply because there are a few unstable people out there. This "stranger" business is a fine line. We can't let fear rule our lives and yet we have to learn to be safe, too. I figure the more chances we have to practice our intuition with people in relatively safe situations (like three o'clock in the afternoon at an open city bus stop), the more finely tuned our intuition will become. This is one of those lines you have to define for yourself and live with what feels right to you.

In Every Tiny Grain of Sand

A Child's Book of Prayers and Praise

collected by Reeve Lindbergh
illustrated by Christine Davenier, Bob Graham,
Anita Jeram, Elisa Kleven

Young or old, Christian or Jew or Buddhist, you can open this book to any page and experience something sacred: simple prayers, poems and words of praise that people have loved and held precious over many, many years. Here is a rich collection of prayers to be uttered when times are good, when times are hard, when there is beauty to be appreciated all around us, when we feel alone or when we know there is a divine being to which we want to express what cannot be expressed in any other way.

In Every Tiny Grain of Sand is divided into four sections: For the Day, For the Home, For the Earth and For the Night. There are various selections from the Christian and Jewish, Hindu, Navajo, Bahá'í and Gaelic traditions, as well as from the Upanishads, Angelus Silesius, Lao-Tzu, Robert Browning and Christina Rossetti—and the list goes on and on—all seventy-seven collected by Reeve Lindbergh when she asked friends and friends of friends to tell her their favorite poems and prayers.

If truth be told, this is a book for all ages. Adults will likely find themselves copying down their favorites to tape to the mirror or on a dashboard, while children who grow up with these beautiful prayers and poems will likely be spiritually connected to the sacred by the thread that runs through all of them. (3 yrs.–adult)

If our children are the recipients of some kind of verbal cruelty or violence, our behaviors are even more critical. Violence begets violence—in word or deed—unless the feelings that arise around the incident are truly acknowledged and the child is comforted. As parents, when another child (or adult) does something cruel to our child, we have the opportunity to teach our children how to stop the cycle of violence. Offering our compassion and comforting our children for as long as they need it—which may be for weeks, off and on, depending on what has happened—we teach our children to respond to cruelty with love. Rising up in anger (though this may be how we wish to act) teaches our children to meet violence with anger instead of love. To stop the cycle of violence so prevalent in our world we have to realize that people hurt other people *because* they are hurt themselves. We must find it in our hearts to meet their hurt with compassion—all the while protecting our child (and ourselves) from further abuse. If we can create a safe harbor for our children to bring their pain, they won't need to inflict their pain onto the world. We will transfer our peacemaking skills to our children, and soon they will be working their peace in the world.

This may sound incredibly idealistic, but I have seen these ideas work magic in schools where teaching emotional intelligence is an integrated part of the curriculum. Children whose emotional needs are met have no reason to seek revenge and no reason to be the schoolyard bully. Children learn better, act better and become kinder people when they grow in an environment that places a high priority on responding compassionately to their emotional needs *and* where adults model this behavior in their own lives.

It's like that beautiful old song about one small voice making a voice for change. Change happens when we can rise above the hurt, hold it and make a place for it and then meet it with love. In essence, we must practice cultivating compassion, which is in some ways much easier to accomplish in the context of a family than in the larger world, because we already love our children. Compassion is based on love. Having compassion for those who hurt others (including ourselves and those we love) is challenging; but every time we model this behavior for our children at home, we empower them to use this behavior in the world. Kindness spreads like ripples on the water just as easily as anger does. And we all have the power to exercise kindness, if we so choose.

Anno's Journey

by Mitsumasa Anno

Picture a wordless book packed with so much detail that it is like a treasure hunt every time you open it. *Anno's Journey* is just that, following a certain traveler from his arrival on the shores of a medieval country to his eventual departure, pages later. The reader's perspective is that of a flying bird, looking down at a myriad of plots unfolding on each spread. The traveler can be found on each page, sometimes effortlessly, sometimes after a search. It's hard to convey how exciting it is to settle down with *Anno's Journey* and try to find "stories" you've never seen before (even after countless readings!) hidden in the fine detail. Certain people show up several times throughout his journey, while there are various characters from nursery rhymes and fairy tales and even history who pop up now and then. (The book includes a list of what to keep your eye open for, if you want help.) The pointing-to-and-naming opportunities are virtually endless, making this one of those sublimely versatile books.

Whenever I run across *Anno's Journey* while I'm dusting our family's bookshelf, it is like finding an old friend who beckons me to stop and reacquaint myself, whereupon I forget time and linger longer than I would have ever dreamed possible. Without fail, anyone to whom I've shown this book and taken a minute to point out a little of its detail and wonderful continuity ends up enthralled! (1½ yrs.–adult) (Be sure not to miss another fabulous book by this author, *Anno's Counting Book.*)

The Old Woman Who Named Things

by Cynthia Rylant
illustrated by Kathryn Brown

Some would say that Cynthia Rylant is fast becoming the Margaret Wise Brown of our day. And by that I mean that she seems to see right into the hearts of children and writes stories that speak to their own special sense of innocence and curiosity in a tone that is neither lofty nor patronizing. Her stories both soothe and help children learn more about how to be a good person, a person unique unto his- or herself but also kind and worthy. *The Old Woman Who Named Things* is a precious example of Rylant's extraordinary talent.

The story goes like this: an old woman has outlived all of her friends. This makes her sad, so she starts naming all the things she knows will outlive *her.* She has a house named Franklin, a chair named Fred and a car named Betsy. One day a tiny brown puppy shows up at her gate looking hungry and very lonely. She feeds the puppy and shoos him away, knowing she can't bear to keep anything that she might outlive. Day after day, the little puppy comes for his meal and a bit of affection. The old woman gives him both, but never does she give him a name. Eventually, the puppy is a dog, a dog with a big heart and no name. But then one day, when he doesn't come, the old woman looks sadly out her window wondering what happened to "her dog." The days go by and she can't find him anywhere. Finally she takes the huge step of going to the pound to look for him. While there, the man asks her what her dog's name is. "Lucky," she replies, thinking how lucky she has been in her life to have had so many things to love. Lucky comes running at the sound of her voice and so begins the rest of their life together—a life in which Lucky has a name and a home.

The Old Woman Who Named Things is one of those books that your heart is always happy to read. (2½–6 yrs.)

Tips on Helping Children Cope with People They "Hate"

♡ Acknowledge that nobody likes everyone. Acknowledge that it is okay not to like someone *and* that we still need to act respectfully toward this person in our words and actions. Give your child helpful examples of how to translate "acting respectfully" into their real life. Encourage kindness. Try to help your child decipher what makes her feel so strongly about this person. Listen carefully as your child speaks about the "enemy." Ask open-ended questions that allow your child to say more than "I hate Joey!" (Often our response to our children's strong words closes them off to further discussion. Who wants to hear a child say she hates someone?) Usually, when a child expresses such a strong feeling she has a good reason. Sometimes she is feeling disempowered or particularly frustrated. Perhaps the dreaded child teases your child or hurts her in some way. Does your child feel left out? Or does the hated child have something your child wants (more friends, toys or power)? Once you understand the source of your child's feelings, it is much easier to help her scope out a strategy for dealing with that particular child.

Occasionally, children find themselves in situations that require an adult's intervention. It may be that you need to step in and do something to protect your child, to be your child's advocate. You may need to talk to the "hated" child's parents or teacher. If you are talking to the parent, tread gently and try to open the door for understanding. Rushing in with words of recrimination will only create more problems. Trust what your child tells you *and* find out as much as you can on your own. If the problem is at school, explain what your child has told you and then listen to the teacher's perspective on the situation. If the issue is with the teacher, you may wish to hear as much as you can about the teacher's perspective without fully explaining your child's perspective. Try to find out the facts before saying or doing too much. As parents, we need to honor our child's true needs. When she is feeling hurt in a situation, it is easy for the "mother bear" instinct to rise up and cause us to solve problems with a roar and a swat. But often this creates more problems for her than it solves. If we can detach ourselves emotionally from the situation, we have a much better chance of seeing a true path to walk. Sometimes that path involves teaching her more skills to deal with a difficult person and sometimes it means severely limiting her exposure to the person. At times, it involves doing both. Without all of the facts, it is hard to know which path to walk.

If the child that bothers your child is someone with whom many children have trouble dealing, try to find out more about her life at home. Often these "difficult" kids are exactly the children who need special understanding. Perhaps she has a problematical situation at home, or someone she loves is going through hard times. If we can explain to our child, "Julie is sad because her grandma is sick and maybe that is making her act unkindly," we offer our child an opportunity to show compassion rather than aversion. A little bit of understanding can go a long way in easing harsh circumstances.

♥ Invite the "enemy" home for milk and cookies! Many a problem on the playground or at school can be solved by a short period of one-on-one time away from the larger social situation. If you do this, organize the visit to include a delicious snack and plenty of close supervision. Have in mind a fun activity or two that allow the children to engage each other, but not be forced to get along if they are having trouble. A new package of clay or a couple of bottles of bubbles can go a long way toward defusing tense circumstances. Plan to make the visit short and fun, thereby allowing the children to meet each other in a new way without involving too much risk.

People

by Peter Spier

Books' popularity comes and goes in households, but if you happen on one that keeps everyone's interest for several years, you have found a gold mine. In our home, this book's popularity did not ebb for about eight years. From the time my first child was two we were able to find countless things in this book to talk about. Several years after that, she was still intrigued and frequently asked that we read it. And what is so wonderful is that as she got older there was *still* plenty in it to interest her.

Peter Spier has created a masterpiece with this intricately illustrated book about people. One could just stare at the pictures forever. *People* (written when the world's population was smaller than it is now) is about the differences among the four billion people inhabiting the planet, and the message is that those differences are wonderful, that they make life exciting. From the page showing different-looking mothers with babies, to the page of eyes, to the page showing the different kinds of games different cultures enjoy, to the page devoted to numerous theological beliefs, this book is good for hours of reading and fantasizing. Words don't do it justice. You and your child have to sit with it and take in the illustrations, little by little, grasping in the process the enormous truth that we are all unique—and how perfect it is that we are. (2½–10 yrs.)

When we meet someone who is from another country, I encourage my children to ask questions and be curious. The man who tunes our skis every year is from Switzerland. Heidi and Aidan have learned from him that he grew up speaking a special dialect that is only spoken in a small valley in Switzerland. He told them that in school he had to speak German and learn French and Italian, too, a fact that leaves Heidi and Aidan awestruck. He has explained to us that the Swiss constitution is based on the Constitution of the United States, which amazed Heidi, since she knew that Switzerland was older than our country. In the course of our few conversations with him in his store, he has opened up a whole new world to my children. They now talk of wanting to visit his valley to hear his language spoken. These random conversations may not seem like much to an adult, but to a young child they can be the first steps toward embracing all people from around the world.

Whoever You Are

by Mem Fox
illustrated by Leslie Staub

Whoever You Are is one of those books that can give you goose bumps because it tells of something genuine and important, something that everyone—young and old—should know. Truer and more precious words were never spoken than those that communicate to our young ones that there are children just like them all over the world. Their skin may be different, as might be their homes, their schools, their land, their lives, their words. But inside their hearts they are just the same—smiling, laughing, hurting. In times when our world is so small thanks to what the news brings into our homes every day, but yet so immense when we realize the vast gulf among cultures, books such as this are treasures for they boil us down to the one thing we all are: human.

The detail in *Whoever You Are* is worth taking the time to appreciate. The children at the book's beginning grow up; there are girls looking in from the outside on a classroom full of boys in another part of the world; and an Eastern European mother and child have a shrine to an ancestor on a wall. There is so much to notice and appreciate and wonder about in this book—just as there is so much to notice and appreciate and wonder about in the world. (3–6 yrs.)

This Land Is Your Land

words and music by Woody Guthrie
paintings by Kathy Jakobsen

In a time when we and our children tend to get from here to faraway there by airplane, we miss seeing the landscape, smelling the air, feeling the wind, sensing the feel of a place. This book goes a long way toward getting our feet and our hearts and our understanding back on the ground.

In richly detailed double-page spreads, we see a guitar-toting Woody Guthrie roaming and rambling on the ribbon of highway, under that endless skyway. We see pastoral scenes; we get glimpses of California to the New York island, from the redwood forest to the Gulf Stream waters. We see vignettes of landmarks and scenes that are part of our past and present—Mardi Gras in New Orleans; Mesa Verde, Colorado; the Statue of Liberty; a space shuttle launch; Dust Bowl refugees; Old Faithful; homeless people camping out under a bridge; a rodeo; a totem pole in Ketchikan, Alaska; the Grand Canyon. Over time, you and your child will have found yourselves curious about the drawing of this site or that and may have chosen to talk about it or look up more information in the encyclopedia.

This Land Is Your Land was written in 1940, as Woody hitchhiked in the dead of winter from Los Angeles to New York City. It is an extraordinary example of what he believed a folk song is: it's "what's wrong and how to fix it or it could be who's hungry and where their mouth is or who's out of work and where the job is or who's broke and where the money is or who's carrying a gun and where the peace is." (3+ yrs.)

The Paper Princess

by Elisa Kleven

A little girl draws a beautiful paper princess, but before she completely finishes her creation, the wind whisks the princess away. After many adventures, the princess flutters down to the ground one day, where she meets a sad little boy. He had been drawing a present for his sister and the drawing has just blown away. The paper princess offers him her other side and so he draws a beautiful meadow there. He gives the princess to his sister and watches a joyful reunion and, lo and behold! the little girl and the princess rejoice to see each other again!

What a lovely story! I can never decide whether I like the story or the illustrations the most. Kleven's art is a cross between painting and collage that results in pictures filled with exceptionally bright colors and plenty of detail. This would be a wonderful addition to your family's library. (3–7 yrs.)

Sometimes in the course of life, our children witness people being cruel or violent to each other. When they are older and in some school situations, this can, sadly, be a common, sometimes even daily, occurrence. When it occurs while they are very young, we hope always to be with them so we can comfort them and offer some kind of explanation—not that there ever *is* an adequate explanation for cruelty.

If our young child witnesses someone being cruel or violent, we must choose our words carefully to leave him feeling both safe and empowered. Unfortunately, all of my children and I have seen parents being unbearably cruel to children, most often in stores. We've witnessed other types of violence, too, but somehow the cruelty of parents to young children stands out. I'm not talking about parents who are simply disciplining an unruly child, but rather parents who are unduly harsh, humiliating or verbally abusing to a child. My response has always been to first assure my child that this behavior is quite simply *wrong* by saying something like "I wonder why that adult is speaking so cruelly to that child. No one *ever* deserves to be spoken to that way. That adult must really be angry or hurt inside to feel like they need to talk that way." I try in a gentle, simple way to leave the door open for compassion, both for the child and for the abusing parent. If there is a way to kindly intercede on the child's behalf, I always try to speak up, though sometimes, depending on the situation, I am a bit hesitant to do that, as I worry about the reprisal the child might be subjected to after I am gone. I want my children to know that other people need to speak up when injustice is being done, yet I try to be careful about further endangering the child. Often, angry parents can be distracted from their vicious tirades by a compassionate comment—a comment that affirms how hard it is to parent and yet somehow affirms the child, too. "Boy, waiting in line with toddlers can drive you batty. They sure love to run around just when you need them to stay still. I'll be happy to hold your place in line for you if you want to let them wander a bit and get the wigglies out."

Once we are away from the situation, I tend to ask my child lots of questions. Do you think that mommy is having a bad day? How could she have handled this situation more kindly? I wonder what it feels like when someone yells at you that way? What would you do if someone yelled at you that way? How would you feel? I wonder if the child was acting badly in the store because he was feeling bad inside? What can we do to help make people feel better? It always amazes me how wisely my children respond to these types of questions. I know that a give-and-take like this helps them learn a little bit more about how to respond in difficult situations; but more important, they come to understand how hurting people almost always leads to more hurt, which leads to even more hurt. In the end, everyone is seeking revenge instead of reconciliation. These questions help my children understand why it is so important to seek compassionate responses to our intense feelings rather than blindly raging at people when we are angry. When my children were small, they did a lot of listening and not a lot of talking during these discussions, but by the time they were four or five, they had quite a lot to say.

When the Wind Stops

by Charlotte Zolotow
illustrated by Stefano Vitale

The sun was setting, and so the day was ending. The little boy had played in the garden with his friend, drunk lemonade in the hot sun and had finished the day with a book on his father's lap. Now the moon was out, and his mother had come to tuck him in. "Why does the day have to end?" he asks her. "So night can begin," she says. He asks the predictable question "Where does the sun go when the day ends?" and his mother tells him that the day doesn't end—it begins somewhere else when the sun begins to shine there. "Nothing ends," she says.

Now, it's fairly unbelievable to a young boy that nothing ends. But Mother goes on to answer all of his questions. The wind doesn't stop; it goes on to make the trees dance somewhere else. When the waves break on the sand, they are sucked back to the sea into new waves. When the storm is over, the rain is made into other clouds that will make other storms. Nothing ends. It begins in another place or in a different way. From day to day, season to season, everything comes full circle. There is continuity in all. And when the sun wakes you, the moon will be beginning a night somewhere far away.

This is a lovely, profound, reassuring book. Its story shows a sacredness in the ordinary, the sacredness from which we humans have become so detached as we scurry about our lives. It is simple yet immense, perfect for a child, and just as perfect for an adult who yearns to experience and celebrate the wonder that truly flows all around us. (4+ yrs.)

Somewhere in the World Right Now

by Stacey Schuett
illustrated by Janice Lee Porter

I remember finding this book right around the time Elizabeth was beginning to grasp that we humans are literally not the center of the universe. We'd already enacted the "Earth revolving around the sun" exercise (she, holding the basketball, which was the sun; and I, trotting around it, holding a Ping-Pong ball, Earth). For all of the light that was shed on the subject, *Somewhere in the World Right Now* really did help to make the concept more believable.

Here is a quiet journey around the world in which the reader touches down in all sorts of places at the same moment in time. In Great Britain, a baker puts bread into his oven in the wee hours of the morning while mice hunt for crumbs. In Africa, elephants sleep standing up, swaying from side to side. In India, dawn is breaking as a rooster crows. In the Himalayas, farmers leave for the fields to tend their crops, while in Siberia, people are buying food for their midday meal. You get the idea. Eventually, we come to Massachusetts, where a child has just gone to bed and where lights are going out all over the city, and the day we've been following around the world ends.

Deep and rich colors go into the illustrations on every page. Brief yet descriptive text says just enough to let you know what's going on in each place. It's always a good thing to be gently reminded that each one of us is part of a much greater whole, and this book does a fine job of doing just that. (4–7 yrs.)

Those bedtime heart-to-hearts with a child can be extraordinarily profound, as any parent knows. It is in those soothing, winding-down moments that important questions arise from the hearts of our young ones, and our answers (or admission that we don't have the answers) come from a pure and quiet place within our own selves. It is the time when our defenses and tensions are down, when we're likely to be exhausted enough to have only enough energy to be our true selves, and say the truth as we know it in our hearts. It is a very special time—a time that begs us to discuss those deeper questions of life. Often these questions have no answers, but rather lead to mysteries to be pondered. "What does it feel like to go to bed hungry and know that tomorrow you might still be hungry? Can you be happy when life is like that?" "How does it feel to live in a country where girls don't matter as much as boys? Why do people think that?"

Hope

by Isabell Monk

Hope is not only the name of the young girl in this story; it is what this remarkable story is about.

Every year Hope comes to visit her vibrant Aunt Poogee, learning more and more about the history and love in her family. On one particular trip, Aunt Poogee's old friend Violet makes a comment that sends Hope spinning. What did Violet mean by "My goodness . . . is that child mixed?" Aunt Poogee first tells Hope to ignore Violet's hurtful comment, but Hope can't seem to let it go. What does it mean? Later that night, as Aunt Poogee puts Hope to bed, she tells her a story, a story that explains what "mixed" means and why Hope should be proud of it. Aunt Poogee talks about the faith it took for her immigrant great-grandparents to leave their homeland and come make a new life in America. She talks about the faith her slave great-grandparents had to hold to know that a better day was coming. She tells Hope about the faith of her white grandparents who worked so hard for civil rights so that all people could read and vote in this country. She speaks about the faith her parents had to marry because they loved each other, a faith that allowed them to look forward to a future when people are simply human and are not defined by the color of their skin. Aunt Poogee's healing touch shows Hope that the next time someone asks, "My goodness, is that child mixed?" she can stand up and in a loud, clear voice say, "Yes, I am generations of faith mixed with love! I am Hope!"

This book is so incredibly special. Every child, every classroom, every library in the country should have it. The beauty of the story, unlike so many stories with a "message," shines strong, belonging in all of our children's hearts. (4–9 yrs.)

When my children were young, I loved finding ways to help them make connections from their world to faraway places. Eating foods from other countries, reading stories about children from other cultures or even shopping in stores that carry traditional items from the other side of

the world—each of these activities builds bridges of curiosity and interest about others. Often, we will read about another culture's holidays
and make our own version of these celebrations. With friends, we have
had huge bonfires and danced around an enormous Swedish Midsum-
mer's Day pole. We've had many a high tea, in keeping with English traditions. Our ten-course teas became marvelous yet lighthearted
opportunities to teach manners. Another borrowed custom that has
become a favorite happens on November 11, Martinmas. That day we
take a lantern walk in gathering dusk, honoring the Frenchman Saint
Martin, the patron saint of beggars. Since our city has so many homeless people, these walks offer a natural conversation bridge to the hardships of being homeless. My kids love making various types of candle
lanterns and then walking through the park at dusk with their friends,
singing songs of peace and friendship. There are so many beautiful customs around the world; I love to let my children have a small taste of
them at home, even if they can't travel across the world to experience
them in person.

The Little House books

by Laura Ingalls Wilder

Can this series possibly need an introduction? It is quite possibly the
most read-aloud set of chapter books in America. My family has read
the Little House books out loud at least four times. Each time we all
look forward to our nightly sessions on the couch, snuggled together,
absorbed in Wilder's rich descriptions of her pioneer childhood. We
experience famine, hard work, grasshopper plagues, sleigh rides,
laughter and the melodies of Pa's fiddle. The stories speak of love, integrity, ingenuity and courage. They make a powerful statement about
what families can be. (4+ yrs., or as soon as a child can sit through a
chapter book.)

Mental illness is something that is often shunned in our culture. For a variety of good reasons, parents often shield their children from relatives or people they know with mental illness. And while we always want to protect our children from potentially violent people, allowing them to interact with people with other forms of mental illness can produce a wonderful opportunity for our children to develop tolerance for differences in others.

When Becca and Laura were little, I had a friend who had significant mental difficulties that made coping with life hard for her. She was definitely an odd person to be around, but she had a heart of gold. Her eccentricities made the girls feel uncomfortable sometimes, and yet I know my friend had a profoundly positive influence on them. Over the period of a few years, my friend helped them to see that she was much more than just her diagnosis. She was a caring, witty, intelligent woman *and* she had many peculiar ways of dealing with the world. They might not have picked my friend as *their* friend, but as they grew older, I think knowing her helped them to look more deeply into people and develop compassion for those whose lives were more difficult than their own.

 Children Just Like Me

A unique collection of children around the world

by Barnabas and Anabel Kindersley

Chock-full of photographs of children, this book is packed with information and insights about what makes youngsters tick in such varied places as Mongolia, Rajasthan, Ajllata Grande, New Mexico, Sulawesi and Western Australia. We meet Yannis from Greece, Daisuke from Japan, Taylor from New York and many more. There are children from both industrialized and developing nations, children from busy cities and remote rural communities and children from tribal cultures. Most live with families, but Suchart, a novice monk, lives in a monastery, and Tadesse, an Ethiopian boy, lives in an orphanage. We meet their siblings, mother and father, learn how the family makes a living and see their home. We learn a bit about their religion, find out about the food they eat and their favorite games. One of the best things about each child's colorful and double-page spread is the close-up photograph of them in unassuming, everyday attire, with their autograph—often in an alphabet new to us.

Here is a book that can live on your coffee table and be perused countless times. (5+ yrs.)

When dealing with difficult situations or people, help your child learn to breathe. When they are upset or frustrated, let them cry the tears they need to cry and then encourage them to breathe deeply to clear their hearts. Breathing is such a simple yet potent opportunity to reconnect with our inner selves. And every problem feels more manageable when we feel connected to our innate wisdom. When situations require our children to act with kindness or special understanding, they will be much better able to do this if they first calm themselves. Teaching them to breathe deeply at moments like this gives them a lifelong skill for finding inner peace.

Celebrations

Festivals, carnivals and feast days
from around the world

by Barnabas and Anabel Kindersley

What child doesn't love a festival? Celebrations are a way we bring joy to our lives and build community. All over the world people celebrate the changing of the seasons, their specific religious beliefs and the bravery of their people. They honor their history and their culture. Festivals are the way we celebrate ourselves. *Celebrations* is a virtual feast for the eyes, capturing the world through a child's eyes.

Each page is filled with gloriously smiling children from all cultures, short explanations of the holiday and many small photos that provide a glimpse into the essence of the holiday. What a beautiful way to raise our children's cultural appreciation of the glories of our neighbors around the world. The striking visual format makes this book highly appealing to children of many ages. Younger children love to look at the pictures and be read short segments of the book. Older children are fascinated to read the book themselves. (5+ yrs.)

Young children discover what is true about the world by watching how we interact with the world. Do we get angry with bad drivers and yell at signals, or do we exhibit patience even when things are trying? Do we place blame on others when we, ourselves, need to be accountable? If we wish our children to learn to treat people with kindness and respect, we must model this behavior for them. Even on the days when we are tired or everything has gone wrong, we are responsible for our behavior. When we take our frustrations out on retail clerks or service helpers without apologizing for our unkind words, we teach our children that only certain people are worthy of respect. We teach them that it is okay to be rude to get what they want, and that, in fact, getting what they want is *more* important than how we treat people.

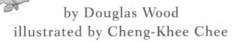

Old Turtle

by Douglas Wood
illustrated by Cheng-Khee Chee

For all who are impassioned for a world of peace, this book is for you. For all of you who yearn to give your children a deeper understanding of the earth and our relationship with all the beings who inhabit it, this book is for you.

Old Turtle is a powerful and exquisite fable for children and adults. Told wisely, yet with a simplicity, innocence and freshness that reach deep into the heart, it is for those who have chosen to know God through the people they meet and through the natural world around them. It begins with an argument about who God is and ends on a note that will touch your heart, leaving you with a smile and with hope.

The artwork is remarkable. The watercolors are exquisite, beautiful, mysterious, translucent, crystalline and somehow spiritual all at the same time. This is an extraordinary book. (6 yrs.–adult, and collectors of all ages.)

Material World

A Global Family Portrait

by Peter Menzel

Material World is the most eye-opening, human, absolutely stunning book! It would be a wonderful thing if every child in America had a chance to spend some time with it. It is, quite simply, amazing!

Simple in concept, but exquisitely executed, this book is a gigantic photo-essay on families. Photographed outside their homes with all their worldly goods, these are average families from countries all across the earth. Brief text and a table of statistics elaborate how this family fits into their world. From the detailed statistics, we learn about the family and their country. These statistics range from area, population, life expectancy and literacy rate to household size, most valued possessions and wishes for the future. The comparisons between countries are fascinating. We get an intimate glimpse into daily life from the text and the photos. We see the people at work and how their children spend their day. We see what their homes are like and what the earth looks like where they live: the poverty, the affluence, the dignity, the smiles. We see the threads that bind our humanity together, the beauty inherent in the incredible diversity of life on our planet. The photos in this book will likely fill your heart with smiles and your eyes with tears. My children have spent hours poring over the pictures in *Material World*. They ask questions and study the world map trying to understand where these families live. The book graphically illustrates the astounding basic material discrepancies that exist on the planet today.

The conversations I have been trying to have for years are now surfacing because the kids are bringing things up instead of me. "Why is their most valued possession a donkey?" goes a lot further than the starving children in Africa routine. "Why do they only want a future and not stuff?" opens up the discussion of what war is really about far better than my restricting the conversation to how they play with their toys. My daughter commented that these are not just poor children in another country, they are children just like her, only different; they play, they sing, they look happy, they have families.

This book brings the whole glorious world into focus. It speaks of diversity and the true dignity of being human. Through pictures it talks about what makes us rich. Is it money or is it love? *Material World* is not a children's book per se, but it is certainly one that children relate to. It is truly astonishing. (All ages.)

Dear Friends,

There's this fax machine across from my office here at Chinaberry. Its proximity has made life easier for all of us on this side of the building. The only glitch is that we have to be careful not to send something with Wite-Out on it, as this apparently damages the mechanism. Fair enough. We can handle that.

There's a problem, though: I dread using it because for one reason or another, about half of my faxes get error messages and I have to resend them. And perhaps resend them! Its temperamentalness is frustrating and maddening. I'm now to the point that I actually scowl at the machine as I approach it or walk by.

Now, if I were hooked up to some sophisticated monitoring equipment, it wouldn't be a big surprise to see it indicating a rise in my blood pressure and increased stress when I enter the fax room. It's that scowl of mine that concerns me, though. I know that it's neither good for me nor for those near me to carry around such animosity, but on some level I also know that it's not good for the fax machine, either. The concept of animism is not the issue here. It's just that it's always seemed common sense to me that carrying around negative thoughts is harmful to everyone and everything around you.

My mixed feelings about this fax machine brought to mind a conversation I had with a friend who is a computer programmer/troubleshooter. Over the course of a month, he witnessed an experiment conducted in a psychology class at a local state university. Eight students who owned their own computers and who were willing to keep them at the school for a month were recruited for this experiment. The computers were from different, but equivalent, manufacturers, and had the same memory capacities. Four of the computers were kept in one room and four in another room.

Throughout the month, the students would do their normal computer work in those rooms. They were told to keep a daily journal of their computer's performance, recording, especially, error messages, glitches, lock-ups, crashes, things of that sort. The journals were not shared with anyone during the experiment.

Unbeknownst to the students, each day the experimenters would enter each room for five minutes. In one room they would spend the time thinking dark and negative thoughts, making hostile gestures and screaming and cursing. In the other, their thoughts and actions were entirely the opposite. Never, however, would they touch a machine.

At month's end the journals were studied. The results were astounding. The computers in the "dark" room experienced a poor performance three times as bad as those in the "light" room. A similar experiment with plants exhibited even worse results in that three of four plants in the "dark" room died and the one that survived showed no growth. The "light" room plants all flourished.

Now, I can't vouch for this experiment's ability to pass rigorous scientific muster, but it seems to me that the findings must contain some truth. If one's being on edge, angry and negative can affect a computer's ability to perform well and a plant's ability to thrive, then consider a bigger picture. With all of the frustrations and stresses and negativities that can easily pull us off center in our busy lives, it's especially crucial that we keep the space around us clear and as pure as possible. And nowhere is this more important than in our families' lives. Having our computers lock up or crash is one thing; having our children absorb our anger and negativity just by

being in the same room with us is another. Recognizing that we are con-
stantly surrounded by less-than-soothing events, man-made conveniences
such as our fax machine that suddenly become man-made inconveniences,
and other frustrations that abound in daily living, we need to be ever aware
that negativity can creep into our lives at any moment. We must choose to
be peace bearers and we can make that choice by the way we react to what
is happening around us. The poet Wallace Stevens put it eloquently when
he wrote: "It matters immensely. The slightest sound matters. The most mo-
mentary rhythm matters. You can do as you please, yet everything matters."
The next time I go to use the fax machine I hope to remember that wher-
ever I go and whatever I do, the way I do it matters, for it is up to me to cre-
ate sacred space wherever I go.

Traditions

The Threads That Weave

Our Lives Together

The best things you can give your children,
next to good habits, are good memories.
—SYDNEY J. HARRIS

Parents are the gatekeepers of family traditions. We choose what to celebrate, how, when and why. Whether these family customs have to do with birthdays, holiday celebrations, vacations or even simple Saturday morning pancake feasts, traditions build bonds and memories. They can be the cement that glues a family together, allowing them to flourish in the good times and survive the rough ones. Nowadays, families come in all shapes and sizes, but no matter what our family constellation is, we can create traditions that strengthen our relationships and evoke happiness. A wise friend of mine once said that happy families make lots of happy memories. She's right. Families that genuinely love and respect each other enjoy family members' company. They do things together that make memories and bring back smiles. They often have long-standing family jokes, and small, rather silly traditions that they vigorously claim and defend simply for tradition's sake.

Children can latch on to these family customs with a ferocity that always amazes me. They insist that we do something again and again just because it is the way we have always done it (even if they don't completely love what they are doing). One example of this that always makes me chuckle is my family's habit of going out for breakfast on Christmas Eve morning. Every year, my children and I trek down to Pike Place Market, our local farmers'-artists' market, to buy salmon for our Christmas dinner feast. This has always been a fun way to fill that excruciatingly long day of waiting and make it pass a little bit faster. To avoid the last-minute shopping crowds, we always arrive just as the market is opening. Motivating my children to get out the door that early had always been a formidable task, though, until one year I said, "Let's have breakfast at the market before we do our shopping." The minute I mentioned breakfast out (a rare occasion in our family) they began throwing on their coats and were ready to go! On the way, I mentioned we would have to be frugal and order something inexpensive. "Fine, fine" came the shouts from the backseat. Who cared what we ate? The surprise treat of eating out was all that mattered. Upon arrival, we perused the menu of a small café and decided upon oatmeal and hot chocolate—a choice that allowed all of us to eat for less than twenty dollars. Thus began a long-standing custom. Year after year, we make our trek to the market, eat our oatmeal and purchase our fish and a couple of loaves of fresh bread from the bakery. Then, after a quick jaunt through the artists' stalls, we are on our way back home. But the thing I find so humorous about this is that for all those years, my kids didn't enjoy the oatmeal we'd been ordering! It was covered in nuts and fruits and all kinds of mixed, hard-to-decipher delicious goodies, and they'd just wanted the plain oatmeal they got at home. Nonetheless, year after year, they ate it without a fuss simply because it was what we do on Christmas Eve. It wasn't until many years later, when my husband decided to come along and then absolutely refused to eat oatmeal, that our traditional menu was abandoned and we began to order what we individually liked. The tide of tradition was so strong, it carried my children straight past food they hated, just for the sake of doing what had always been done. Tradition is certainly a powerful phenomenon, but one that my husband so aptly showed us must be ready to adapt to the times and the people at hand.

Clearly, we mustn't hold on to something simply because that is what custom calls for, but rather wisely choose our traditions to suit the needs of our family. We stand ready to adapt when times change and hold on to the meaning of the tradition as the specifics of the event evolve. The birthday party that was a grand success for a five-year-old can become rather stale for a ten-year-old. And yet, with simple fine tuning, the basic choices we made for how birthdays are celebrated in our family can hold for the length of our child's life. How we celebrate anything is an opportunity to express our family's values. In most situations, our child will follow our lead and be quite happy with our decisions. So it is up to us to make choices that reflect what is in our hearts. For example, I want my children to grow up to love and care for the earth, so when it comes time to fill birthday party bags, I look for something special that helps my children and their friends interact positively with the earth. Laura and Heidi have fall birthdays, so we generally include a few daffodil or tulip bulbs among the treasures. Aidan's birthday is in the spring, so his bags often have a small plant or packet of seeds.

My husband and I decided long ago to forgo as much commercialism and materialism as we are able to in our family celebrations. We make our valentines and grow lush baskets of Easter grass. At Thanksgiving, we make fresh cranberry sauce and pumpkin pie starting with a sugar pumpkin, so our children can clearly identify the connection between what they are eating and the origins of that food. We find all kinds of things to celebrate—the solstices (with candles in the wintertime, and a sun cake in the summer), Fat Tuesday with homemade doughnuts, May Day with bundles of flowers secretly left on neighbors' doorsteps. There is no end of things to celebrate, and my children are happy to make a tradition of it all. They are delighted to participate in the celebrations of other families who happen to have different backgrounds. They have greatly enjoyed being included in their friends' Hanukkah and Passover celebrations. They come home with eyes bright, full of questions and possibility, wanting to know more about what they have experienced.

Every family chooses its own traditions, from simple to complex, and children love them all. It is up to us as parents to choose what best suits our desires. Our own family's birthday celebrations start the night before with the traditional birthday poem.

A Verse for the Night Before the Birthday

> *When I have said my evening prayer,*
> *And my clothes are folded on the chair,*
> *And mother switches off the light,*

I'll still be _____ years old tonight.
But, from the very break of day,
Before the children rise and play,
Before the darkness turns to gold
Tomorrow, I'll be _____ years old.
_____ kisses when I wake,
_____ candles on my cake!

(*from* Festivals, Family and Food, *see page 135.*)

Upon waking, our birthday child finds a specially decorated birthday chair that is his or hers to sit in for a week. Dinner is her choice of menu, always ending with a homemade cake. For parties, we have chosen simple at-home affairs, often with the same activities year after year. Slumber parties and "events" (such as bowling or gymnastics) were things we told our children to look forward to when they grew older—a sort of coming-of-age acknowledgment when they were ten. The simple at-home parties remain fun because the parties grow with the child, evolving through the years. I have learned that it isn't what we do or how much we do at the parties that make it a success, but rather our intent. We have chosen these simple celebrations, but we watch our friends construct much more elaborate schemes with great success. In the end, what matters most is the act of celebration and the happy feeling behind it, not the specifics of how we are celebrating it. Most birthday children love any kind of party that focuses on fun and on them.

When designing traditions for our families, we must look back to our childhoods and to the present to know the needs of our current situation. Consider closely what made happy memories for you and then find ways to create traditions effused with those same loving feelings for your child. If you use the possibilities inherent in a child's love of tradition to strengthen the love and joy of your family, you will never be sorry.

Books can be great anchors for family traditions because they are always the same—comfortable words and illustrations that bring joy, especially if they are saved just for certain occasions.

Tips for Successful Birthday Parties

♥ Know your child. And know yourself! Some children (and parents) are much better suited, temperamentally, to large, chaotic celebrations than others may be. Birthdays are high-stress times for young children. Generally, they have been waiting so long for their birthday and with so much anticipation that they can hardly contain themselves. It is perfectly normal for a birthday child under the age of six to burst into tears at some point during her party—or, worse yet, turn into some kind of horrible demon you have never seen the likes of before and never will again. I remember going to a brilliantly planned, highly creative birthday party for a five-year-old, put on by a mother who couldn't have cared more about her child. This party was a true extravaganza—lots of kids, lots of parents, lots of sugar and lots of incredibly fun but challenging games. When it came time for the birthday girl to have her turn at one of the games (the old drop-the-clothespin-in-the-milk-bottle trick), the skill level required for the game was suddenly way beyond this child's capability. (On any other day she could have mastered it with ease.) All of a sudden, this normally delightful girl simply fell apart. Her marvelous birthday celebration came to a sudden halt as we all watched aghast as the poor, overwrought child grabbed the clothespins and the bottle from her mother and ran, shrieking, at top speed around the yard. The mother, not thinking, joined in the chase. For five long minutes the two chased each other around and around the yard, never thinking to stop. The poor child, the poor mother—what a heart-wrenching scene. After the mom finally reached the child to gather her up in her arms, it took many long minutes of full-fledged screaming on the girl's part before she could calm down enough for the party to resume. It was a truly agonizing event to watch and I can only imagine how it felt to be that young girl (or the mother!). Clearly, this party was too much for her young self. So remember, if your child is timid, particularly sensitive or emotionally intense, a busy or loud party will quite possibly cause her to fall apart. If, on the other hand, you and your child love big events and your child has an adaptable temperament, go for it. There's nothing quite like a big birthday bash. Just know that the more elaborate the party, the higher the risk that a young child will emotionally disintegrate.

There is an old rule of thumb that many parents abide by: invite one guest for each year of your child's life. You may wish to disregard this bit of parental lore, but it is nice to know about before you invite fifteen three-year-olds over to your house and wonder what happened. We have followed this rule with various exceptions for all four of my children's parties and it has worked quite well for us.

Explain your expectations of your child to your child clearly and firmly before the party. "When your guests arrive, you must . . . After you open your friend's present, look her in the eye and say . . . When it is time to leave, make sure you say good-bye to your friends and thank them for coming. . . ." or whatever your expectations might be. Knowing the expectations ahead of time helps your child prepare for what could be a scary moment. Birthday party manners are new to young children and they must be taught. This goes for when your child is a guest, too. You might also want to explain the format of the party so your child knows when to expect to open presents and when to expect to play. The birthday children have enough to concern themselves with without getting overexcited about the order of events. If you show your child that you have a plan and then gently but firmly carry out the plan, you are much more likely to avoid the power struggles so common at young children's parties.

Playing noncompetitive games greatly reduces the party tension for preschoolers, especially those who tend to become overexcited, anyway. Our family has taken many of the old standard birthday party games and with slight adaptations made them noncompetitive. For example, we transformed musical chairs into musical pillows. We start out the game with a pillow for everyone. When the music stops, each child plops down on a pillow. After each round, we remove one pillow and keep all the children. By the end of the game, all participants are piling (carefully!) onto one pillow. This version has provided our children with plenty of giggles and fewer hurt feelings. With a little creativity most games can be transformed into win-win situations where "everyone giggles and everyone wins," to quote Shel Silverstein.

Try not to feed young children too much sugar without first putting some nutritious food into their stomachs. Either plan your party di-

rectly after a normal mealtime, or serve a meal during the party before you serve your cake. Too much sugar on an empty stomach
makes it harder for some young children to maintain their party
manners. A couple of cute cookie cutters turn peanut butter and
jelly sandwiches into haute cuisine; add a few starry apple slices
(cut horizontally instead of vertically), string cheese and a small
handful of trail mix and you have an easy, nutritious lunch.

Remember to provide a balance of activity. Too much running
around *or* expecting too much calm behavior from young children
will most likely lead to mayhem. A quiet game followed by a rowdy
game; opening presents followed by cake and ice cream. It isn't necessary to keep kids highly scheduled for the entire party. If the children know each other, they will quite likely enjoy a chance to play
together, but be ready with some extra games just in case things go
awry. Seek a balance that works for your child and your home. The
smaller your space, the more structure you will probably need to
survive with your sanity intact.

You might want to decide on something special that will define a
tradition for your family's birthday parties. In one family I know, the
father creates the most elaborate cakes—beautifully decorated
works of art, every year something completely new and different. In
our family, tradition demands an elaborate treasure hunt. Each year
we design a hunt that lasts for quite a while and has the kids running hither and yon (inside, outside, upstairs, downstairs) in search
of those all-important party bags. I've been told over and over
again by many of my children's friends (and by my children) that
the treasure hunt is the best part of our parties. Having a signature
event helps brand your family party style in your child's mind, building happy memories and strong family traditions.

The concept of party bags has grown to amazing proportions in the
twenty years I have been a parent. What used to be a simple bag of
treats and perhaps a small toy can now be a major expense, depending on what you choose to put in the bags. Don't feel as if you
have to keep up with the Joneses, but rather do something creative.
A fifty-cent bottle of bubbles, a blown-up balloon and a whistle pop
can be a perfect collection of party favors for a four-year-old, if
you take the time to blow bubbles and have a whistle parade during
the party.

While it is often nice to give children choices in their lives, too many choices on special days like birthdays or holidays can be emotionally overwhelming. This is a time to remember that *you* are the parent. Be in charge, but be kind. Let your children have the fun of participating, but don't give them complete control of the party. (There is plenty of time for this when your child is older.) If children create too many specifics in their imagination, chances are you won't be able to live up to their expectations and you stand a strong possibility of disappointing them. Ask them one or two things, such as what kind of cake and ice cream they want, and then plan the rest on your own.

And remember, there is no rule that a child has to have a birthday party every year. Sometimes, a quiet celebration with just family is the best party ever. But bear in mind, your children will come to expect what you have done in the past. (Long live traditions!) So be ready to field some reluctance if you step out of the norm. And at the same time, trust yourself to know what is best for your child for any given year.

It's My Birthday

by Helen Oxenbury

It may be my imagination, but it seems as if the best-tasting birthday cakes we've had while celebrating our children's birthdays over the years are the ones that they have helped make. My favorite thing of all is not working in or being in a kitchen whose every last inch of counter space has been devoured by the debris of cooking. But there is truly something special about the mess that is left after a good, old-fashioned stint in the kitchen with your toddler. When your child's next birthday rolls around, try making the cake together if you don't already. I guarantee it will add a sweet, new dimension to the special day.

This story is a twist on the Little Red Hen, in which all the animals were eager to have some of the cake she was baking, but were unwilling to help her with the process. Here, a little androgynous-looking toddler sets about making a cake because it's his (her?) birthday. He needs some eggs, and the chicken volunteers to get some. He needs some flour, and the bear heads home to get it from his house. The child needs butter and milk, too, so the cat raids its family's refrigerator to get some. And so on. Once all of the ingredients are assembled, the whole eager crew hunkers down to make the cake. And even though there is a moment of uncertainty about who's actually going to get a piece of it, they all do, in the end.

This is a simple and sweet book infused with a wonderful spirit of friendship and cooperation—and dessert! (18 mos.–3 yrs.)

Scary, Scary Halloween

by Eve Bunting
illustrated by Jan Brett

This simple story is mainly visual, although the opening verse helps to set the mood:

> *I peer outside,*
> *there's something there*
> *That makes me shiver,*
> *spikes my hair*
> *It must be Halloween.*

Yes, we see witches, goblins, ghosts romping through a field. But the illustrations also include indications that these are real, live, excited humans just having fun with it all. Throughout the progression of the story, the action is being viewed from nearby shadows by mysterious green eyes, which provide a delightful surprise at the end of the book. The text is rhyming and simple and the illustrations are richly colored, providing a wonderful balance between the delicious scariness of Halloween and the outright fun of it all. You might not be able to stash this away eleven months of the year; it will be right out there with all the other favorites. (2½–5 yrs.)

Somebody Loves You, Mr. Hatch

by Eileen Spinelli
illustrated by Paul Yalowitz

Mr. Hatch is a lonesome soul. Retiring yet kindly, his unexciting existence is about as bland as it gets. No circle of friends embraces him, and vice versa. But that Valentine's Day when the postman delivers a big package with a note saying "Somebody loves you" changes things forever.

Awestruck that someone actually noticed him enough to *love* him, for heaven's sake, Mr. Hatch lets down his shy defenses and opens up to everyone around him, because, of course, anybody could be the mysterious source of that package. Touched by the wonderful spell of feeling loved, he smiles for the first time the townspeople can remember. He opens up, he feels accepted by people, they respond in kind and Mr. Hatch acquires a glow to his face thanks to the warm glow in his heart. Life is good, as it is meant to be.

But when the postman returns one day with the ominous news that he had unfortunately misdelivered the "Somebody loves you" package of several weeks ago, bereft Mr. Hatch hands over the box. Life returns to the ho-hum, day-in, day-out existence of prepackage days. Mr. Hatch goes back to being the lonely soul he's always been. (Note that the illustrations have gone from lifeless color to vibrant and now back to lifeless.)

But the townsfolk have seen his light and you will see that nothing is the same after that. The story ends in a fine way and the bottom line is that everyone is worthy of love and can feel that love in a tangible way.

This book transcends its Valentine's Day theme; it is wonderful for any day of the year. (4–7 yrs.)

Traditions appear in many forms. Certainly, they don't need to be attached to holidays, though we tend to focus more attention on our holiday traditions. Regular Wednesday-evening trips to the library for story hour and Dad's Saturday-morning pancake feasts offer just as much opportunity for creating positive family traditions as the holidays offer. In some ways, since these traditions tend to be less formal, they can feel easier to maintain. After all, less emotion ends up being attached to which day we trek to the library than on whom we invite to Thanksgiving dinner. With a little bit of effort on our part as parents, we can create nonholiday-oriented traditions that strengthen our family bonds and yet allow us to relax, rather than adding stress to our lives. The trick comes in knowing what you enjoy doing and finding a way to include your children in the process. Do you love to bake? Sunday evening Make-Your-Own-Pizza parties might be a perfect family tradition where each person gets to roll and design their own perfect pizza. Like to garden? The planting (and nurturing) of a bean tepee could easily be a favorite annual tradition.

For years, my family had the tradition of "family night." Every Sunday at four o'clock we knew the rest of the evening was devoted to family. We did all manner of interesting things—from winter sunset picnics at the beach to dipping candles. Over the years, we tried all kinds of crafts and activities. We explored unique restaurants, and observed unusual natural phenomena (like watching the wild salmon run up a creek near our home). What we did wasn't the point; the tradition was about spending focused time together. As the kids grew older and more able to do physical things, this tradition evolved away from Sunday evenings and more toward the serious outdoor adventures that my husband and I enjoyed before our children were born. Other families I have known have had this same idea and translated it in their own way to make their family traditions. One had their family meeting followed by a special dessert every Tuesday night. The meeting allowed for better communication and problem solving for positive family dynamics and the special dessert meant fun to the kids. Another friend devotes Friday evenings to playing games as a family. A yummy dinner, followed by a cozy hour of playing in front of the fire, makes their weekend begin with a focus on family. Whatever traditions you choose matter little, as long as they create an opportunity for togetherness. With all the pressures of today's lifestyles, designating time simply for fun and togetherness is a must if we want to create a healthy family.

The High Rise Glorious Skittle Skat
Roarious Sky Pie Angel Food Cake

by Nancy Willard
illustrated by Richard Jesse Watson

When is the last time a member of your family asked you what you wanted for your birthday and you said something like "Oh, nothing. I already have everything I need"? When pressed by your child for some ideas anyway, then you come up with "Why don't you make me something? I like things you make for me the very best." (Remember when you were a child and you simply couldn't believe how boring an adult's life must be not to answer such a question with a whole list of "wants"?!) If any of the above sounds familiar, this book will hit delightfully close to home within the first several pages. It is the story of a ten-ish-year-old girl whose mother finally answers the what-do-you-want-for-your-birthday inquiry with a request for a birthday cake made from the same (never-written-down) recipe her own grandmother invented long ago. The cake, you see, is dangerous. In her journal, she had penned, "It is irresistible to man and beast, woman and bird. I fear it may fall into the wrong hands." This is followed by a clue to where the complete recipe may be found. Our child heroine quietly stays up all night baking the cake for her mother.

The detailed and colored illustrations on every spread are just amazing. There is ample to look at and the book's feeling is joyful and down-to-earth. (And yes, the recipe is included!) I know one young woman for whom this cake has been a tradition for over ten years.

Its text is substantial (it will take about thirty minutes to read it aloud), and the book is great for girls or boys who still enjoy being read to. (4+ yrs.)

When it is time for gift-giving on any occasion, consider making and giving coupons to your children. The sky is the limit. "This coupon good for one breakfast out with Dad." "This coupon good for staying up late on one weekend night." "This coupon good for one bike-riding afternoon with Mom." What is so wonderful about coupons is that they can so easily translate into time spent together with loved ones, rather than just another *thing* to accumulate. We started this tradition early in our family and it wasn't too long before we parents started getting lovingly scrawled coupons from the *children*. It is a sweet way to teach that gifts of self are often so much more meaningful and fun than gifts that originate in the wallet.

The Country Bunny
and the Little Gold Shoes

by Du Bose Heyward
illustrated by Marjorie Flack

All the other bunnies laugh when Cottontail says she will grow up to help Grandfather Bunny deliver eggs to children for Easter. They tell her to leave such tasks to "great big men bunnies like us," and to go home and care for her twenty-one children. But when the time comes for wise Grandfather Bunny to select a new Easter Bunny, he chooses Cottontail because he needs someone who is clever, wise, swift and kind, and he sees that Cottontail's experience as a mother has given her all of these qualifications and more. The country bunny is given a very difficult task on Easter Eve. The reward for her help is a pair of little gold shoes, which she hangs in a special place on the wall of her country house, symbol of her self-confidence and achievement.

This is a lovely book to bring out every year at Easter, or anytime your children need a boost in confidence to make their dreams come true. It is suitable for young ones, yet sophisticated enough for eager readers who may wish to try the words on their own. (4–8 yrs.)

Rechenka's Eggs

by Patricia Polacco

Here is a story especially meaningful to those who celebrate spring-time or Easter with the coloring of eggs.

If you or your family has had the experience of working with Pysanky (eggs painted in the elaborate Ukrainian style), you will feel a kinship to Old Babushka, known throughout all of Moskva for her beautifully painted eggs. *Rechenka's Eggs* is steeped in tradition, with ingredients that make for an enduring classic. When Babushka takes time from her egg painting to aid a wounded goose, she also opens the door to a series of small miracles and to good fortune.

The stunning, detailed and deeply colored illustrations comple-ment this timeless story of the mysterious ways in which kindness is repaid. An especially beautiful lesson for your child about how what goes around comes around. (4–8 yrs.)

Michael Hague's Family Easter Treasury

collected and illustrated by Michael Hague

Michael Hague, illustrator extraordinaire, has collected and illustrated thirty-two of his favorite texts and poems about Easter. In a balanced combination of religious and secular stories, he has captured this mag-nificent time of rebirth with the same kind of lush illustrations that have made him famous.

Some all-time favorite poems and stories found their way into this collection. The book is divided into four sections: A Time of Faith; A Time of Rebirth; A Time of Celebration and A Time of Love. Through these four sections children come to understand the deeper spiritual meanings of Easter. Hague has chosen to include stories and poems about the journey the earth is making at this time. This offers children a concrete way to see the miracle of death and resurrection that lies at the heart of Easter, since the earth is re-creating the same process at Easter time. While Easter can be confusing to young children, this book helps them to understand the transformational process of death and resurrection as they watch their garden go from winter to spring. This is truly a lovely book in all ways! (All ages.)

The Holidays

The holidays. Say those words and a flood of varied emotions emerge. Rare is the person who can approach the holidays without a pile of emotional baggage in tow. Some of us are busy trying to make the perfect holidays for our children. Others of us are plagued with the guilt, remorse and uncertainty of how to best deal with the complexities of our own extended families. Some of us are so completely overextended at this time of year that we hardly get a chance to sit down. Whoever the person, the holidays always seem to hold some dissonance. We want magic, joy and love to abound in our homes, and yet with our conflicting, confusing feelings, we may get lost or even sometimes immobilized by our uncertainty. For some, the whole season can sometimes feel like a pile of "shoulds"—things that, when they all are completed, leave us feeling completely exhausted and unfulfilled. If we want to find the peace and magic of the season, we must somehow learn to let go of these "shoulds" and create our own way to celebrate, the way that suits us perfectly. We have collected some suggestions that make the holidays work better for us. These are just ideas—springboards for your own revisioning of a magical celebration.

♥ First of all, make a list of everything you think you have to do (i.e., the "shoulds") and examine each one carefully. Choose to do only the ones that bring your family joy. If certain activities are emotionally draining or you do them only because someone else thinks you *should*, rethink them. It is *your* energy—spend it on the things that nourish your soul. It takes great courage to say "no" to "shoulds," but the rewards are enormous.

♥ Focus on the holiday season rather than on the particular day, especially with Christmas. If you have spent weeks singing carols together as a family or making homemade gifts and decorations, there is less emphasis on Christmas morning and more on the meaning of the season. Celebrating the whole season—Advent through Epiphany—takes the focus away from the gifts and allows the soul to fully rejoice in the inner beauty of the season. Find little, simple rituals (e.g., lighting a candle every night or reading a special story-book such as *The Christmas Storybook*) to acknowledge the sacred-ness of the season.

Rather than feeling as if you have to spend more money than you have or want to spend, find ways to give of yourself. A gift of time or an outing may mean much more to someone than yet another thing. Teaching a skill (like cooking or sewing) is fun for both par-ties and costs nothing to give.

One family we know forgoes all gift giving to their friends and loved ones (except a simple gift or two for their children), takes the money they would spend and donates it to people less fortunate than they are. Each year they donate their Christmas money in their loved ones' names. One year, this family actually took two weeks (almost their entire year's vacation) and spent the money they would have given in presents to take themselves to a rural vil-lage in Central America to help with the hard physical work of hand digging a new water system. What a gift for all concerned!

Genuinely attempt to not overschedule yourself. Most of the joy in the holiday comes from the quiet moments spent with those you love. If you are busy running from party to party and making sure you hit every store in town to find the "perfect" gift, chances are you will end up tired and grouchy rather than filled with the joy of the season.

The holidays are a wonderful time to clearly define what makes your family special. Your children will learn at least as much from your saying "no" to them at this time as they will gain from the temporary pleasure of a "yes." Show them what makes your family special by actively choosing to live your values. Help them to under-stand why you choose to do things the way you do and buy the things you buy by talking about the reasons behind your actions.

Take time for creating magic. The holidays allow our children to be-lieve in the unseen world. They take us out of our ordinary time and space and allow us to hope for miracles and magic. This ability to believe, to hope, is fundamental to our lives. Nurture your child's sense of wonder. Believing in elves and other magical beings builds our child's sense of imagination. Leaving little notes or treats from these special beings throughout the season nourishes our children's sense of the possible. (They also help to diffuse the incredible anticipation of "*the* day.")

Elijah's Angel ☆

A Story for Chanukah and Christmas

by Michael J. Rosen
illustrated by Aminah Brenda Lynn Robinson

This beautiful and loving book is a gift to both Jews and Christians. The book leads us to a deeper mutual understanding and appreciation of each religion's winter celebration.

Michael's and Elijah's lives came together some time ago, but it wasn't until the year that Christmas Eve and Chanukah fell on the same day that these two friends formed the bond of love and understanding that is tangible in this story. Michael is a nine-year-old Jewish boy, and Elijah, an African American barber and woodcutter, is a Christian man in his eighties. On the day that Elijah gives Michael one of his carvings, an angel, the boy must learn how to accept it without feeling that he is compromising his religion by bringing a graven image into his house. As the story and their friendship develop, we see Michael mature enough to view and love the angel as a sign of Elijah's affection. With his parents' guidance, Michael understands that this beautiful, hand-carved, black-faced angel is but a symbol of their friendship, and knows that the perfect gift for Elijah will be the menorah he made at Hebrew school. And, given with joy, it is accepted—and used—in joy.

This story is based on a real Elijah, a barber and renowned woodcarver in Ohio. The text eloquently evokes the odd combination of confusion, love, admiration and excitement Michael feels as he takes part in creating a path of understanding between himself and another, and their two religions. It is a joyful story of two people who are able to look beyond—and remain true to—their religions and see the thread that winds through them both. (5+ yrs.)

Holiday Spirals

Here is a quick and easy holiday craft that, while simple to make, adds extraordinary beauty to your home. All you need is a needle, thread, scissors, paper (colored origami paper, gold paper or slightly stiff paper all are good choices) and tape. Simply cut out a circle of paper—four to six inches in diameter. Then with scissors, gently spiral your way to the center of the circle, cutting a quarter-inch in from the outside of the circle as you spiral your way in. Once at the center, leave a half-inch-wide center piece and use a needle to attach a knotted thread to the center. Make the thread long enough to dangle from your ceiling at a pleasant height. Attach your spiral to the ceiling with tape.

We dangle spirals all over our home and let them dance and sway in the gentle breezes of the blowing furnace. You can also hang them high above a lighted candle (high enough that it won't catch on fire) and have the spiral spin continuously. These spirals are especially pretty when made with gold or silver paper, as the metallic sheen of the paper glimmers in the light.

The Family Treasury of Jewish Holidays

by Malka Drucker
illustrated by Nancy Patz

What a lovely, lovely book this is. It is for everyone—not only Jewish families, but for any family interested in learning more about Jewish culture. It is truly a feast for the eyes and the soul! Taking us through the wheel of the Jewish year, author Malka Drucker discusses ten significant holidays. Each one has its own section, relating in simple language the meaning and historical significance of the holiday. The book tells how each holiday is celebrated and includes a special story or two that relates the deeper meanings of the holiday to a child's life. Drucker explains the special items for each holiday in a way that expresses what is sacred about each, and yet enlightens the child about what can often seem like a mystery to a young mind. She includes simple, inexpensive family crafts, games, songs and recipes for special foods associated with each holiday. Everything is here to capture the joy and meaning behind what is sometimes an unfathomable experience to a young child, making this book a special way to learn about one's family traditions.

Beautiful watercolors enhance almost every page, making the words come alive. *The Family Treasury of Jewish Holidays* is a book to return to again and again. When your children are young, introduce the holidays ahead of time by reading the stories and singing the songs. As they grow older, add the crafts and the more meaningful sections about the history of the holidays. In this way, the book grows as your family does. (All ages.)

HAPPY HOLIDAYS

The Christmas Story Book

collected by Ineke Verschuren

The Christmas Story Book has been my family's favorite Christmas book for many years. Each early December we lovingly haul it out of the basement to set it beside the couch for the Christmas season. All of the children treasure the stories and eagerly look forward to our evening reading sessions.

This is a book unlike any other I have seen. It gathers stories from all over the world, some familiar, most unfamiliar, and divides them into five sections: Advent, the birth of the Child, Christmas night, Christmas around the world, Christmas to Epiphany. The anticipation of reading the stories in order is delicious, as it seems to prolong the Christmas season and allows us to ponder the deeper meanings of Christmas as the weeks go by. Celebrating Christmas for six weeks instead of a few days helps to take the focus away from the one day of presents and allows us to behold the sacredness of the season. Each story in the book contains a deeper truth that helps children learn the many facets of the Christmas spirit. In this all too material world, it is wonderful to find a book that speaks to the holiness of the season without seeming too preachy.

The Christmas Story Book contains truly beautiful Christmas stories (it does not contain any illustrations, however—only stories) and each story is labeled, identifying its age-appropriateness. (4+ yrs.)

The Christmas Miracle of

Jonathan Toomey

by Susan Wojciechowski
illustrated by P. J. Lynch

This is a remarkable tale about the true spirit of Christmas. It is the story of a man whose last name is "Toomey." But, since he never smiles or laughs, and since he keeps completely to himself, the children of the village have come to call him "Mr. Gloomey." They don't know the truth, but the reader soon finds out that he is simply a profoundly sad and lonely man whose wife and baby died within days of each other years ago, essentially taking his own life with them.

One day there is a knock at his door and two newcomers to the village stand before him: the widow McDowell and her seven-year-old son, Thomas. In the process of moving their belongings here, they have somehow lost the very special set of Christmas figures that her grandfather had carved for her when she was a girl. With Christmas now only days away, she was hoping that this woodcarver the villagers had mentioned to her might be able to carve a set for Thomas and her in time to celebrate the holy day. Gruffly, he agrees to do what he can in the time he has. The only problem is that Thomas is determined to sit beside him and watch, offer suggestions on how to make each figure as extraordinary as the ones he remembers and ultimately (and unwittingly) open Toomey's heart in a way it hasn't been open since before his family died. At first, Toomey resists. But as the days pass and Thomas and widow McDowell become more and more at ease with the woodcarver's ways (and vice versa), things begin to soften. This is a stunning story about what Christmas does to people's spirits. It is not the story of Christ's birth, but it is the story of the rebirth of three unsuspecting people and how a simple request can lead to a miracle that opens hearts and allows us to see the goodness that is all around.

The Christmas Miracle of Jonathan Toomey speaks to the child, mother and father in all of us. It speaks to the lonely and deserted part of us, as well as to the hopefulness and innocence that abide in our hearts. The rich and realistic watercolor illustrations make the story as real as a story can be. It is an experience that will stay with your family a long, long time. (3+ yrs.)

Letting Go

Sometimes my unbound enthusiasm can make me go a little bit overboard during the holidays. My mind, buzzing with creative ideas, keeps coming up with just one more thing to cook, to make and to experience, until I am simply exhausted, thus losing the fun of the holidays by trying to do too much. I have bestowed on myself the huge responsibility of making the holidays magical for my family. This responsibility used to be a joy back when our family was smaller and the children were younger. But our increasingly complex lives now make this joy feel more like a chore. The paradox is that the very things I like the most about Christmas—the magic, the surprises, the joy—were being destroyed by my best efforts to make sure they happened! It has taken years, but I have finally learned that the less I do and the more I can just be present in the moment, the more likely it is for my mythical, *magical* Christmas feeling to appear.

So if you find the holidays somewhat lacking or even forced (as if you have been trying too hard for too long), try simplifying what they mean to you. Identify the essence of the holiday and make sure to choose activities that celebrate the true meaning of the day (or days). Once I simplified my expectations, my true desires seemed much more manageable and made much more sense to me because they were now undeniably heartfelt.

> And you know the funniest thing is, once we started really focusing on what Christmas truly meant to us, our material wants diminished and all the magic I was seeking flourished in our hearts quite by accident.

The Donkey's Dream

by Barbara Helen Berger

Most of us who celebrate Christmas will agree that there is a certain magic to Christmas Eve. Even if we can't quite put it into words, *something* happens when the sun goes down on December 24.

For those of you who feel a reverence for whatever is special in the air, this book will warm your heart and make you smile. It is about the donkey that carries the pregnant Mary to Bethlehem. With the precious load on his back, he dreams that he's carrying a city with gates and towers and temple domes, a ship, a fountain, a rose "soft as a mother's touch and sweet as the sleep of a baby" and a lady full of heaven. (The illustrations are of each of these visions, which are symbols given to Mary by "tradition," as explained at the end of the book.) Upon finding a cave, the lady goes in while the man removes the tired donkey's saddle and sees that he has water. In a while, a baby's cry is heard in the quiet night, and the man whispers for the donkey to come. There, the donkey sees the lady on a bed of hay, with his saddle as her pillow. She smiles and says, "Come see what we have carried all this way, you and I."

The softly hued color illustrations are a fine match for this romantic story of the Nativity. (3–8 yrs.)

The Clown of God

retold and illustrated by Tomie dePaola

This well-loved story takes place during the Renaissance, and the illustrations of the scenery, clothing and customs of the period reflect a certain whimsical authenticity.

It is about a street urchin named Giovanni who devotes nearly his entire life to bringing joy to people through his superb juggling. As time wears on, and the rigors of old age prevent him from performing flawlessly, he puts away his juggling balls and roams the Italian countryside. On a cold winter night, he finds himself on the doorstep of a church in which worshipers are celebrating Christmas by placing gifts in front of a statue of the Madonna and Child. Giovanni, concerned by the Child's stern facial expression, decides to attempt to make him smile by juggling in the quiet of the empty church later in the night. The rest is the Christmas miracle, which shouldn't be spoiled for you here.

This is a book my children have asked me to read back-to-back-to-back in one sitting. There is something magical and captivating about it. Perhaps it is the innocence and pure heart of a man who knows the greatest gift he can give—and then gives it. (4–8 yrs.)

 ## Night Tree

by Eve Bunting
illustrated by Ted Rand

This is a book that, in its own way, gets down to the nitty-gritty of the true spirit of the season. It is the story of a family's annual Christmas ritual of sharing their joy and goodwill with the animals of the forest at the far end of town. Narrated by the eight-or-so-year-old boy, the story is told simply and from the heart, while the illustrations are rich, festive and nighttime-dark.

It is the night before Christmas. Two children and their parents, bundled up against the biting cold, drive past the brightly lit store windows and straggling shoppers to the place where they spend every Christmas Eve. Their faces shine, the excitement is contagious and we aren't quite sure what they're up to. Tromping into the forest near where they've parked, they're carrying a box, a lantern and a blanket. A few minutes more of walking brings the family to a tree that they greet as if it's an old friend. " 'Here's our tree,' said Dad. 'It's grown since last year,' I say. Mom puts her hand on my shoulder. 'So have you.' "

In the box they've been carrying are popcorn chains, apples and tangerines with strings on them for hanging, balls of sunflower seeds and pressed millet and honey—all for hanging on the tree. Shelled nuts, breadcrumbs and pieces of apple go underneath the tree for the little creatures who can't climb very well. Then out comes the blanket, mugs and thermos of hot chocolate—enough to keep everyone warm while they sing some Christmas carols in the still night air. As this lovely ritual comes to a close and the family heads back to their truck, the boy turns his head for one last look at the tree, which, for now, has folded itself into the darkness. Yet, on the last page, the reader sees scores of animals approaching it and tasting its delights. What a sweet tradition—for all concerned! (3–7 yrs.)

A Midwinter Tree

Making a feast tree for the birds and small woodland animals that live by our home has always been one of my children's most treasured holiday activities. They love the whole process—making the food, decorating the tree and then watching through the kitchen window as the little animals eat their treats. We usually make our tree for the birds out of our own Christmas tree after we have dismantled it, but most any tree will do. We drag it outside to a sheltered spot in the backyard where we can unobtrusively observe the animals' doings and then decorate it with all kinds of yummy bird and squirrel treats. This is a fun activity that preschoolers manage with ease. In case you are interested in trying this out for yourself, here are a few ideas on how to decorate your tree.

♥ Strings of Popcorn—All you need to make this welcome delicacy is plenty of freshly popped corn (omit the butter and salt) and a needle and thread for each person. Knot the thread and then carefully push the needle through the popcorn. Some young children have trouble making these, as the popcorn needs to be threaded with a light touch or it tends to crumble. You'll have to judge your child's dexterity level. Some enjoy this activity greatly; others find making popcorn strands tedious. Our family has found that if we appoint one person to read aloud and have the rest of the family stringing, our popcorn strings grow much longer with *much* less effort. We have tried stringing cranberries but the animals in *our* area, anyway, don't seem to care for them.

♥ Peanut Butter Pinecones—This treat is always the first to be eaten by the birds at our house. They're simple to make and a big hit with the preschool crowd. Be forewarned, these can be a bit messy to make but are always worth the effort. You'll need pinecones (most any kind will do, the more open the better), string, peanut butter, birdseed and sunflower seeds. To begin, knot a string loop on the cone so it is easy to hang the finished product on the tree. Next, mix the seeds together and pour them into a shallow pan (a pie pan or a small roasting pan will both work well). Slather pinecones with peanut butter, using a knife or your fingers to gently push the peanut butter into the cracks. I tend to assign this task to the oldest child, if she is willing, since it is the messiest and small children have trouble getting enough peanut butter on the cone. If there are no older children available, an adult might want to do this. And last, roll the cone in the seeds, trying to get as many seeds as possible onto the peanut butter. (Many two-year-olds are fabulous at this messy task!) It should look like one big blob of seeds when you are done.

♥ Fruit Strands—Slice apples and oranges in rounds and string like the popcorn.

♥ Suet Balls—For this nutritious tidbit, ask the butcher for suet. You will need to have a few empty paper egg cartons on hand, as well as some birdseed and a bit of yarn or string. To begin, melt the suet over low heat (be very careful with the hot fat and young children). Add in an equal amount of birdseed and stir. Gently stir the suet-birdseed mixture as you pour it into the egg holes in the egg carton. Make a loop of yarn or string and place it into the melted suet mixture. (This is a great job for three- or four-year-olds.) When the suet cools, the yarn will become the handle with which you hang the suet on the tree. Some people like to add some peanut butter to this mixture for extra nutrition. Allow the suet to harden and then gently peel away the egg carton to hang the suet balls on the tree.

♥ Once you have gathered enough goodies to decorate your tree, make it an event. (For inspiration read *Night Tree* by Eve Bunting, page 129, or *The Tomten* by Astrid Lindgren, page 132.) After you decorate your tree, don't forget the ground-feeding birds. Leave a few peanut butter pinecones and some extra birdseed on the ground for them to nibble, too.

The Twelve Holy Days

Something that has helped my family remember the spiritual meaning of the Christmas season is to extend our celebration to include the twelve Holy Days (and nights) between Christmas and Epiphany. These long, dark nights always have a deep magical feel to me, as if the earth is holding them sacred, too. Long ago people used to pay close attention to their dreams on these nights, as each dream was said to portend the special meaning for the month that correlates with that night in the coming year (i.e., the first night correlates with January; the twelfth night correlates with December). I have told my family this legend and we take special care to record and think about these dreams. Through this, we find meaningful ways to connect with our inner lives. On Twelfth Night we have a special celebration with a Three Kings Cake. We bake an uncooked bean into our cake, and whoever gets the piece with the bean is the king or queen for the year, a title that bestows great honor and good luck in the next twelve months! Then we make a grand procession and bless our previously cleaned home with burning frankincense. We parade through all the rooms, opening closets and little cubby spots, making sure every corner of the house is blessed. Then we move outside and bless the front door. We take chalk and write C + B + M (the initials of the three kings) and the year to show the angels that our house has been blessed. This is an old-world custom your family is sure to enjoy. Children love leading the procession and being the ones to bestow the special blessings upon the home. We find this a lovely tradition that lets us internalize the deeper meanings of Christmas long after the commercialism of Christmas Day has past.

The Tomten

by Astrid Lindgren

The Tomten is a magical book experience that leaves the reader wondering—in an enchanting "what if?" way. It is the story of a gnomelike old fellow who is rather like the unseen guardian of a snow-covered farm. Swedish in origin, the legend gently and simply tells of the little character who makes his quiet rounds at night, when the animals are quiet and the humans are sleeping. Moving in the moonlight and the bitter cold, he visits each farm animal and talks to it in "Tomten language, a silent little language" that the beast can somehow understand. His message is one of acknowledgment and hope, such as "Winters come and winters go. Summers come and summers go. Soon you can graze in the fields." We follow him on his rounds, even into the house to gaze at the sleeping family members. He leaves tiny footprints in the snow sometimes, too. There is a quiet, underlying sense that all of those the Tomten visits are safe and cared for in a good and mysterious way.

The artwork has a dreaminess to it, perfectly complementing the story. Try to remember how much fun it was to wonder if animals really could understand what you were saying or thinking, as a child. Try to remember what an unforgettable feeling it would have been to imagine a kindly little character "watching out" for your home while you slept. If you can, then you can understand the magic in this book. *The Tomten* is wonderfully rich with Swedish tradition. (3–6 yrs.)

Who Is Coming to Our House?

by Joseph Slate
illustrated by Ashley Wolff

"Who is coming to our house?" ask the animals in the stable one night. Only the mouse is absolutely sure that they're in for a visitor, but all he can answer is, "Someone, someone." Despite this vagueness, each of the creatures knows that room has to be made, that things have to be cleaned up. The ram offers to dust the beams, while the chick pecks the debris in the earth off to one side. The spider spins a new web, the duck lines the crib with eider and the hen lays an egg. Now things are ready and the animals wait expectantly. Ah, but it is dark, notes the cat. And the rat is still not convinced that anyone is coming at all. All of them are clustered at the stable's door, watching, waiting.

And here they are: a man, big-bellied woman and donkey. They seem to know this is the right place for them. There is a birth, and the next thing we know, everyone and everything is gathered around the baby. Wondrous, gentle facial expressions complement the very heartfelt "Welcome to our house!" that greets the new family. And outside, under a bright star, shepherds start to arrive.

This is one of those very special books where less is more. A simple text accompanies lovely woodcut illustrations that clearly convey the wonder and joy of the first Christmas night. (2–5 yrs.)

Take Joy!

The Tasha Tudor Christmas Book
Songs, Stories, Poems, Things to Do
for a Family Christmas

by Tasha Tudor

Christmas wouldn't be Christmas without digging this book out of storage once a year when it's time to start "getting into the spirit." Veritably packed with Christmas stories (from Hans Christian Andersen to Charles Dickens to O. Henry), poems, carols, lore and legend, it is illustrated with well over one hundred pictures in full color or black and white—all aglow with the tenderness, reverence and beauty for which Tasha Tudor's work is known.

Ms. Tudor couldn't resist including a chapter on Christmas at the Tudor cottage, and has shared with her readers many traditions, recipes and ideas for indulging your family in the coziest, most joyful ways. There is even an index—which may come in handy if you want to look up how to make marionettes or find out more about Sweden's Festival of Light.

Festivals, Family and Food

by Diana Carey and Judy Large

If you love the seasons, celebrating and food, this is the book for you! Full of old-fashioned, wholesome fun, *Festivals, Family and Food* provides an amazing variety of seasonal activities. A quaint English book (which is sometimes a bit hard to track down), it offers all kinds of fun, simple ideas that are completely new to American sensibilities and plenty of ideas that are familiar, too. The pages are filled with craft ideas, stories, poems, songs, recipes (given in European measurements), decoration ideas, activities, dances, party tips, teatime celebrations—all with a seasonal theme. Rich in folklore and traditional children's lore (the knowledge passed from child to child—which seems to be sorely getting lost as children play more and more inside their homes instead of out on the streets), this book has enriched my family's life in more ways than I could ever say. Many of our favorite traditions are based on ideas I read about in this book. Flowerpot ice cream for birthday parties, the birthday poem, star apples, our favorite Halloween poems, giving gifts to the fairies, hot cross buns on Good Friday—I could go on forever. We owe so much of the richness of our lives to this book. Even just taking the time to read and see how much there is to celebrate when you orient your life around the seasons could change your parenting outlook forever. Life gets so much more fun when we feel connected to people, to our community and to the earth around us. This book offers the key to just that; it shows us how to reconnect to things lost, not nostalgic old times past that have no meaning, but to the realness of life, to the things that make us feel truly alive.

When I was a child, Christmas wasn't Christmas to me until all the presents were opened and we were on our way to my Auntie Barbie's house. Once there, after we finished greeting the hordes of relatives that awaited our arrival, I would soon sneak off with a couple of pieces of my aunt's famous fudge. Lying under the Christmas tree, I would savor each bite of sweet heaven and enjoy the lights and chaos around me. Though we don't travel to my aunt's house each Christmas, my children and I still savor the feeling of lying under the beautiful Christmas lights and eating fudge. If you want, here's the recipe so you can, too:

Auntie Barbie's Fudge

1 large can evaporated milk
4 1/2 cups sugar
1/2 pound butter
3 cups semisweet chocolate chips
10 oz. small marshmallows
2 tsp. vanilla
2 cups or less chopped nuts (optional!)

Put milk and sugar in a heavy-bottomed pan. Bring to a boil and let it boil with enthusiasm for ten minutes, being sure to stir *constantly* the entire time it is cooking. Remove from heat, add butter and chocolate chips. Stir until melted. Add remaining ingredients and stir until as smooth as possible. Pour into a ten-by-thirteen or nine-by-twelve pan (if you want thicker fudge). Let set at room temperature for three hours before cutting. Caution: this fudge may be addictive.

This is the best creamy stuff. I never make it with nuts. (They ruin the consistency for my tongue, but my aunt wouldn't eat it without them. She always makes a batch of each type for the nut lovers and non-nut lovers of the family, kind soul that she is!) If the fudge ever comes out grainy or runny, it's because you didn't heat the sugar/milk mixture correctly. This recipe requires a lot of diligence in the stirring department!

Heart to Heart

Dear Friends,

While on vacation a few years ago, our family had an opportunity to go tubing down a remote river in Central America. This was a trip we'd planned months before, and wouldn't you know it? That proverbial nightmare of the evening-before-departure crisis had happened: Elizabeth had broken her elbow in a freak accident jumping over Evan's Lego city. Determined not to let a broken elbow stop us from this tubing adventure, we blithely wrapped her cast in plastic to keep it dry (don't let anyone tell you that works!) and finally launched down the river. Our family of four and our guide were on our way.

For a couple of miles, all went smoothly. The water was as warm as bathwater and the only sounds were of birds and cicadas. I pinched myself to make sure the experience was real. It was that surprise four-foot waterfall and the following rapids that broke the spell. Being the first one over the waterfall (and having been thrown out of my tube), I knew Elizabeth (who wouldn't be able to maneuver well because of her broken elbow) and her dad, immediately behind me, had little chance of making it to calm water safely. Yet, there was absolutely nothing I could do. Scream at them to watch out? Sure, I did that, but they couldn't hear me above the roar of the water. Position myself, clinging to a vine, to help out in whatever way I could when their battered bodies eventually floated by me? Yep. That panicky, hopefully once-in-a-lifetime feeling of being completely at the mercy of a bigger force while watching my ten-year-old being carried downriver by the raging water is something I'll always remember. (Part of that memory is the sight of good ol' responsible Elizabeth, remembering to hold her arm high to keep her cast out of the water, appearing as a disembodied plastic-covered cast bobbing up and down in the water.) It was one of those instances that seem to take eons to unfold. I saw her helplessly heading toward me in the rapids. I reached out to grab her as she was swept by.

While I gripped a vine for all I was worth with one hand and clasped her good arm with the other (holding on tighter to both than I've ever gripped anything!), I was able to keep her from continuing downriver. In the end, and several hundred yards later, we dragged ourselves onto the bank as transformed (at least temporarily) people. Our tubes were gone. We didn't know where we were, our bodies were bruised and we could hear a large animal lumbering in the brush nearby. I'm not sure what my children will think when they look back on that day twenty years from now, but I've had a glimpse of something unforgettable and it will stay with me until my dying day.

I'll remember that there are only a few things in life that really matter, no matter how many times I hear differently from other people, from advertisers, from "experts." These things have to do with the love and appreciation that surface especially when life is uncomfortable, when I am stretched to my limits, when I must be focused enough to identify what is "clutter" and what is not, then to drop the clutter and deal with what is left: the essence.

A parent doesn't have to have a near-death experience tubing down a river to know how uncomfortable life can be, how frequently we can reach those limits. It is just so easy to get caught up in the process and forget the real issue—the essence. To put this in a seasonal perspective, it is difficult to keep focused on the innocent joys that can make up the holidays when we allow commercialism to twist its spirit into such a monster of materialism. It is difficult to remember that the season's essence, peace on earth and love of our fellow humans, is exemplified not by the number of gifts meted out, but by the loving manner in which we continue to deal with life when it is uncomfortable. My hope is that in the midst of the hustle and bustle of family celebrations, you have some glimpses of what really and truly matters in the long run, and keep your focus right here. If it makes it any easier, simply envision your child being swept helplessly down a river. That should do it.

Smiles, Giggles and Belly Busters

How Humor Makes Life Richer

*Humor is a presence in the world—like
grace—and shines on everybody.*
—GARRISON KEILLOR

f there's anything that can make a bad day better, it's
humor—especially humor dispensed with a hug. I remember how a good dose of laughter came to my rescue
a long time ago, when we still lived in rural Maine. Becca was five,
Laura two and we lived a half an hour away from any little friends. It
was another of those "Will winter *ever* end?" days—way too cold to be
outside for very long. The sky was gray *again*. Oh, how my soul longed
for a warm, sunny day. But no, it was winter still, with no end in sight.
I love the seasons, but I was raised in California and this was March,
after all! My bones were singing "Spring" and the world was saying
"Not yet, honey."

My husband worked long, long hours then, and my days at home
with the girls sometimes felt like an eternity. I loved being with them,
but none of us could stand being cooped up inside. I needed action
and so did they. On this particular afternoon, moods were headed
downhill fast; we were clearly on the way from bad to worse. Our little town of a thousand people didn't offer much in the way of enter-

tainment. A person could go to the post office or take a walk. If you were really desperate, you could always drive out to get gas and buy a pickled egg from a jar. We had already done everything but buy the egg and none of us was brave enough to try that. We were stumped.

For lack of anything better to do, I settled the girls onto the couch and started reading Dick King-Smith's masterpiece, *Babe*, a perfect first chapter book for young listeners. Becca was old enough to love a simple chapter book, but Laura could not sit still at this age. Nothing held her attention except moving—until we started reading *Babe*. With Becca cozy next to me on the couch, and Laura circling close beside us on the floor with her toys, I read and we laughed. And after a pause to catch my breath, I read on and we laughed some more. Something about that farmer, his two-word sentences and that endearing little pig just charmed our hearts. We read and laughed all afternoon. Even Laura finally abandoned her toys and crawled up onto the couch, rapt. *Babe* was so hilarious we could hardly stand it. After an hour and a half, when my voice was hoarse from overuse, I tried to stop, so I could start cooking dinner. That idea was met with a resounding "*No!* Please keep reading, Mommy." And so I read more. I read until the sky was dark. The dinner hour came and went with no dinner made and still we read and laughed our hearts out. We laughed so hard that afternoon, the muscles in our stomachs ached for days. After hours of reading, we finally finished the book, ate peanut butter sandwiches for dinner and headed straight to bed, giggling all the while about that plucky little pig. I have treasured the memory of that day ever since, for I have never laughed so much in my life.

I also learned a powerful lesson—even the grimmest day can be salvaged by a dose of humor. The trick is learning to find humor in things that are truly funny, rather than indulging in cheap humor that tries to be funny by taking little bites out of the soul. Finding this balance, though, can be ever so tricky, especially with young ones. If we can learn to laugh at our own foibles rather than making fun of someone else's, we have acquired a tool that can help us through even the darkest of days.

Children who are just learning about the world are often very literal in their interpretation of things. They are simply so busy making sense of the world that they often don't stop to consider that someone is making a joke, even a joke that is intended to make them feel better. Children tend to accept our words at face value, until they learn not to.

I still vividly remember being confused by certain types of humor when I was very young. One Saturday afternoon my dad and I were walking around town doing errands. I was four or five at the time, and, in my eyes, my father was a giant. He walked with strong, purposeful steps and I felt like a little mouse scurrying along behind him. On this particular day, my dad was in a hurry, and I simply couldn't keep up.

Finally, after what seemed like endless minutes of literally running after him, I whined, "Dad, I'm tired!" What I wanted was for him to slow down a bit, but my dad was on a mission. In an effort to keep me walking, he joked, "Glad to meet you, Tired, my name is Jim." I had heard this joke before, so I knew he was trying to humor me, but inside I burned with indignation. I was *really* tired. I needed to slow down. I was asking for his help and he was ignoring how I felt. Or so it seemed to me. (In truth, of course, he was just trying to use humor to motivate me along, but I failed to see anything funny in his words.) This was just a small incident, but it has stayed with me—a lifelong reminder of how it feels to be unheard and unseen. My dad certainly didn't mean to hurt my feelings that day, yet I think of that tired little girl even now when I'm tempted to tease my own kids out of moods or needs that don't happen to coincide with my own.

I was lucky, because my parents' humor was, for the most part, harmless. They didn't use sarcasm or derisive humor, and so, as a child, it never occurred to me to make jokes at another's expense or to cut my friends down to size with sarcastic remarks or caustic wit. I learned about sarcasm the hard way. At eighteen, when I met the man who would eventually become my husband, I was shocked by what he considered funny. He'd grown up in a family of competitive punsters, where no comment was ever safe from ridicule. What they considered humorous seemed downright mean to me. Why would anyone say such hurtful things to the people they loved in an attempt to be funny?

Being smart myself, and wanting to fit in, I was soon tossing puns around with the best of them, but something in my heart didn't feel quite right about it. Why was this funny? Why did I have to take a jab at somebody else in order to feel clever myself, or to make people laugh?

Before long, I gathered up my courage and started to object to my boyfriend's idea of "funny." I urged him to soften his caustic, yet witty, edge. For years we argued about it. After we married and our kids were born, we argued more. I could see no reason to expose a child to this kind of humor. And he thought (rightly so) that I was just trying to control him. After all, he should be able to laugh and be funny in whatever way he wanted. I hated watching the hurt look on our children's faces as they tried to understand their father's jokes. It seemed that every time they accepted his comments as "humor," a little part of their hearts had to harden up to handle the joke.

Fortunately, I married a wonderfully sensitive man, a man who loves our children with the same kind of ferocious intensity that I do. Over time, he saw for himself how sarcasm hurt our children's hearts. How each time they absorbed the biting edge of a sarcastic comment, it chipped away at their trust in the world. How cynicism and sarcasm slowly stole away their innocence and eroded their belief that words work and that people are meant to be kind to each other.

By examining his own feelings when he was about to say something cutting, my husband realized that his sarcasm was actually rooted in the pain and hurt of his own childhood. And he learned that when he finally dealt with that pain, he no longer wanted to hurt others with his words. It's been a beautiful thing to watch. As he has worked to heal his own heart, my husband's humor has been evolving into the kind of loving, lighthearted humor that opens hearts.

It's a radical thing to say that we need to protect our children from sarcasm and other forms of biting humor, but I fully believe that this is true, especially while they are young. By the time they are in middle school and the world has lost some of its sparkle, maybe you can throw a touch of sarcasm their way, though I am not sure why you'd want to. Remember, instead, how tender our children's souls are. Honor their openness with your kindness.

I find that it's as important to be careful with my words when I'm being funny as when I'm disciplining my children. As we choose what to laugh at in our daily lives, we teach them how to view the world. If we can laugh at ourselves, but not at others, we lay a foundation for compassion. And aren't we all trying to teach our children a sense of kindness and respect for others? The world will give our children plenty of opportunities to learn about meanness and unnecessary cruelty. Even if we, as parents, never utter a sarcastic word, our children will surely experience sarcasm's bitter taste. Every time we flick on our televisions, we are inundated with sarcasm and cheap humor; the culture is saturated with it. And yet, even though sarcasm may be a fact of life in our culture, we don't have to model it ourselves. We can open up a world of healthy, hearty laughter to our children just as we can choose whole wheat bread over white. We can point out life's absurdities and take ourselves lightly, without stealing a laugh at someone else's expense—and what a gift such humor is to our children, who, after all, like nothing better than to laugh. The kinder we are, the more our children learn to respond to others with kindness. Our own behavior is our children's first and primary experience of how the world works. Why wouldn't we want that experience to be as kind and gentle as possible? There is plenty of time for the world to toughen them up. For now, let's nourish our children's hearts and keep them pure, so they will have the strength to respond with love when life gets hard.

In this chapter you will find several books sure to get a chuckle and some ideas that will have the whole family laughing.

It's funny how children can take something so normal and turn it on its head. Suddenly, with a new twist, life has a touch of humor where none was there before. Take trash trucks, for example. When Evan was about two years old, he began his career as an avid vehicle lover. Trucks, tractors, utility company "cherry pickers," cranes, headache balls, you name it. It if was big or loud or scary-looking, he loved it. Our garbage truck came every Thursday. Somehow, he could hear it from blocks away, so he was out in front of the house bright and early—still in his soggy nighttime diaper—waiting for the crew as they lurched toward our end of the block. It was the high spot of his week and every day he asked if *this* was the day the garbage truck would come. Six days out of seven, the answer was "No, Evan. Six more days." (Or five or four or whatever.) And so, Evan learned to count backward—from six to one—*well* before he felt inclined to count forward! You just had to chuckle at a boy who cared more about trucks than breakfast!

The Very Hungry Caterpillar

by Eric Carle

With vibrantly colorful illustrations and die-cut pages, this book dramatizes one of nature's most common yet beautiful marvels: the metamorphosis from caterpillar to butterfly. But there is a sense of the outrageous along the way and perhaps that has a lot to do with why this wonderful book has endured for so many years. You see, the tiny and very hungry caterpillar that hatches one Sunday morning at the book's beginning somehow knows it must eat to grow in order to undergo the transformation into a butterfly. It's just that after he eats his way through the pages, devouring all of the *right* things (plums, strawberries, apples) and is still hungry, he begins to choose all of the *wrong* things: salami, watermelon, etc. It does not take too long before our little green friend is a much bigger green friend and ends up with a tummy ache, a concept that young children find rib-tickling funny—when it's in a caterpillar who has eaten with no discretion. All does end well, but not before you have covered a lot of delightful ground: the book also introduces sets of up to ten objects and progresses through the days of the week and colors, too.

Pretty darn near a "must-have" of a book. You will get tons of mileage out of it. (15 mos.–4 yrs.)

Look Out, Bird!

by Marilyn Janovitz

It all begins when snail slips off the vine he is climbing and hits Bird. Bird then flies and frightens frog, who jumps and topples turtle, etc., etc. This chain reaction continues until moth flutters and startles snail, who then starts to fall again and yells, "Oh, no! Not again! . . . Look out, Bird!"

This book is so simple to describe and yet it is so dear to behold and experience with your child, who, it is almost a given, will soon learn to shout out, "Look out, Bird!" at just the right time in the story.

This is one of those books you buy for the younger sibling but that everyone ends up enjoying.

Frisky and buoyant, Janovitz's pen-and-ink/watercolor illustrations are a delightful complement to the lively and rambunctious story. (1½–3 yrs.)

How long has it been since you laughed one of those full-bodied belly laughs? You know, the kind that offers complete emotional release. How about your kids? How often do they laugh like that? Probably many times a day, if they are like most kids. Most children have the gift of laughing with their whole heart and soul. If your days ever seem long or overwhelming, take a hint from your child: look at the world with laughing eyes. Laughter really is the best medicine. And there's nothing quite like giving *and* receiving a slobbery raspberry on the tummy to get you to giggle!

Splash!

by Ann Jonas

Here is a lively book for families with children of more than one age, for there is much to do and see on every page. The story is quite simple—a girl sits beside her pond and counts all the animals that are there at a time. Each page shows different animals falling in and climbing out of the water. Some are happy to be there, while others are not!

Splash's whole concept is quite engaging. Wildly colorful, it captures the eye of any toddler, who will happily look for fish and frogs and dogs and turtles and cats, any of which may be in or out of the water at any given time. Older children who are learning to count or do simple addition will love the challenge of figuring out just how many beings are in the water at any given time.

Believe it or not, it is rare to find books that entertain a very young listener and, say, a six-year-old at the same time because their tastes are so different! *Splash!*, though, bridges the gap beautifully. (1½–6 yrs.)

The Jolly Postman

And Other People's Letters

by Janet and Allan Ahlberg

There is something about this book that has to be experienced in order to be understood and appreciated, but I will do my best to explain its magic.

The Jolly Postman has delivered the mail, but it is not just any old mail. It is mail that familiar fairy-tale characters have written to each other.

What did Goldilocks write to the Three Bears? In sevenish-year-old penmanship on hand-decorated stationery, she's written:

> Dear Mr and Mrs Bear and Baby Bear, I am very sory indeed that I cam into your house and ate Baby Bear's porij. Mummy says I am a bad girl. I hardly eat any porij when she cooks it she says. Daddy says he will mend the littel chair. Love from Goldilocks. P.S. Baby Bear can come to my party if he likes. There will be 3 kinds of ice cream and a majishun.

Stuff the letter back into its envelope and go on to read one for the Wicked Witch, which turns out to be junk mail perfectly fit for a witch: a flyer advertising such things as an easy-clean, nonstick cauldron, cup and sorcerer tea service (it washes itself!) and the Little Boy Pie Mix (for those unexpected visitors when the cupboard is bare). There are six letters in all, to various fairy-tale celebrities.

Now, without exception, adults who see this book for the first time are bewildered about what age a child would enjoy it. The characters are known to virtually all little children, but the subject matter at times is humor that seems meant for a more mature audience. Let me tell you that *also,* without exception, eighteen-month-olds as well as seven-year-olds thought this book was magical; they latched on to it immediately. (1½–7 yrs.)

Frog Goes to Dinner

by Mercer Mayer

This book came close to falling apart from too many readings in our home.

It is wordless—the illustrations giving new meaning to the saying: "A picture is worth a thousand words." There is simply so much expression and action in the pen-and-ink drawings that this outrageous story is delightfully and abundantly right there before your eyes!

Frog Goes to Dinner is about a little boy who goes to a "fancy restaurant" with his family and is distressed to find that his pet frog must have sneaked into his pocket before leaving home. Frog sneaks out of the pocket onto a tray passing by with a tossed salad on it, and that's when the fun begins. Before long, it is the rest of the restaurant that is distressed, but the rest of us can't help laughing aloud. Frog's antics and everyone's reactions to them make this book quite an escapade. A *great* wordless experience! (2–5 yrs.)

I've noticed on days when my kids are out of sorts and nothing is going right, a sudden touch of humor can surprise them into changing their attitudes. At times like this, I rely on my "Mommy Monster" persona to save the day. For example, if my kids are being uncooperative about picking up their messes, all I have to say is "Do I need to find Mommy Monster to *make* you clean up this mess? You know how Mommy Monster feels about little children who leave messes on her floor." Generally, the minute I say this, my kids break into giggles and get to work picking up. But if not, out comes the dreaded Mommy Monster, who is nothing more than me with a loud, gruff voice, walking around, waving my arms wildly, saying, "Who made this mess?! Do I need to eat this mess or is someone going to pick it up? You know how I love crunchy, colorful Legos!" (At which point I pick up a Lego piece and pretend to gobble it up.) The slight tension of "Is Mommy really a monster?" is both funny and motivating enough to get them to work. If for some reason this doesn't work, Mommy Monster picks up the smallest child and turns him upside down and pretends to prepare to eat him. My kids are just in a fit of giggles by this point. The giggles inevitably break their spell of noncooperation and they get down to work. A friend of mine does a similar act, only she becomes the Italian hausfrau (yes, you read that correctly) who speaks in a wildly garbled pseudolanguage. As she screams her unintelligible madness she frantically gesticulates toward whatever she wants her children to do. Suddenly, her children are madly picking up to avoid the wrath of this wild woman. A little humor can go a long way on a cranky day.

Sheep in a Jeep

by Nancy Shaw
illustrated by Margot Apple

Oh, there is a near-magical quality to those tongue-twisting, silly books, however maddening the words are to get out of your mouth. But then, that is half of the fun! Children love it when their adults make fools of themselves, but when the fool-making happens in the coziness of a reading chair, it is even more delicious for them.

This is a rollicking, rhyming foray into a meadow with five sheep who happen to have a jeep at their disposal. Text is simple:

Beep! Beep!
Sheep in a jeep
on a hill that's steep.

The rest of the story, as simple as it is, merely describes in rhyme what happens when the jeep breaks down, the sheep give it a push, the driver doesn't look where he's steering, the jeep ends up in a puddle, etc. The sheep will endear themselves to you from the beginning, and become even more appealing as the story progresses. This is a silly, simple book with delicate and expressive colored pencil illustrations. A fun introduction to rhyming. (2–4 yrs.)

Mama Don't Allow

by Thacher Hurd

Nearly any child appreciates the devilishness of the alligators in this story. Down in Swampville, young Miles, of the 'Possum family, got a saxophone for his birthday. But while he is learning to play, those who can hear him must tolerate more than anyone should ever have to. It turns out that the alligators are the only creatures in town who *will* listen to Miles and the band he's pulled together, and the lot of them are asked to play at the Alligator Ball on the riverboat. You've never seen such goings-on, such partying, such fun. But that is just the beginning of this adventure, because the alligators' intentions turn out not to be the loftiest when midnight snack time rolls around.

Watch for facial expressions in the lively and vibrantly colored illustrations. But most of all, be a sport and don't be afraid to belt out the rambunctious song that is the namesake for the title. (Music arrangement is included. You can hunt and peck your way through it.)

This story is a happy combination of humor, intrigue and suspense—on a child-size scale. (2–5 yrs.)

Rabbits Galore

A Six-Book Set

Black and White Rabbit's ABC, Gray Rabbit's 123, White Rabbit's Color Book, Brown Rabbit's Day, Gray Rabbit's Odd One Out, Brown Rabbit's Shape Book

by Alan Baker

As a rule, I avoid books whose sole purpose is to teach. Not that I mind the teaching, it is just that a book needs to do more than teach a few facts to hold my interest. Consequently, a color/number/ABC–

type book really has to stand out for me to take much note of it. Having said all that, you can guess the following books are pretty special, and you are right.

Two particular traits make these books exceptional. First are the remarkably engaging illustrations. The second is the text. Each book is about a cozy little bunny who is doing things that relate to whatever concept the story is about; so the book is really a story that talks about a concept, rather than the concept being the sole focus of the text. For example, in the color book, Rabbit finds three tubs of paint and proceeds to bathe in each of the colors, making all the colors of the rainbow and a big mess in the process. In the number book, Rabbit has great wads of colorful clay, which she keeps molding into different lively animals: eight rumpeting, trumpeting elephants; nine spotted, dotted bugs and ten squeaking, peeking mice, which at the end of the day left one weary, bleary rabbit fast asleep. And so on, a book for each concept. By the end of the book, these little rabbits feel like personal friends. Not precisely funny per se, this series will bring a smile to your face because of the books' subtle and sweetly absurd humor.

I don't have a clue as to which of these books is the best; they are all wonderful! (1½–4 yrs.)

Bathroom Humor

Don't be surprised if sometime between the ages of four and six your child suddenly gets enamored with what our family calls "bathroom humor." Children this age seem to be utterly fascinated by incredibly horrible jokes involving all sorts of natural bodily functions. Different parents handle this in different ways. When Becca and Laura were little, I didn't really want to listen to these jokes and my husband, who worked long hours, wasn't often home when they were awake. Consequently, I said they could tell all the jokes they wanted but just not in my presence. That is when they got dubbed "bathroom jokes" because these two silly little girls would run into the bathroom to tell each other their ridiculous jokes. (My favorite was: "Want to hear a dirty joke? Pig fell in the mud!" Now how that elicited as many laughs as it did, I have *no* idea, but they could laugh over that silly ditty for hours.) Since their dad is home more now, he has been around for Heidi's and Aidan's bathroom-humor period. He happens to love these kinds of jokes, so he joins right in. (Arg . . .) If you are of the opinion, like many parents are, that these jokes are in poor form, my advice is the old adage: "Least said, soonest mended." If your children know these jokes will cause a dramatic response from you, they are much more likely to continue telling them in your presence. If they get little reaction, the bathroom-humor phase will probably slip away over time.

If You Give a Mouse a Cookie

by Laura Joffe Numeroff
illustrated by Felicia Bond

This seems to be one of those books you can read a million times and never feel like hiding from your child so you won't have to read it yet *again!* It is a fine book to consider when a young child's birthday looms on the horizon. It's practically fail-proof!

This is the story of a boy who makes the mistake of giving a mouse a cookie. (The mouse is quite adorable.) Now, if you give a mouse a cookie, he's going to want some milk. (We see the boy getting the mouse a glass of milk.) But then the mouse will probably ask for a straw. (The boy gets a straw.) When he's finished, he'll ask for a napkin. Then he'll want to look at himself in the mirror to make sure he doesn't have a milk mustache. (The boy gets a napkin and holds the mouse up to the bathroom mirror so he can see himself.) This goes on and on, one thing leading to another, the boy getting deeper and deeper into this craziness, the house getting more and more into a state of disarray. Eventually, the story comes full circle, and the endearing mouse, who is thirsty, needs a drink of milk. And, of course, if he asks for a glass of milk, he's going to want a cookie to go with it. (By this time, the boy is completely exhausted, and the kitchen is a mess.)

Text is sparse and that is perfect because the colored illustrations have enough detail to keep you completely in touch with the outrageousness of this irresistible story. (2–5½ yrs.)

The Piggy in the Puddle

by Charlotte Pomerantz
illustrated by James Marshall

What I want to know is how you could ever resist a book that starts out like this:

> *See the piggy,*
> *See the puddle,*
> *See the muddy little puddle.*
> *See the piggy in the middle*
> *Of the muddy little puddle.*
> *See her dawdle, see her diddle*
> *In the muddy, muddy middle.*
> *See her waddle, plump and little,*
> *In the very merry middle.*

In the course of the story, a little piggy's whole family—father, mother and brother—admonish her to use soap. But in the end, they all succumb to the delight that every pig dreams of: wallowing in the mud.

While the plot is one virtually any little child will delightfully relate to, the book's main appeal lies in the silliness of the giddy text and the just-as-ridiculous illustrations. If you bothered to mouth the words of the text offered as an example (above), you'll probably recognize immediately that this book will tickle the funny bones of anyone reading and listening to it. (2½–6 yrs.)

The Wheels on the Bus

A Book with Parts That Move

by Paul O. Zelinsky

So you already know pretty much how this song goes, right? There are the wheels that go round and round, the doors that go open and shut, the people that step out and in, the driver that says, "Move on back," the windows that slide up and down, the wipers that go "swish swish swish," the riders that go "bumpity bump," the babies that cry, "waah, waah, waah!" and the mothers that go, "shhhh shhh shhh." Now picture movable tabs that cause the wheels to go round and round, the doors to open and shut—and go down the line—even to the point of a mother "shushing" her baby by moving a finger in front of the baby's face *while the baby's eyes follow her finger!*

This is a pop-up book to end all pop-up books. Everyone who sees it is enthralled not only because it is such a mechanical wonder, but also because the bright pastel artwork is so detailed and eye-pleasing.

You'll have to be the judge about whether or not to delegate the tab-moving job to your child; they can be stiff at first, but the pages are on extra-heavy stock. Plan on singing the song slowly in order to give you time to "do the tabs." (2½–6 yrs.)

You're on the thousandth reading of a book you and your child have known by heart for months. Every single word is predictable and you could tell this story in your sleep. And your child could tell it to *you!*

When it gets to the point that you feel as if you really do have to shake things up just this once to keep them from getting stale, try substituting really outrageous words for some of those in the story. If, for the thousandth time, you are about to read that the moon rose over the mountain, try having the moon rising over the . . . oh, I don't know . . . *refrigerator!* See what happens. I'll bet on a brief startled reaction from your child (or, okay, maybe an admonishment to just stick with the real words, Daddy!) and then a belly laugh. For both of you.

When I did this with my young children, it always elicited howls of delight and then their own ridiculous contributions shouted out. To this day, whenever I see *The Very Hungry Caterpillar,* I remember how (with all due respect to its author, Eric Carle) we occasionally had that caterpillar eating not the watermelon, cherry pie and sausage shown in the book, but rather the dump truck, food processor and fireplace that just happened to pop into our minds. And for all my silly distortions, the book became even more of a favorite "Can we hear it one more time, this time the 'real' way, Mommy?" book.

Could Be Worse!

by James Stevenson

A well-done, funny, rambunctious and utterly zany story can't be beat and James Stevenson is just the author to do one. *Could Be Worse!* is an expertly woven yarn about one grandpa whose stock answer to any little complaint is "Could be worse!" and grandkids, Mary Ann and Louie, who think that's a pretty lame comment and are overheard by Grandpa saying so.

What happens the next morning? Grandpa spins for them an outrageously far-fetched bad luck story that supposedly happened last night. A large bird pulled him from bed, dropped him in the snow-covered mountains where he met an abominable snowman, but he eventually ended up in the desert where he almost got squished by a giant something-or-other, but got kicked into the clouds by a huge ostrich . . . got the picture? It gets crazier and crazier and sillier and sillier until the end, whereupon Mary and Louie give him a predictable taste of his own medicine: "Could be worse!"

Stevenson's whimsical watercolor illustrations are just as absurdly wild as this story. I can't tell you how many times we've read this book over the years. It's lovably crazy. (3–5 yrs.)

The Funny Little Woman

by Arlene Mosel
illustrated by Blair Lent

If you read this book one time, you will read it many. There is just something so deliciously suspenseful yet cheery and innocent about it. Prepare to ham it up while you are reading and you will find that your enthusiasm, along with the dramatic illustrations, will make *The Funny Little Woman* well loved by your child.

It is a Japanese folktale of a woman who loved to laugh. She "tee-hees" her way though everything—even her encounter with the traditional bogeyman-type characters, the "wicked Oni," who, by the way, are so outrageous-looking that children *love* them. Captured and called into action to use a magic paddle to make rice dumplings for the whole lot of wicked Oni, she not only manages to find humor in the situation, she finds her way *out* of the situation, much to the dismay of the lumbering and not-too-clever monsters. Triumphing over bizarre odds and through the Swiss cheese–like tunnels under the earth where her captors have taken her, our heroine emerges with enough aplomb—and humor—to spare for all of us. (3–6 yrs.)

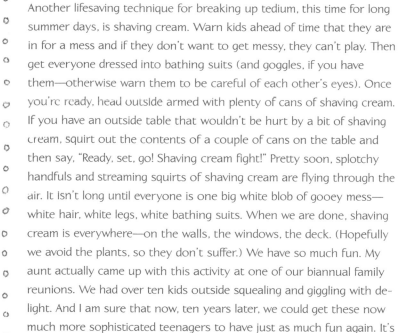

Another lifesaving technique for breaking up tedium, this time for long summer days, is shaving cream. Warn kids ahead of time that they are in for a mess and if they don't want to get messy, they can't play. Then get everyone dressed into bathing suits (and goggles, if you have them—otherwise warn them to be careful of each other's eyes). Once you're ready, head outside armed with plenty of cans of shaving cream. If you have an outside table that wouldn't be hurt by a bit of shaving cream, squirt out the contents of a couple of cans on the table and then say, "Ready, set, go! Shaving cream fight!" Pretty soon, splotchy handfuls and streaming squirts of shaving cream are flying through the air. It isn't long until everyone is one big white blob of gooey mess—white hair, white legs, white bathing suits. When we are done, shaving cream is everywhere—on the walls, the windows, the deck. (Hopefully we avoid the plants, so they don't suffer.) We have so much fun. My aunt actually came up with this activity at one of our biannual family reunions. We had over ten kids outside squealing and giggling with delight. And I am sure that now, ten years later, we could get these now much more sophisticated teenagers to have just as much fun again. It's such an emotional release to just let go! And the best part of all is that with a quick hose job, everyone and everything cleans up with a minimum of work.

Cloudy with a Chance of Meatballs

by Judi Barrett
illustrated by Ron Barrett

This is the wild tale of a small town that never needed any grocery stores because three times a day some sort of food came down from the sky. It rained things like juice, snowed things like mashed potatoes and peas, and sometimes the wind blew in hamburgers. People could listen to the weather report and find out what was going to be for dinner! Why, they even took their plates and utensils with them when they left the house—so they could "catch" a bite! There was an occasional Jell-O sunset and, yes, "lambchops, becoming heavy at times." This sort of silliness goes on and on until one day the weather takes a turn and it becomes clear that all of the residents from the town of Chewandswallow should relocate. Things do settle down with more normal weather, but not before you and your child will hoot with laughter at the wonderful outrageousness of the whole affair. Its line drawing/watercolor illustrations are absolutely, enchantingly funny. (3–7 yrs.)

 # Rotten Teeth

by Laura Simms
illustrated by David Catrow

It all began with show-and-tell in Mrs. Swann's first-grade class in New York City. As in most first grades, show-and-tell was a very important part of the day. Poor Melissa was sure there wasn't a thing in her home that qualified as interesting. What could she bring? When it came time for her show-and-tell day, she was stumped. Like most intelligent girls, she decided it was time for help. So she called on her superintelligent older brother, Norman, to offer his wisdom. She wanted to bring something really special, something everyone would love. And what did thirteen-year-old Norman suggest? A bottle of rotten teeth! You see, their father was a dentist who worked out of the home. Way in the back of his office was a large bottle filled with all types of rotten teeth. And so, off Melissa went with her bottle of teeth and a plan to give every child their very own rotten tooth.

As you can guess, things didn't quite go as planned. The kids were happily horrified and the teacher, well, she wasn't so pleased. But not surprisingly, from that day on, Melissa's show-and-tell day was a well-known event!

David Catrow's boisterously entertaining illustrations are the perfect complement to this wonderful story. He captures the charm and humor of every moment. And just as a minor detail, it might make the story even better to know that it is a true one! (Of course, the names have been changed to protect the innocent.) (3–7 yrs.)

The Mysterious Tadpole

by Steven Kellogg

I can't think of one person who has seen this book in our house and has not fallen in love with it and wanted a copy for their own family.

This is the story of Louis, a young boy who gets a "tadpole" for his birthday. The "tadpole," though, ends up being a cousin of the Loch Ness Monster: too large, when grown, to be contained even in the junior high's swimming pool, but oh, so lovable! The hoops Louis must jump through to keep his tadpole well fed, and eventually well hidden, are simply hilarious. Facial expressions, detail, delicious understatement—they all add up to a book that has become a classic. It belongs not only on a child's bookshelf, but on the bookshelf of anyone who occasionally needs a good laugh. That might sound weird, but nearly any adult will get a kick out of the humor in *The Mysterious Tadpole*. (4–7 yrs.)

When children get grouchy, it's a powerful thing to help them gain the self-awareness that they are in a bad mood. Sometimes a touch of humor helps them learn this. When Heidi was young, she and her dear friend Emily used to play "Sourpuss Hats." I think the game started because one day Emily's mother had asked Emily if she had put on her sourpuss hat because she was so cranky. Emily (and then Heidi) quickly adopted this idea. They found real hats that became their official sourpuss hats, which they donned whenever being a sourpuss was warranted. With hats on their heads, they stomped around the house with dour looks on their faces, making various grumbly comments. It was hilarious for all concerned. But the best part was the holdover for when they really *were* grouchy. All we mothers had to do at this point was say, "Do you need your sourpuss hat? You're acting mighty grouchy right now." And the girls would giggle and somehow the grumpy mood was magically transformed. They started this when they were two or so, and still to this day, nine years later, if they are in a grouchy mood, they both break into a smile at just the mention of the words "sourpuss hat." It's astonishing what a little good-hearted humor can do to save the day!

Six-Dinner Sid

by Inga Moore

Every time a stray cat wanders into the neighborhood and lets us pet it and maybe accepts a nibble of a treat from us, I wonder how many other of us well-meaning characters have done the same things for it that day. Probably plenty, judging from how fat they frequently are. I don't know if this is the first book ever written about such clever felines, but a cat who divides his life among six masters is surely the makings for a great story. Why, even self-proclaimed cat *non*fans I know had their socks charmed off by Sid, the hero of this book.

Sid lives on Aristotle Street. In fact, he lives at number one Aristotle Street, number two, three, four, five and six Aristotle Street. Each homeowner thinks Sid considers that house his home, so, in each place, Sid gets his own special bed, his own favorite food and exhibits his own idiosyncratic way of being present with the master. In one place, he's full of mischief; in another, he's the watchcat; in another, he's all sweetness and light. Six different times a day, he makes appearances at the houses on Aristotle Street and assumes six different identities. Like I said, we've got a scam going here.

Only, the whistle gets blown when Sid develops a nasty cough and he's hauled to the vet, yes, six different times. An alert doctor who notices that all the owners of these sick cats live on Aristotle Street puts two and two together. With the wool no longer over their eyes, the neighbors agree to join forces and feed Sid only one dinner (catch the scene of Sid hissing at his one measly bowl of food), so he's off to Pythagoras Place, where the pickins might be better once again. They indeed are, and you'll see how.

Delicate yet colorful pastels comprise the illustrations on each page, and the text is brief. Sid's facial expressions are not to be missed. (3–7 yrs.)

Beware of Boys

by Tony Blundell

Take a little boy walking alone through a forest and a hungry wolf who carts the boy back to his cave and you've got a fairly predictable plot, right? Wrong. Boy is nonplussed by his predicament and you can practically see the wheels churning in his head. Convincing Wolf that a cooked, not raw, Boy-meal would be much tastier if Wolf spent a little time with preparation, Boy sends him on a "shopping" trip for the ingredients for Boy Soup. Here's the recipe: "One boy (medium-sized), one large iron pot, one ton of potatoes, one oodle of onions, one wooden tub of turnips, one cartload of carrots, one packet of fruit chews, one well-ful of water, one barrel of bricks, one trowel. *Method:* 1. First catch your boy. 2. Wash him thoroughly, especially behind the ears. 3. Place him firmly in the iron pot. 4. Add water, potatoes, onions, turnips, carrots and fruit chews to taste. 5. Sit on the barrel of bricks and stir with the trowel until Thursday."

Wolf thinks it sounds mouthwatering, and scurries about gathering these ingredients. But he forgets the salt. (Which wasn't on the list, actually, but that's part of Boy's plan.) One thing leads to another, and, well, you get the picture. In the end, it's the ridiculousness of the ingredients and all of the midstream recipe changes (instigated by the ever-so-clever boy) that enable Boy to make a safe getaway to his home. This is a clever, detailed, funny book. It's a real winner with kids. Its illustrations are colorful and big, while the text is perfectly brief and understated. Wolf's rather pathetic countenance toward the book's end (after he's hauled in tons of ingredients and been tricked into letting Boy escape) even stirs up compassion for the wily fellow. (4–8 yrs.)

Dear Friends,

As I write this, not too many summer vacation days have elapsed since school let out, and the whole concept is still a rather novel idea for Elizabeth and Evan. One of the manifestations of this is that Elizabeth, due to the principle of the thing, is determined not to get out of bed earlier than 11 A.M., or change out of her pajamas before 2 P.M. (even if it turns out to be torture to do so!). To Evan, it means prowling the neighborhood in search of some unsuspecting yard work–type person whom he can babble at and "entertain" while the poor soul is trying to do his work. Today, though, there's no reason for Evan to leave the property, because that lucky guy happens to be right here in our yard, attempting to fix our sprinkler system. This fellow, Greg, sounds sidetracked, though. Instead of quietly going about his sprinkler repair work, I can now hear him and my husband (who left work early today in order to fix the toilet's broken sump pump in the backyard and who has obviously recruited Greg to help him) grunting and making heaving, male-bonding-type noises and grumbling about water pressure and sump pumps.

Pajama-clad Elizabeth recently decided to start collecting coins, and has cornered Evan within earshot of my computer and is attempting to get him to go fifty-fifty on a two-thousand-year-old Ancient Roman "Hail Caesar" bronze coin for $9.95. (But, Evan, it's two thousand years old! Two thousand! From when Rome was cool!) Evan doesn't bite, all he wants is to enlist poor Greg's help in tearing up the deck in order to find an heirloom gold locket of mine that was accidentally dropped between the cracks a few weeks ago during a special ritual we had on his seventh birthday. In the meantime, Elizabeth badgers me until I make the coin-ordering phone call, and my poor husband emerges from an unsuccessful sump pump repairing endeavor to inform me that it feels as if a Santa Ana is moving in. (This is a Southern California weather phenomenon during which the winds blow in off the desert, rather than the ocean, bringing heat and smog and bizarre ions onto the scene for a few days, causing PMS-like symptoms to surface in every human being, in varying degrees.)

My husband finally goes back to work, but not before asking me to take a whiff of him and assure him he doesn't smell like a sewer (which, by now, is the only thing his sense of smell can detect). It isn't long before Elizabeth has exploded a water balloon in the house, by accident of course. (Gee! I wonder whom she was planning to hit with it! Could it be a seven-year-old boy whose name begins with "E"?) When she's decided she's tormented Evan enough, she'll come back in and turn on some questionable, to my ears, music and finish reading the less-than-fine literature (not a book from Chinaberry!) that she started in bed this morning. And Evan? Well, as soon as Greg leaves to go get some needed parts, he'll be in here asking if he can conduct an experiment with sphagnum moss in the bathroom or else set up his rock-selling stand at the end of our street. (Question of innocent passerby: "How much is this rock?" Evan's answer: "Well, you see . . . , it's real gold and it's ten dollars, but if you really want it, I'll give it to you for free.") And if he doesn't get anyone to buy the rock, but still feels he needs a little extra cash, he'll systematically loosen his already loose baby bicuspid until it falls out during his bedtime story tonight so he can trade with the tooth fairy for some fast, hard cash. (I'm not making this up; he has done this before. And just for the record, the tooth fairy also brings a pretty feather or a seashell.) All this activity "went down" during a several-hour stretch one afternoon as I attempted to meet a deadline for work.

Now, I don't know about you, but I sure enjoy days that run smoothly. I have a tendency to resent the sort of shenanigans of humans and nature that upset my momentum and equilibrium: the broken sump pumps, the burst water balloons, the sibling bickering, the Santa Anas and all the little *problems that throw me off of my routine. Each one of these could appear as an obstacle to happiness and serenity if taken at face value. It's when we can muster a light heart and appreciate the variety that we can see and feel the rich texture of life shining through. It's when we can step back and see that the "whole" (living and growing with a family) is so much bigger than the sum of its parts (the little hassles we encounter endlessly) that we can know how very special this experience of parenting really is. It's rather like the difference between a scrumptious salad consisting of many ingredients with contrasting tastes and textures, which you might ordinarily shy away from if you had to eat each item separately (like marinated beets or radish sprouts!), and a salad consisting of iceberg lettuce, period. There's simply no comparison between a parent who is learning to be comfortable among things she can't easily control, and one who can't find humor in much of anything. Now, I'd better go check up on that sphagnum moss experiment.*

Ties That Bind

Friends and Family

Being deeply loved by someone gives you strength;
loving someone gives you courage.

—LAO-TZU

f there is one thing our extended families offer us, it is the opportunity to learn compassion. Whether it's through the model of their loving actions toward us and our human frailties or through the process of healing our wounds from childhood when our relatives acted in less than compassionate ways, the lesson is always there. For some of us, our feelings about our families are complicated. We want to just love them and accept them for who they are, but often, their very humanness makes this difficult. We love them and sometimes we hate them. Or, perhaps, we hate them and sometimes we love them. However we feel, the ties that bind our hearts are strong. As adults, one of our jobs is to come to peace with our relationships with our families in whatever way we can. We have to find a healing balance between acceptance and reality.

Perception is everything when it comes to healing our relationships with people, in general, and our families in particular. I remember one day when a new perception brought about radical healing in my life. Becca was eight months old. I was walking in the back door of our home after running a bunch of errands. Becca and I were completely content in the glowing warmth of the spring sun. The air was heavy with the scent of an ancient purple lilac that bloomed along our fence. It was one of those perfect moments in life when everything feels just right. With Becca balanced on my left arm, I stood on the porch holding some stuff, including my knitting project, in my right arm. I was in a bit of a hurry to get inside, as our errands had taken longer than I had planned. Instead of putting the knitting down to negotiate the key in the lock, I stashed the knitting under my left arm and leaned forward to fuss with the key. As I jiggled it, Becca moved unexpectedly, and knocked the precarious balance of all my cargo out of whack. Suddenly, in one of those slow-motion moments of horror, I watched my knitting needles head straight for Becca's face. "Her eyes, her eyes!" I thought. "I've blinded her." In the next instant, time stood still as I assessed the damage—a small puncture wound half an inch below her right eye. Poor, surprised Becca screamed in pain. I stood petrified by the thought of what could have happened. Shaken to my core, I dropped everything except Becca and rushed inside to comfort her.

She was soon soothed by my ministrations; I, however, was not. All I could think, over and over again, was "How could I have been so stupid not to anticipate this possibility?" The "what ifs?" of the situation overwhelmed me. All I wanted in the world was for Becca to feel loved and be safe, and here I was, *her mother*, hurting her! I was utterly devastated. I walked around listlessly, literally in shock, for hours. I tended to Becca's needs, but I had no clue how to tend to mine. In all my heart, I never knew that *I* could ever be the one who would hurt my child. Naïve though I was, I always thought the purity of my love would protect us from harm. Suddenly, I saw that my love wasn't enough. I wasn't in control of everything. The unexpected could, and seemingly would, happen and Becca could be hurt.

A couple of hours later, a revelation brought me out of my shock. I realized that sometimes people just hurt other people and that sometimes love isn't enough to stop them from hurting each other. I knew what had happened between Becca and me was an accident because I was in a hurry and I didn't stop to think about what could happen as I acted. But in that moment, I clearly saw the connection between hurts that happen accidentally and hurts that happen when people are out of control and their anger or pain overtakes their behavior and makes them do the unspeakable. I knew from my own experience as a child with an alternating abusive, loving mother that acts of rage that arise out of nowhere are confusing to a child. Suddenly, my whole worldview changed. I realized that my mother, as much as she hurt me over and over again throughout my childhood, loved me with as much intensity and passion as I loved Becca. She just couldn't control her rage sometimes; and sometimes, I felt the brunt of it. I was awash with both compassion for the pain that lived inside my mother that caused her to hurt me and a sense of thankfulness that even with this pain she could love me in her own distorted way.

This revelation was like an angel reaching down from heaven to offer me a path toward healing. My new perception of my mother altered everything. It didn't take away my pain, but it opened my heart toward understanding. I realized that my mother hurt me, not because she didn't love me, but because she didn't know how *not* to hurt me. Her love and her lack of control were separate facts. I now understood how she could both hurt me *and* love me. I saw that while I couldn't eradicate the truth that she had hurt me, I could work to heal. I could learn to forgive. And from that moment on, I vowed with the deepest part of my heart that I would do everything I could to heal myself of all my wounds, in order to stop the abuse that was the legacy of my family. Great-grandma to grandma, grandma to mother, mother to me, we all were wounded. And if I didn't do something soon, right here, right now, I, too, could be hurting Becca in ways I didn't understand.

That lucky day, knitting needle and all, changed my life forever. It was at this moment my true journey as a parent began. I saw how vitally important it was for me to work on myself (on my demons, my dragons, my pain and my rage) so I could more purely express my love to my child. My new perception gave me the strength to face myself head-on in hard times. It gave me the understanding that Becca's and my relationship was really about both of us and what both of us bring to the situation. I saw that for me to be the best parent I could be I had to face my pain. I knew if I was going to be of help to Becca as she grew, I had to learn to see with clear eyes, not eyes that were clouded by my own misperceptions and wounds. I had to learn to separate my behaviors from my feelings, and know that while I couldn't control my feelings, I could learn to better control my behaviors.

As Becca grew and did what all young children do—investigate, make mistakes, test limits, etc.—I watched my reactions. Every time particularly strong feelings arose in response to Becca's behaviors (and soon, her younger sister Laura's), reactions that felt out of proportion to her actions, I learned to step aside from my feelings, calm myself down and then examine what was going on inside of me at another, less-charged time. Deal with the child's behavior in the moment and the source of my feelings later, away from my child. Over the years, and with lots of mistakes on my part, I learned that if I was feeling extraordinarily angry, it usually didn't have much to do with my child's behavior, but was more about me. It's so easy to feel angry at a child when what we are really angry about is something else, especially something that is out of our control—a nasty decision from an unforgiving boss, or feeling pressured to get too much done in too little time. Once we can recognize that our anger is about something else, we can protect our child from our misdirected rage. When I learned to identify where my anger stemmed from, I was able to intercede with my behavior sooner. This lent me much more control over my words. I still needed to deal with my feelings, but I didn't need to inadvertently lay them on my child.

This intense self-scrutiny brought many gifts. It made me examine closely not only the wounds I experienced as a child, but the good things, too. It taught me what I wanted to re-create in my own family and what I wanted to leave behind. I had lots of warm memories centered around my mom and making cookies, so I cultivated that. So much so that it seems whenever we are having a hard day, I tend to make a batch of cookies out of habit. It gives me a sense that I can love my children even when I am out of sorts. Over the years, I have learned that no family is perfect. We all have much to learn and much to give. If we can learn to let go of the parts of our parents' behaviors that didn't work and also see and fully cultivate our parents' gifts, our children will most certainly benefit from our growth and our families' wisdom.

As we work to create healthy families for our children and ourselves, here are some book suggestions and practical tips to encourage strong family ties.

Big Like Me

by Anna Grossnickle Hines

The cover of this book is undoubtedly a drawing from a photo in the author's family album: a three- or four-ish-year-old big brother, sitting quietly, gingerly cradling a newborn baby in his lap, proud as can be, and probably making plans to be the best big brother in the world. We have a photo exactly like it, with Elizabeth balancing newborn Evan on her three-year-old lap. You can practically read her thoughts: "I'm going to show this baby what the world's all about 'cause *I'm* the big sister and I already know!"

This book is the chronicle of a year's worth of being a big brother to an infant sister. After the dedication page's illustration of a little boy with ear pressed against his pregnant mommy's belly, we see him, in January, offering the newborn his finger, which she squeezes, and telling her, "Hello baby, little tiny baby. This is me. I'm going to show you everything." Through the months of the year, he shows her what to do with some baby toys, how to sit on laps, the springtime leaves and caterpillars, how to play pat-a-cake, how to fill a cup in the wading pool, etc.

His lessons are exactly what an older sibling of this age truly feels is useful information to a growing baby and indeed it is. Lucky is the infant who has a gentle, older sibling to show her the ropes of life in the first year. As the baby grows throughout the year, her brother introduces her to progressively more complicated aspects of their world, finishing up with gallantly teaching her to blow out her birthday candle and open packages.

This is a sweet and loving book for a new sibling. Keep it in mind for the newest young big brother or big sister in your life. (2½–5 yrs.)

Connecting with loved ones far away

Thanks to our increasingly mobile (and ever-busy) society, more and more children are growing up without the benefits of a geographically close extended family. Long gone are Sunday dinners at Grandma's home, dinners where the tables were crowded with aunts and uncles, cousins and miscellaneous (possibly eccentric) other relatives that built a sense of connection. Relationships with our extended families offer children a sense of context. The stories, the history, the idiosyncrasies that make each family itself help our children define themselves in the context of the greater world. Sometimes, if our relatives are psychologically unhealthy, distance from them can help us create a healthy family. But most times, if we distance ourselves from our kin, our children lose out on a richness that geographical proximity can provide. We can overcome this and encourage closeness with our faraway relatives in other ways.

♥ Weekly phone calls, even if you can only afford a short call, make Grandma and Grandpa an integrated part of a child's life. Encouraging your child to remember to tell Grandpa a funny story that happened that week or to ask Grandma about her adventures with Great-uncle Mark when she was young builds connection. Phone conversations offer children another person to whom to tell their story. Often a child will tell Grandma something she won't tell Mom or Dad. Even if your child is just a toddler, and not quite up to "talking" on the phone, you can hold the phone up to her ear for a minute or two and let Grandma speak to her. Over time, her phone skills will grow. It won't be long before your child sees Grandpa or Grandma as a resource for a tricky how-to question or other bit of trivia. Even if you know the answers yourself, allowing your child the opportunity to ask an older relative is just another way to build a bridge between the generations.

♥ Encourage a written relationship between the generations. When your child draws a picture, ask her what it is about, write it on the backside and then send it off in a "letter" to Grandma. It won't be long before your child will get the idea and let you be her scribe while she dictates letters. If Grandma and Grandpa respond with letters of their own, so much the better. Holiday and birthday thank-you letters are another wonderful opportunity for your child to reach out to faraway relatives. With the advent of e-mail, the written word has gotten even easier. Though to my mind, it still doesn't replace the joy on a child's face when she receives a real letter addressed just to her!

♥ Encourage your child to make presents for the relatives. Taking the time to make homemade expressions of his love strengthens his bond to faraway relatives, especially when your child visits and sees his creations on display.

♥ Give your child a small, hand-size personal photo album filled with pictures of all who love her, or make a collage on the fridge. Photos make names real and prepare children for the times when they see their relatives in person. Telling a story to your child about each photo helps enliven these distant people in your child's mind. Include favorite pets, since children are so often drawn to animals.

♥ Draw on the small traditions of your childhood and attach them to your child's life. For example, when I was a small child, every time I got out of the bath my father took a towel and gave my body a vigorous rub to dry me off. Once Becca was a toddler, I began this tradition with her, calling it a Grandpa Jim rub. The tradition continued with all four of my kids. This little, rather insignificant act helped tie my children to my childhood and build the bond with their faraway grandpa.

♥ Encourage big family reunions. My dad's family has one every other year. My children have grown up knowing their cousins and great-aunties and uncles intimately simply because of this wild (and often intense) week we all spend crammed together in someone's house. Our family has always chosen to keep costs down by not renting a large space, thereby enabling everyone to come. This intense closeness works for us, but I can see how other families might choose a different route. The important thing is to get together long enough for people to relax, tell stories, be silly and have time to play together. We don't do much (except the annual talent show—which has many acts that are hard to call talent and which we wouldn't miss for the world). Mostly we cook, eat and clean up, with occasional forays into the real world for food or entertainment. The point is not what we do, but rather just to *be* together. By the end of the week, everyone goes home exhausted and yet full with a richness that will last all of our lives. My children already talk about bringing their children to the far-distant family reunions, so important have these weeks of family become to them.

Oh, Little Jack

by Inga Moore

Oh, Little Jack is the story of Little Jack rabbit, a sweet little bunny who is just too little to do any of the things he wants to do. He's not strong enough to help his mom and dad in the garden or big enough to control his sister's go-cart. He's too little to keep track of brother Buck's kite and too unsteady to help carry tea to Grandpa. It is not until Grandpa fixes up a tricycle for Little Jack to ride that he finally finds something for which he is just the right size.

Moore has capitalized on one of the age-old struggles of siblings and created an *absolutely* endearing book. The illustrations are soft, warm and homey. They also have a wonderful sense of personality that really captures the essence of the story.

This is one of those books that almost every child will love, but it seems like a must for every younger sibling. There is something truly wonderful about your struggles being seen and understood. (2½–6 yrs.)

I Love My Baby Sister

(Most of the Time)

by Elaine Edelman
illustrated by Wendy Watson

The big sister in this dear book has an infant sibling, whom she really loves. But of course she must put up with the hair yanking, the crying and the diminished attention from parents that usually occurs when there's a new baby. This little girl is the narrator of this book, and innocently leads us through the high and low points of having a new sibling. There is remarkable wisdom in the simple text and illustrations, and that is so much of the book's appeal. (Be sure to note the wonderful illustration of a disaster-area kitchen, with the mom holding the baby and trying to cook, while the caption reads: "Sometimes my baby sister keeps Mother so busy I have to jump around and holler just to get a hug.")

This is not one of those technical books about what it is going to be like to have a baby in the house. There is more heart and soul to it than there typically are in other "new baby" books. Instead, while not pussy-footing around, it tells us cheerfully and lovingly that having a baby sister is fun—and that she'll even be a pal someday—someone "I might even let button me up in the back, where I can't reach." This is a precious book, sparse on text, lavish in the detail of its watercolor illustrations. (3–5½ yrs.)

Grandpa Bud

by Siobhan Dodds

Among all the little pleasures that children love, one is to be in on a joke. This is a story about a series of innocent miscommunications that result in a comedy of errors a child's mind can almost envision happening, but not quite. Grandpa Bud is the only one in the dark, and young ones will revel in knowing just how outlandish the whole situation really is.

You see, Polly calls her grandpa to ask if she can spend the night. The request simply makes his day, and her suggestion that he bake a chocolate cake isn't such a bad idea, either. But in the middle of mixing the batter, the phone rings again. It's Polly. She wants to know if she can bring Henry, who "won't be any trouble," who has a sore knee from doing cartwheels, but who will feel much better with some Jell-O and ice cream, and who can sleep in her bed. That's fine with Grandpa, but while he's busy making Jell-O, the phone rings again. It's Polly. She wants to know if she can bring Rose (who "won't be any trouble"), who happens to have a cold today. Banana sandwiches are fine with her, and she can sleep in Polly's bed, too. That's fine with Grandpa, sport that he is, but his mind is starting to go a mile a minute now, with preparations and such. Polly calls yet again, and asks whether George can come. (He won't be any trouble, either. . . .) Grandpa is envisioning a bed full of four kids and, frankly, a pretty wild night. Only, here's the secret: Henry's a teddy bear with a Band-Aid on his knee; Rose is a pink stuffed animal; George is a toy duck, etc.

Big, bright yet delicately colored illustrations jump out from every page, and large text invites the new reader to give it a try. (3–6 yrs.)

Friendships can be such an important part of a child's life. As parents, we can do much to instill the value of lasting friendship. Making time in our busy schedule for children to play with their friends is one simple way. For some children, regular play dates with one or two favorite friends do more to develop healthy social skills than all the formal classes and preschool classes in which we enroll them. One-on-one, with an adult nearby to help facilitate kind behavior, children learn how to interact in healthy ways. They learn to give and take in small situations so they can bring these skills to the larger world as they grow older.

The Maggie B.

by Irene Haas

Little Margaret Barnstable, about five, six or seven, wished on a star one night for

> *a ship named after me,*
> *to sail for a day,*
> *alone and free,*
> *with someone nice for company.*

And off she went to bed. She awakes to find herself in the cabin of her own ship, the *Maggie B.*, and her nice company is her baby brother, James.

Margaret delights in taking care of the ship, making meals, caring for her baby brother, organizing a picnic, etc., and even painting a handsome portrait of James while he naps on his velvet pillow. She makes stew out of fresh vegetables and fish from the sea and when a storm comes up, she deals with that, too. And her day on the *Maggie B.* comes to a sweet end when she puts James down for the night in her big-sisterly way. This all may sound too simple to be remarkable, but there is just something about *The Maggie B.* that is heartwarming and reassuring.

Its illustrations are lovely, full of detail and exude the pleasure and mutual love Margaret and James share. (3–7 yrs.)

Peter's Song

by Carol P. Saul
illustrated by Diane deGroat

Peter's a pig who's made up a song that no one in the barnyard seems to want to hear. The hens shoo him off, the horse asks him to please sing it somewhere else, even his mother is unenthused enough to tell him she'll listen to it only at some point in the future. Understandably dismayed, Peter decides to run away, so down the road he trots. Before too long, he finds a willing audience—or, rather, duet *partner*—in the form of a frog, Francis John, an undiscovered singer himself. With a new, empathic friend, synergy happens—as it so often does—and Peter now feels so good about himself that he de–runs away back home, for all is now well with the world.

You'll find yourself being called upon to sing often while reading *Peter's Song.* Make up your own tune to Peter's simple ditty and you'll have it made. But the fun really kicks in when pig and frog chime in together because, as Peter's song says,

> *Cause the best part of a song,*
> *oinky oinky oinky oink,*
> *Is when someone sings along,*
> *oinky oinky oinky oink!*

This is a feel-good book whose big, colorful illustrations sport the most endearing, joyful faces. Text is substantial for a picture book, perhaps taking you fifteen minutes or so to read aloud. (3–7 yrs.)

Children love to hear the stories of our past, stories that connect them to the child inside their parent and that speak of precious family history. My husband grew up in a family of four rowdy, astonishingly mischievous boys. Over the years, he has spent hours entertaining our children with the deeds and misdeeds of his childhood. Growing up at the base of a ten-thousand-foot peak, he had plenty of adventures in the wild both with his brothers and alone, getting lost in Hidden Valley, playing "Marines" out in the fields, climbing peaks to gain vast views of the mountains. He tells stories of dog-eating cats and the foot-stomping pony who hated boys. His older brother arranged pranks that would make any mother faint, but that make a great story forty years later! Baby-sitters would lock themselves in the bathroom just to get away from those four boys and cry until my husband's parents came home! Sometimes, I wonder how his parents survived. Those boys found their way into so much trouble on their path to adulthood, it's truly astonishing that they grew up. The thought of my children following in their father's childhood footprints horrifies me (and I think it horrifies them, too, judging from the expressions on their faces when he tells the stories), but what a gift he has given them through the sharing of his childhood! They know Grandpa spent hours with his boys playing catch out in the yard, and that if the boys managed to stay absolutely quiet on Sunday morning, they could miss church (what a feat of self-control that must have been!). My children now have a pretty good idea of what it was like to drive for days across country in the hot summer sun, six of them crammed into a Mustang (with no air-conditioning and without wearing seat belts!) to visit their loud, loving and eccentric Missouri relatives. They know a kind of history no history book will ever teach them. Since we live far from our families, these childhood stories have helped my children feel close to the people they seldom see. The storytelling has shown our children a side of their dad they would never know, now that he is a serious, grown-up doctor who seldom has time for pranks. (Thank goodness!) His stories make him real in new ways.

When we pass down the stories of our family's past, our children feel connected to something big, much bigger than themselves. It's almost as if they connect to their family on a genetic level. No *wonder* we all love potatoes: we're *Irish*, for gosh sake! When my kids learned that my Uncle Tom hid his vegetables in the cuff of his pants so as not to have to eat them, it made them feel just a little bit better when they sat in front of a serving of broccoli that they would gladly have handed down to the dog. Knowing our family stories makes us strong, even if the stories aren't always what you hope for your children. Children hear stories of survival, of the experiences that make us resilient. Of course, the stories we tell have power, so we should make sure we tell them the ones we want them to know. Even horrible events of the past can be told in such a way to show the enduring strength of humans as they endeavor to carry on.

Toot and Puddle

by Holly Hobbie

Toot and Puddle (who are pigs, by the way) live together in a house in Woodcock Pocket. Puddle is a homebody (homepig?) and Toot loves to travel. One day in January, Toot decides to set off on his biggest trip ever. And not surprisingly, Puddle decides to stay home. Still connected in a way only good friends can be, they think of each other a lot, despite their physical separation. While Toot is sloshing around with hippos in Africa, Puddle is pirouetting back on Pocket Pond. When Toot is galloping through the Egyptian desert on a camel, it's maple-sugaring time back home for Puddle and he's wishing his pal could share some pancakes with him. The year rolls on, through the seasons, and every now and then a postcard arrives from Toot. Then one morning in November, Toot wakes up (somewhere in Italy, it appears) and knows that it is time to go home—much to Puddle's delight. The book ends nearly a year after it began, the two friends reunited, life again sweet—sweeter than it's perhaps ever been before. And that's the story—an engaging and charming tale involving two distinctly different personalities.

The detailed and softly colored illustrations invite you and your child to pore over each one and find the subtle humor and charm. A sweet *and* fun book. (3–5 yrs.)

The Milly-Molly-Mandy Storybook

told and drawn by Joyce Lankester Brisley

The Milly-Molly-Mandy Storybook is a perfect book to read to your child the minute she can sit and listen to text without a lot of illustrations. The heroine, after whom the book is named, is a young girl of many-years-ago Britain. (Most of the stories in this collection were written in the late 1920s.) She is six-ish and lives with an extended family in the country. Her joys and challenges and disappointments and adventures are perfectly age-appropriate. Milly-Molly-Mandy tackles things like spending her first night away from home, successfully remembering all of the things on her lengthy errand list, being helpful to her neighbors, attending her first wedding, taking joy in being given trust and responsibility, etc. It is a truly charming book. Gentle, simple, innocent—a beautiful example of the ways in which stories can show graciousness, the exploration of conscience, the realization that comes with maturity that none of us is the center of the universe.

Simple black-and-white drawings can be found every couple of pages or so. This book has an innocence to it that is refreshing and will help keep alive a small child's sense of wonder and belief in the simple pleasures of life. (3–7 yrs.)

Friends

by Helme Heine

There is an exuberance to this book that feels just like the joy you used to experience when you were with your best friend and your parents were nowhere to be seen and everything was going right and you wished the day would never end. There are few who don't fall in love with this book on the spot due to its innocence and lovely and light-hearted watercolor illustrations.

Here is a joyous romp with three characters (pig, mouse and rooster) through a day of hide-and-seek, playing pirate on an old boat, fishing, picking cherries and trying to figure out a way to stay together even when it comes time to go to sleep. Deceptively simple, it is so much more than the sum of its parts. Anyone who has ever had a good, good friend will understand why this book is so well loved.

Friends never slows down till sleep takes over the three best buddies—just as children having a great time never stop until they drop. (3–8 yrs.)

If you have chosen to be distant from your family for one reason or another, your children need not miss out on the loving ministrations of the older generations. Explain your situation and ask a beloved older friend if he or she would be willing to be your child's adopted grandma or grandpa. A friendly neighbor might love to spend time with your child, inviting him over for cookies and conversation or perhaps a short walk around the neighborhood. We live far from all of our relatives and I've been interested to note how each of my children has been unofficially adopted by one of my friends (each child by a different friend). They have formed a special attachment to these adults that helps carry them through hard times. Aidan calls his special friend his fairy godmother. And that is just the role she plays in his life—always adding that little bit of magic that makes life rich.

Mr. Putter and Tabby

a series by Cynthia Rylant
illustrated by Arthur Howard

Just perfect for new readers, these books are a faultless mix of endearing characters, engaging illustrations and relatively simple language. As a parent, I actually enjoy reading these stories over and over again, which certainly *isn't* the case for most Easy Reader books I have seen. There is dear sweet Mr. Putter. He is like a ten-year-old boy (full of mischief and sparkle) trapped in an old man's body. Just to give you an example, in *Mr. Putter and Tabby Pick the Pears*, Mr. Putter wants to pick the pears in his old pear tree, but his cranky old legs can't climb the ladder. *How* can he get those pears down?! Suddenly, he realizes he can make a slingshot out of his underwear and shoot the pears out of the tree. It turns out that he isn't very good at hitting the pears and soon he has lobbed all the windfall apples from his apple tree (he was using the apples to hit the pears) over his house and into his neighbor's yard. Who should appear but his neighbor, Mrs. Teaberry, carrying a big basket of apple goodies. She just couldn't understand why, but that morning when she woke up her yard was littered with apples and she couldn't resist making an apple feast.

If you have a soon-to-be-reading person around the house, you would be wise to stock up on these books. They surely take the edge off struggling with learning to read. Reading *Mr. Putter* books is like having a kindly grandpa living next door: they only make life richer! (3–8 yrs.)

All the Places to Love

by Patricia MacLachlan
illustrated by Mike Wimmer

All the places to love are the ones that surround young Eli. On the day he is born, his grandmother holds him up to the window so that what he hears first is the wind, and what he sees first are the valleys, river and hilltop where blueberries grow. He will be lovingly shown the beauty and simple pleasure in his world, and will grow up knowing that no matter where life takes him, he will always think this is the best place because those who showed it to him love him and these places more than anything else.

Eli grows up on a farm. The sense of purity and innocence of his world is tangible and makes many of us yearn for a life where time is slow and beauty is easy to find in the simplest of things. Eli gets to slosh through the marsh, pick blueberries under a sky only an arm's length away, cross the river to the woods, where he finds a soft, rounded bed where a deer has slept (and it was still warm!). But much more than that, it is the story of a boy whose loved ones take the time to be with him and share the joys that they have found and that have seen them through life.

The possibility that Eli is Everychild lies within all of us, as we bring our babies into the world. So much of what our children learn to love is what they sense gives us our own peace and our joy. Whether our homes are near marshes and blueberry hills or high-rises and community playgrounds, the lovely message in this story is the same. (4+ yrs.)

Difficult relatives can be a wonderful learning opportunity for children. When I was a child, my mother and her mother never saw eye to eye, yet my mother knew how important *her* grandmother had been to her, so she never stood in the way of my relationship with my grandparents. She bowed out so she had little to do with them, but I still was allowed plenty of access. Knowing how my mother felt toward her mother and yet feeling adored by this very same woman helped me to learn that people are complicated. Yes, my grandmother could be very loving to me and yet, when it came to my mother, all I saw was cruelty. The paradox of my grandmother's behavior was actually enlightening. I came to see how people have many facets. Her complexity taught me to be more accepting and often more forgiving of people's weaknesses; additionally, it gave me more compassion toward my mother and her struggles.

A Chair for My Mother

by Vera B. Williams

Here we meet a young girl, her mama, her grandma and an aunt and uncle. The mom works in a diner, supporting her daughter and the grandma. The story starts out, narrated by the girl, with a little background: this family saves her mother's tips and any other coins in a big jar. The plan is to buy the mom a comfortable chair with the money when the jar is full. (Remember, her mother works in a diner, and always has aching feet when she gets home.) The reason there's not *already* a comfortable chair in their home is because a fire destroyed their previous home, a fire described lucidly and in sufficient detail to give this story just the right amount of suspense. The money jar is eventually filled to the brim and the family goes shopping for chairs, the love among them coming through heartwarmingly loud and clear. This wonderful family is so warm, so loving, its feel so delightfully different from the family dynamics we watched in *Leave It to Beaver*.

The vibrant watercolors complement the warmth of this story so very well. (4–7 yrs.)

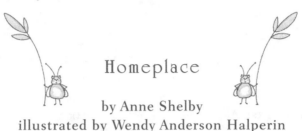

Homeplace

by Anne Shelby
illustrated by Wendy Anderson Halperin

This story begins two hundred years ago, with a great-great-great-great-grandpa. And it ends in present day, with a great-great-great-granddaughter sitting in her grandma's lap. *Homeplace* begins with the clearing of land generations ago, the building of a sturdy cabin, the planting of corn, and babies being put to sleep on a cornhusk bed. The story ends in the present day, in the child's bedroom of that same old house.

The magical part of this book is that it is being told by a grandmother—who was born and lived on this land—to her granddaughter. The story follows the generations and house through their days and changes over the course of a couple of hundred years.

There is a wonderful continuity and good feeling about this book. It gently and clearly evokes a real connection with those who came before us. The illustrations do an extraordinary job of adding to this story. Not only do we get a glimpse of how the house and town evolved over generations, but there are also photo-album–like drawings across the bottom of the pages. This is a very special book that might make you want to live in that very house. (4–7 yrs.)

Day of the Dead

Having grown up next to a Hispanic community, I have always been intrigued with their lively way of celebrating holidays. I especially love the Day of the Dead celebrations. While my family always honored this day (All Souls' Day) by going to church, I always felt we were missing out on something special by not celebrating as our neighbors did. After church, they all seemed to have fun, piling in their cars and heading off to the cemetery for a day of celebration. First they would carefully tend the family plots and then they would have a huge picnic with their neighbors. It was a time of remembering the lives of those they had lost—telling stories, laughing and sometimes crying about old times, and feasting on a gigantic picnic lunch (complete with very interesting skeleton treats—I always wanted some of those!). Children would miss school and whole families would celebrate together the bonds of love that held their loved ones close. As a child, I always longed for our family to have such a celebration, too. I so wanted to hear the stories of my ancestors, of my dead grandma whom all my cousins knew and loved, but of whom I had no memory. I wanted to feel connected to something much larger than my small, three-person immediate family.

Now an adult, I enjoy honoring this day and my relationship to my ancestors. I want my children to grow up knowing a bit of the history that makes our family special. Each year I find a different way to celebrate. Sometimes it is as simple as remembering to tell a story about one of our ancestors, a story that illustrates to my children the strength and determination that is in their genes. Other times, I like to do something a bit more elaborate. One of my favorite ways to celebrate this day is to make a little altar dedicated to my ancestors. I find old pictures of deceased family members and display them all together with a special candle or perhaps a candle for each person. When I sit down to be with these pictures, I light the candles, saying a special prayer for the souls of each of my loved ones. This is especially powerful when I am working through some emotional issue with this person. Both my mother and one of my grandmothers died before I had completed working out my relationship with them. Honoring them with this altar helps me work through my own sorrow. And it has helped my children. Laura was especially close to my grandma. She grieved Grandma's loss for years. Talking and honoring her picture seemed to help Laura work through her grief. One year we even made a pilgrimage to the cemetery where my grandparents are buried. We took old sheets and crayons and made rubbings of the gravestones. Simple as they were, these rubbings were very special to us all.

Our culture has such a hard time with death. We often shelter children from funerals or seriously ill people, thinking it is good for them. But how, when death is a part of all of our lives, can this be good for us? Honoring our ancestors helps take death out of the closet and put it back into proper perspective.

A Song for Lena

by Hilary Horder Hippely
illustrated by Leslie Baker

Young Lena and her grandmother are making apple strudel together. As they work, Grandmother hums a beautiful song from Hungary, the country where she grew up. When Lena asks her grandmother to tell her the story of this song, a tale of compassion unfolds that is good for the hearts of all who hear it.

Long ago, when Grandmother was young and growing up on a small farm, one apple-picking time found her own mother making a special treat: apple strudel. While it was cooking, Grandmother went outside to play with a friend. And as they were playing, the girls came across a hungry old man walking in the fields. He asked them to ask their mother for a bit of bread because he hadn't eaten all day. Instead of bread, though, Mother answered their plea by cutting him a large piece of strudel and sending out a large mug of coffee, too.

The rest of the story comes together in just the way we hope stories of kindness will come together. Although the ending of *A Song for Lena* is one you need to experience for yourself to understand its beauty, it involves the beggar returning through the years and playing lovely music on his violin—music that could be heard in the air during strudel time, even long after the man had come for the last time.

This is a story of love, kindness and of giving from the heart. It is about giving and receiving. The lovely words of *A Song for Lena* are perfectly complemented by Baker's soft watercolor illustrations. They capture the warmth and love of Grandmother's family. And Grandmother's Apple Strudel recipe is also included. (4–8 yrs.)

When Jessie Came Across the Sea

by Amy Hest
illustrated by P. J. Lynch

Reading this book reminds us of how good it is to be alive, to be human, to be able to love. With exquisite words and illustrations, *When Jessie Came Across the Sea* tells the story of young orphaned Jessie as she leaves the loving embrace of her grandmother's arms to travel to America and make a new life for herself as a lacemaker. Given the gift of a free ticket and the offer of a home and a job with a kind widow, thirteen-year-old Jessie knows she must leave all that she loves and risk her fate in a new land. Her warm heart enchants all she meets and soon she makes new friends and is learning a new language. When time passes and Jessie falls in love, she dreams of bringing her grandmother to America for the wedding. Somehow it doesn't surprise us that with hard work and lots of determination, she makes her dreams come true.

This is one of those very special stories that seem to touch the hearts of all who read it. It speaks so clearly about what is true and good about being human that it is hard not to be caught in its enchanting web. The illustrations are an epic in themselves, a perfect complement to a beautiful story. (4–8 yrs.)

Thundercake

by Patricia Polacco

Thundercake is not only full of unforgettable and unrivaled folk-art illustrations, it is also a lively, dear, truly unique story of a grandmother and granddaughter who, knowing a thunderstorm is coming, prepare for it in a comforting way.

You see, while the child is petrified of thunder and hides under her bed during its clapping, Grandma coaxes her out with the promise that while the storm approaches they will prepare "Thundercake" so that it will be in the oven when the rain starts to fall. From the first mention of the muggy, still air at the farm to the moment when the two of them are seen feasting on their cake, there is never a dull moment. Grandma admonishes her granddaughter to pay attention to the thunder only for the purpose of figuring out how far away the storm is, and to move quickly in order to gather eggs, milk the cow and get chocolate, sugar and flour from the dry shed. As they count aloud and the thunder booms and crackles at closer intervals, all that is left is to collect the "secret ingredient." Are you ready for this? Three overripe tomatoes and some strawberries. The two of them raid the garden, then head into the kitchen to complete the Thundercake. Phew! The cake gets into the oven before the storm hits, and the last we see are a joyous old woman and young girl enjoying their little party, and the sound of rain on the roof. Yes, and for you romantics, the recipe for Thundercake is included at book's end. (4+ yrs.)

Every family needs a delicious, foolproof basic cake recipe to draw upon for any festive occasion. Here's a great chocolate cake recipe that you can turn into a German Chocolate Cake, Ice Cream Cake, Birthday Cake, Fourth of July Cake, etc. It all depends on how you choose to decorate it.

Possibly the World's Best Chocolate Cake

2 cups flour
1¼–1½ cups sugar
1 cup water
¾ cup sour cream
4 oz. melted unsweetened chocolate
¼ cup melted butter
1 tsp. salt
1¼ tsp. baking soda
1 tsp. vanilla
2 eggs

Preheat oven to 350 degrees. Mix all ingredients together and beat until *very* smooth. Pour into greased and floured nine-by-thirteen-inch glass pan. Bake thirty to thirty-five minutes, or until toothpick comes out clean when inserted in the center of the cake. Cool completely on rack before frosting.

Frosting:

$^1/_4$ cup soft (but not melted) butter

2 cups powdered sugar

2 oz. melted unsweetened chocolate, cooled

$^1/_2$ cup sour cream

1 tsp. vanilla

Cream butter and sugar until smooth. Add cooled chocolate, sour cream and vanilla. This tends to be a soft frosting; if too soft, chill in fridge before spreading.

Grandad's Prayers of the Earth

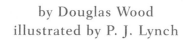

by Douglas Wood
illustrated by P. J. Lynch

This stunning book portrays the deep loving bonds between a young boy and his grandfather. Together they take quiet walks through the Minnesota woods looking at the simple beauties of nature. The boy asks his wise grandfather many questions about the workings of the world. And his grandfather gives him answers that make the world seem just right. One day the boy asks his grandfather about prayers, but instead of explaining, Grandad answers with another question: "Did you know, boy, that trees pray?" Grandad goes on to explain how all things on earth pray just by being themselves. A bird prays when it sings, a tree prays by reaching up to the heavens. The boy wonders about this and then asks about people and praying. Grandad suggests that people pray when they notice the beauty of the world, smelling a flower or watching the exquisite beauty of a snowfall. We pray to give thanks; we pray for others when they are sick or lonely or far away.

Grandad advises that any words said from the heart are a prayer. And when the little boy asks if the prayers are answered, Grandad says, "If we listen closely, a prayer is often its own answer. Like the trees and winds and waters, we pray because we are here—not to change the world, but to change ourselves. Because it is when we change ourselves that the world is changed." The years pass, until one sad day Grandad dies and the boy is lost in his grief; lost until he remembers how to pray. As he goes back out into the woods where he and his grandfather have walked so many times, the boy is reminded of the prayers of the earth and for the first time he is sure he feels them. Suddenly, he is aware of his grandad's love coming through the earth to him.

Each lush illustration captures the wonder and joy of the love between this wise man and his grandson. The paintings are so rich in life, the faces so complete in their emotions.

There is a good chance that simply reading this book will change your life for the better. (5+ yrs.)

Dear Friends,

I've just returned home from visiting my aunt in the Midwest. Born shortly after the turn of the century, Aunt Flo is the closest relative I have left on my mother's side of the family. Over the years, she's accumulated an extraordinary amount of stuff—things that she's kept with her all through her life and things that my grandmother left behind when she died. Except for her clothes, a clock radio or two and a new refrigerator, there is very little in her house that isn't old. Her telephone is even a rotary phone.

On this last trip, she took me around her little house, showing me articles that she thought I might want for my own keepsake collection, articles that might not be there the next time I visit, articles she just might decide to finally dispose of if she ever decides to move to a retirement community. We went through trunks and dressers in the attic, we went through several drawers in the dining room hutch and we went through boxes from shelves high up in the closet. I felt transported to the early part of the century.

The dining room, though, is what held the treasures. She carefully unwrapped some well-worn silver utensils. Tarnished and dented, they'd belonged to my grandmother, a woman who, I've learned over the years, lived a hard life. She unwrapped two more items, a hand-painted creamer and sugar bowl. The bowl's rim had countless small chips around it, I suppose from the thousands of times a spoon was thrust in for sugar and nicked the edge occasionally. These had been my grandmother's wedding presents. Pretty and utilitarian at the same time, they had obviously not been put away for special occasions; they'd been used constantly, along with the silver utensils. When I touched each of these items and paused for a moment, I felt as if I were touching much more than old pieces of kitchenware. I felt as if I was somehow connected to lives that managed to make it through losing loved ones in the Great War, to lives that survived and didn't survive polio and whooping cough, to lives that coped with the Depression and with the earthshaking effects of World War II. I felt connected to lives in which there was a certain harshness yet sense of community and simplicity born of necessity. Whatever thread it is that weaves itself through generations and connects us was alive and almost breathing in these well-worn and no longer perfect articles that had been stashed away for decades.

Yes, I said, I'd love to take these home with me. And even though I thought I'd been sensibly discriminating, I found myself at the airport with an extra suitcase of things my aunt wanted me to have. Pristine-condition silver candy dishes, lead-crystal bowls, silver candlesticks, etc., that looked as if they'd never been used. And now "we're" all home. I've polished the silver and washed everything else in preparation for putting it away. But I can't bring myself to put those dented silver utensils and that sugar and creamer set where their history, their soul, their imperfections will sit in a dark, solitary place behind the doors of my hutch. For, just as the Velveteen Rabbit became "real" only after it became well worn and well loved, these items are real, dents, nicks and all. No, I was going to use these pieces, make them a part of my family's everyday life and be reminded of my grandmother's strength and courage every time I used them.

With this decision to use these well-worn pieces, I began to think about the imperfections we all have. Just as my favorite articles brought back from the Midwest are the ones that have obviously been through a lot and were very much a part of someone's life, it is often the dents and the nicks that bring out the beauty in us, that give us depth, that make us strong, that test our values and insist that we live them if we are to be true to our higher selves. It is the challenges in our lives, the times when we've struggled, when we've righted a wrong, when we've looked at, instead of away, when we've been compassionate and perhaps ended up with some battle scars in the process—those are what make us real. In a time when it's drummed into us that we can "have it all," that we can create the perfect life for ourselves, that our children can be brilliant and successful (and healthy and beautiful and popular) if we just raise them the right way, it's easy to be intolerant of that which isn't flawless. But life is a journey of peaks and valleys, joys and sorrows, perfect times and imperfect times, and each one of us is a tapestry created by what we've lived through. Just as my grandmother's well-worn utensils have an authentic and deep-seated beauty to them because they were often used rather than tucked away for special occasions, the love we create in our families is often stronger and more resilient and more enduring if we accept others' imperfections as part of what makes them beautiful—and real.

My hope is that you find something you can make real, that you use—and keep using throughout the year—a special article you've stashed away, that yes, you may even chip or dent in the process. But years from now, it may be a profound gift to someone who may hold it and sense that it was part of a real family's life—and all the laughter and tears that make a family a family.

Learning to Be Human

Living with Our Foibles

To do for yourself the best that you have it in you to do—to grit your teeth and clench your fists in order to survive the world at its harshest and worst—is, by that very act, to be unable to let something be done for you and in you that is more wonderful still. The trouble with steeling yourself against the harshness of reality is [that] the same steel that secures your life against being destroyed secures your life also against being opened up and transformed by the holy power that life itself comes from. You can survive on your own. You can grow strong on your own. You can even prevail on your own. But you cannot become human on your own.

— FREDERICK BUECHNER

My home is in the midst of a major remodeling project right now. Our normal twenty-four-hundred square feet of livable space has been reduced to about five hundred square feet. When we started, I didn't ask how long this disaster would take to repair. (Our hundred-year-old house was literally falling into the ground and seriously unsafe). I don't think I wanted to know. I just packed up our stuff, moved into what we lovingly call the compartment (two rooms at the back of the house and one bedroom upstairs with a war zone in between them) and adjusted. It's been thirteen months now and there is no end in sight. We've been cooking on a hot plate, the grill and occasionally in an oven far across our property. We use tubs to collect water from the shower to do the dishes. Heating is marginal, at best. It's been rough.

Since we started remodeling, we've had many houseguests (gatherings that we've enjoyed greatly, but that have probably stretched our guests' concept of acceptable hospitality!). We've sent one daughter off to Argentina for her junior year abroad and another back to college. I agreed to work on this book and my husband took on new responsibilities in his work. Life is nuts.

Right now, it's just the four of us: Heidi, Aidan, Steve and I, surviving in the compartment, and things are tight. Since I work from home and my work involves a lot of "stuff" (i.e., boxes and boxes of books arrive every week), it sometimes feels as if I am being suffocated in this small space. And while I'm normally a pretty chipper person, lately I've been feeling mighty cranky. I keep struggling to smile and endure with a positive attitude, but really and truly this situation is taxing my patience. Every day I wake up with new resolve to face this remodeling with a smile and make the best of it; at the close of every day, I lie down in bed completely exhausted, wishing it would all be over *now!* I am constantly overwhelmed by the sense that life is asking too much of me, and this doesn't make me feel as if I am the best mother I could be.

Lately, it seems as if I am always saying "no." "No, I am too tired"; "No, there isn't any space"; "No, it will make too much of a mess." "No, no, no," when what I really want to say is "yes." "Yes, go ahead and make a cake (even though you'll have to bake it in the workshop)"; "Yes, use glitter to make valentines (even though it means getting the vacuum cleaner out of the one overstuffed closet we have left for our mountains of stuff)"; "Sure, invite your friends over; who cares if there are four rowdy boys romping about in this small space when it's raining?" But instead of saying "yes," I say "no" just to survive. And I feel guilty. I feel guilty because I want to give my children what they want (when it is reasonable), and what they are asking for *is* reasonable, under normal circumstances. I keep thinking, "If only I could just give a little more . . ."

But I can't. I can't give one little bit more this week. My life has pushed me right to the edge of myself and I am learning that sometimes I have to say "no." Being a "can do" person, it's hard for me to surrender to this idea. Can't I do everything? I have always assumed that giving so much was necessary. But you know what? I am finding just the opposite to be true. I am finding that my kids are thanking me more when I do say "yes." They are appreciating the little things in life more, and so am I. Just this morning I woke up to the puppy (oh yeah, I forgot to mention we added a puppy to our chaos this Christmas!) barking to be let out for his morning potty run. Heidi was reading silently in her bed while Aidan lay in his, singing an original little ditty: "My mommy is the best mommy in the whole wide world. I bet every boy wants my mommy to be his." As I lay there, soothed by the sense that all was right with the world (but still not wild about the thought of getting up to go outside with the puppy), the kids, of their own accord, took it upon themselves to escort him out for his early morning walk. They simply slipped out of the bedroom quietly to let me sleep! What magic was at work this day?!

It is amazing to me that just when I am feeling my worst, over-stressed self, my children somehow remind me that things are not so bad, that they love me no matter what. Their caring shows me that we are doing this family thing together. I help them; they help me. Together we are learning how to love each other a little more each day, even when times are rough. They give; I take. I give; they take. We've learned to look at each other and know when to extend that extra hug. In the last week, I have had more little handfuls of flowers, hugs and extra kisses than I could count. Have they learned to do this from me? I don't know, but I do know that they have learned to give of themselves when it is necessary and to care deeply for each member of our family. What a gift!

Moments like this make me feel incredibly blessed, even with all of the chaos around me. The hard work of parenting, the day-in, day-out work of being present for my children's needs is teaching us *all* how to be better people. I can admit now that I can't be perfect (something I constantly strived for in my early years of parenting). I can see now how I can't be everything to my children and that that is *okay*. By not being *everything*, I allow my children, my husband, my friends and our extended family room to give, too. There is room for all of our gifts and we *all* have the support we need to learn from our weaknesses.

Each of us is born into this world with gifts to give and lessons to learn. Maybe these are the two greatest blessings a family can offer to each other—the room to let our individual gifts blossom, and the support to help each other strengthen in the ways in which we need to grow. As we make our way through our lives, like pilgrims on a journey of the heart, each of us moves toward greater wholeness. When we make room in our hearts for each other's foibles and take the time to applaud each other's kindnesses, we make it easier on ourselves to find that wholeness. Our love for each other provides a safe container in which to grow, offering safe passage on this rocky road of life.

Teaching our children to be the most they can be not only involves teaching them manners, but also involves showing them heroes of all kinds overcoming the eternal obstacles of life, big and small. What follows is a list of books and suggestions that encourage the development of the full breadth of your child's humanity.

Transforming Mistakes into Opportunities

Making mistakes is inevitable. Learning to accept these mistakes—ours and our children's—is a humbling, yet powerful practice. If we can come to view mistakes as opportunities to learn, rather than as some horrible events, mistakes become teaching moments for us all. Blaming, condemning, overprotecting or overcompensating, only teach our children to blame, condemn and be afraid and unsure of themselves. Viewing mistakes as a chance to learn helps us all move ahead with new information.

When our children err, many things can be at work. Sometimes we learn that our expectations of their behavior are set too high, given their age. If this is the case, we learn more about what a two- or three- or four-year-old is capable of and we graciously lower our expectations to match his development. Other times we learn that we have not provided him with enough information to accomplish the task before him. If this is the case, we can correct his misstep and ours with a simple statement. "Glue works best when spread in a thin stream, not in giant globs. Here's a damp sponge to wipe up that extra glue." Relaying non-judgmental information is so much more helpful than berating him about a mess. Sometimes children do "interesting" things (that parents reference as mistakes) simply out of curiosity. Who would have guessed that pouring a bottle of shampoo down the toilet would cause a problem? Certainly not a two-year-old. But a two-year-old definitely might think to do such a thing. (Pouring is fun!) It's easy to lose patience with such behavior, but in reality, small children *don't* know any better. This is another instance when information is more powerful than emotion in teaching children how to behave.

Children (and most adults, too) make more mistakes when they are tired, hungry, angry, hurt or otherwise out of sorts. When physical and emotional needs aren't met, it's hard for anyone to behave. Knowing this, we can try to address our child's needs promptly so we don't allow the situation to get out of hand. If, for some reason, we can't correct the situation (say, we are minutes away from home in the car), we can apologize and *acknowledge* his needs. Letting him know that we are aware that he is hungry but that food is still minutes away (or whatever) may help him be patient. (It may not if he is feeling too desperate. But at least it helps him know that a solution is on the way, and that may help *you* stay calm so your energy isn't escalating the situation.) Later, when his needs are met and he is feeling better, we can take the time to explain how hitting his brother when he is frustrated because he is hungry is a mistake. Consistently using this approach teaches children to have faith in us. When we know they are hungry and we say we can feed them in five minutes and then we do, time and time again, they learn to trust us. This trust will help them develop the patience to wait, even when they are feeling distressed by their physical or emotional needs. They won't feel as if they are forced to act rudely to have their needs met. Remember: this is a process. You begin with the toddler and (depending on your child) you see the results over time. Some children are able to master this type of self-control much earlier than others. But with a consistent, patient approach, most children do master it eventually.

Most parents make their fair share of blunders, too. I know *I* do. A day seldom goes by that I am not apologizing for some mistake I have made. If we can learn from our mistakes rather than criticize ourselves or get defensive and blame someone else (usually our child or partner), we model for our children the process we want them to learn when faced with a difficult situation. The more direct responsibility we assume for our mistakes, the more personal responsibility our children learn to take. And since personal responsibility leads to positive solutions, the happier we all will be.

Say Please

by Virginia Austin

Sometimes it seems that we can get awfully mired down in the process of teaching the necessary courtesies of "please" and "thank you." So when a book like *Say Please* comes along, it's like a breath of fresh air because it takes you out of your own situation and puts you in someone else's. Young Tom's, to be exact. Not pedantic, not didactic, not cloying or patronizing, it gets at the issue in a sweet, unassuming way that is just innocent enough that "please" and "thank you" might become a part of your child's repertoire a little sooner for having read it.

This book shows how young Tom goes about his day, a day that happens to involve interacting with a handful of animals. There's his dog, who barks, "Woof woof," as he looks expectantly at Tom while he holds the ball. And there are the ducks, who "Quack quack," as they follow him while he eats a sandwich. The cat says, "Meow meow," as he holds a glass of milk. Etc. In each case, Tom knows that the animals are asking for something: "Throw my ball, please," or "May we have some bread, please?" or "May I have some milk, please?"

When Tom brings his favorite book to Auntie Bea, she knows that he'd like her to read him a story. So when she reminds him about saying "please," he says, "Woof woof, quack quack, meow meow, please, Auntie Bea!" It shouldn't be any great surprise that his "thank you" is prefaced by the same animal "words" when they are finished reading the book.

Both silly and sweet, *Say Please* is a gentle book about gratitude for the very young. (2–4 yrs.)

Cinderella

illustrated by K. Y. Craft

In this classic of all fairy tales, K. Y. Craft has taken what may be the most common of all children's tales and turned it into an unmistakable masterpiece. The story itself is beautifully retold, based on Andrew

Lang's and Arthur Rackham's (two master storytellers) renditions of this ancient tale. The words speak of higher truths, of acting with faith and compassion and finding the true desire of your heart as a result. Cinderella is the model of goodness and forgiveness; the beauty of her heart is what makes the prince love her. She is rewarded by her fairy godmother for her kindness. Our children could do worse than to model their hearts after the goodness of Cinderella. Craft has taken this profound tale and added her own remarkable touch with elaborately detailed illustrations so gorgeous you can't help being moved. They are truly radiant.

Cinderella is a story meant to bring hope to our hearts when life is hard; it is meant to show us how, in the end, God rewards us for our goodness. What a beautiful message to give our children as they navigate their way through a world that seldom rewards what is good. (3+ yrs.)

Children need heroes. If we fail to give them real heroes, they will gladly seek out their own in the form of rock stars and superathletes with questionable morals. One of the most powerful things we, as parents, can do (besides be living examples of what we hope to teach) is offer them stories of *real* heroes. Offer them stories that will give them a model of courage so that when it comes time for them to be heroes in their own lives, they will have the inner fire and fortitude to do so. Stories of saints, freedom seekers and ordinary people doing extraordinary things all feed the soul fire burning in our hearts. This is what makes us strong in times of adversity and keeps hope alive.

Strega Nona

by Tomie dePaola

Strega Nona, the legendary wise woman of a small medieval Italian village, cures everyone there of toothaches, warts, etc. It's really quite amazing. Everyone reveres her as her eccentric self scoots around town, healing this, helping with that. Strega Nona's magical abilities also extend to the magic pasta pot, which produces pasta when she utters a certain chant. Preparing to go off on a little jaunt, she leaves harmless and bumbling Big Anthony in charge, but with the admonishment not to even *think* about messing with the pasta pot.

As you might guess, here is the story of the day Big Anthony messed with the pasta pot and how it went berserk, spewing pasta through the streets of the village. *Strega Nona* has become a classic and probably not just because its illustrations are perfectly delightful. I am sure the book's well-loved status comes at least in part from the fact that Big Anthony, in his own way, is Everyhuman—stepping beyond his boundaries for one reason or another, having things backfire on him and learning a lesson. Lucky for him, there was a Strega Nona to save the day! (3–6 yrs.)

 # Perfect Pigs

An Introduction to Manners

by Stephen Krensky
illustrated by Marc Brown

Without pushing its luck and getting too deeply into obscure etiquette, this book covers everything a child has to know to be well mannered by almost anyone's standards.

And, it's funny. Cartoon-style drawings of pigs doing do's and don'ts make the message move right along. The book is divided into the following chapters: At All Times, Around the House, With Your Family, On the Telephone, During Meals, With Pets, Giving a Party, Going to a Party, With Friends, At School, During Games, In Public Places.

This is a remarkably comprehensive book, with chapters covering manners in the home, on the telephone, during meals, in public places and so on. Its "trick" is the use of humor rather than the oh-so-logical approach of trying to get children to understand that other people will enjoy being with them more if they have good manners. (3–7 yrs.)

Teaching children manners in our daily endeavors, no matter how small, is ever so important. When my children were small, they *loved* to answer the phone. They couldn't wait for the phone to ring so they could run and be the first to pick up that magic tool of communication. (It really must seem remarkable to a small child to hear the voice of someone they love come out of a phone receiver—how *does* Grandma fit in there, anyway?) They watched with interest when I talked on the phone and wanted to partake in the fun themselves. Once they started showing interest in answering the phone (which, for my kids, was around two or two and a half years of age), I considered it crucial that they learn how to answer the phone politely. I could easily imagine the person on the other end spending long minutes in a perpetual holding pattern, wondering if my child had really gone to find me or had just set the phone down to go play. In order to avoid this scenario, I made sure my children knew exactly how I wanted them to answer the phone. A small voice exclaiming "Hello, this is Aidan" alerted the caller that a young child was on the line. Once they mastered this initial response, I taught my children what to do when I was not in the same room with them, although I tried not to be out of earshot when they were nearer to the phone than I. If the phone rang, I gave them a chance to answer all by themselves, but then would quickly walk into the room and make sure their manners were on track. By explaining these simple skills, and encouraging my children to follow my expectations, they all became proficient phone answerers in a relatively short period of time. I benefited because I could trust that I would receive my phone calls, and my children benefited from the many kind conversations my friends and relatives graced them with when they answered politely.

Emma Bean

by Jean Van Leeuwen
illustrated by Juan Wijngaard

Meet Emma Bean. She's a stuffed rabbit who took shape one summer night as the moonlight streamed through a window into a room where someone was sewing. Remnants from long-ago dresses, black buttons and rags for stuffing were all she was on that night. But when baby Molly took her first breath, it was as if Emma Bean took hers, too, and two lives thus merged. With a lifelong friendship set in motion, such things as being sat on and spit up on and being the taster of foods and getting the shot first at the doctor's office became Emma Bean's reason for being.

The stuffed bunny accompanies Molly through life, a journey not only through time, but also to the heart. It is about the unconditional love Molly has toward her tattered, now-whiskerless, stained and worn-out Emma Bean, who probably can't be repaired yet again to look like new, but is perfect just the way she is.

This is a wonderful book. And if you think the story sounds heartwarming, wait till you see the illustrations. On every spread throughout there are paintings so lifelike that they catch not only every physical detail of Molly and Emma Bean, they catch the spirit, too. (4–7 yrs.)

Marry the Disturbance

Recently I went to an evening of brilliant storytelling by Laura Simms. In the midst of this astonishing night, one line stood out above the rest, staying with me for days. Laura was in the middle of telling one of those classic shipwrecked-sailor stories in which a man must use his wits to overcome obstacles and demons and to somehow find his way out of impossible circumstances so that he may return home. Danger and peril mark every turn he takes. In the middle of the story (when the man was asked to marry a demon's ugly daughter or lose his life), Laura paused to say, "Whenever you are on a journey, you must marry the disturbance." Marry the disturbance? Wow! Now *there's* an idea! What did she mean, exactly? I carried those words around in my heart for a few days, knowing they were profound and wishing to understand them better. The whole idea of "marrying the disturbance" struck me deeply.

How much of our lives do we spend running away from or trying to otherwise escape the disturbances of our lives? For most people, the answer is "a lot!" What does it mean to "marry the disturbance"? My sense is that it means to take our troubles to heart, to accept what is, to simply *be* with what is. Instead, many of us try to change others so we don't have to experience our disturbances. I thought of how easy it is to discount a child's feelings or try to tell her that she isn't feeling the way she is obviously feeling, just to move forward with the day. "Oh, you fell down; you're okay now." Marrying the disturbance in this instance would require a different response. It would mean stopping what I was doing and consciously acknowledging what was really happening. "Yes, Aidan, you fell and it hurts. I'm so sorry you are in pain." (Even though he has been crying for what seems like an inordinate amount of time over a little thing.)

Who am *I* to determine how long is enough for someone else to cry over his pain? Is not my job as a mother to be there as a kind witness to the pain and a source of comfort; not lending undue attention, mind you, but offering just simple comfort? How long would he really cry about a little owie if I held him close on my lap and didn't say anything, if I just listened to his woes and offered him my heart? Would it take all day? Can I do this without reserve?

It is so easy to make judgments about what another person needs, but is this supposition really ours to make? I don't think so. In parenting, part of teaching our children to have compassion and understanding for others comes directly from our ability to offer compassion and understanding to our children. I had this experience yesterday with Aidan. He and Heidi had been playing peacefully all afternoon. Suddenly, something shifted. Heidi was mad and poked Aidan roughly with a stick. Aidan came running downstairs hurt and indignant, crying inconsolably. Immediately I picked him up to hug and hold him while he tried to tell me what had happened in between his tears. When he was done talking (but was still crying), I tended to his little bruise by rubbing a dab of aloe vera on it and then gave him another big hug. We talked for a bit more, he doing most of the talking, me doing most of the listening. As he talked, his crying gradually intensified. At first I thought he was really making a big deal out of a little thing. I encouraged him to go sit in the chair by the fire and wrap up in a blanket, hoping the cozy warmth of the fire would help him feel better. But after a couple minutes of this, tears still streamed down his face. I walked over and sat down on the arm of the chair, resting my head on his little head as he cried and cried. Suddenly, the real story came out. All day, things had been going wrong. Heidi's small push was the last straw. Things he had made at school had been taken away or destroyed by others. When Heidi got mad and hurt his feelings upstairs, it was just too much. He wasn't crying about Heidi. He was crying about a whole day's worth of frustration. If I had somehow silenced him, or told him he was okay before he really was okay, all those tears would have been left bottled up inside. But by creating a safe space and actively listening to his tears, a whole day of frustration was resolved.

When our days are rushed and harried, it's hard to allow our children enough space to feel the intensity of their feelings. Crying children slow us down. They make us late. And sometimes, they even make us mad. Children experience their emotions on a pure, in-the-moment basis. They have no trouble "marrying the disturbance"; they *become* the disturbance until they are on the other side. And then, when they are on the other side (if they are truly allowed to experience their emotion), they let go of it. They move beyond the trouble.

Obviously, as adults, we can't throw fits the way a small child does, but we can allow ourselves to embrace the obstacles in our own way. Maybe in the process, we will find that the disturbance is actually the universe's way of trying to bring us a gift. This certainly was true in the story Laura Simms told—underneath the smelly, ugly veil that hid the demon's daughter was the most beautiful woman in the world. The sailor found his way home a rich man—rich in gold and in spirit.

Little Red Riding Hood

retold and illustrated by Trina Schart Hyman

Never have I seen a more beautiful rendition of *Little Red Riding Hood* than this version by Trina Schart Hyman. Her retelling modernizes the language yet loses none of the deeper symbolic meanings. Her wolf captures, both visually and in words, the dangers of wandering off your life's spiritual path. He is quite a convincing salesman for the ease of the material world! The illustrations are lavish watercolors with richly detailed borders in a cozy, old-fashioned style.

Reading it aloud to our children offers that ever-important but gentle reminder of what is truly important in life. (4+ yrs.)

Animalia

by Barbara Berger

A rare and wondrous collection, *Animalia* offers thirteen miraculously illustrated stories about saints and sages whose lives are a powerful example of how we may live in harmony with the animal world. The word "animal" comes from the Latin *anima*, meaning breath, life and soul. Imbued with just such meaning, this tender book (meant for children but really for all of us) speaks volumes about learning to live with true compassion, gentleness, respect, selflessness and love. It is a book that illuminates both the eyes and the heart. In fact, the paintings have a luminescent quality that makes them seem to glow from within. I've had *Animalia* for nearly twenty years and still I am astonished by its timeless wisdom every time I pick it up to read again. (5+ yrs.)

Best Loved Stories in Song and Dance

audio recording by Jim Weiss

In these three wondrous stories, Weiss lifts us from "here" and sets us down in the midst of the characters' lives, offering not only noble adventures, but also a deeper understanding of the worth of the characters' journeys. The volume includes: "The Twelve Dancing Princesses," who quietly go to bed in a locked room of the palace each night, yet greet each dawn with shoes whose soles have been freshly worn out. Who can explain the mystery? "The Sleeping Beauty," from the pen of the French master Charles Perrault, is the immortal tale of a beautiful princess, an evil fairy's curse and a brave prince. It offers one of literature's most satisfying endings. "Snow White and Rose Red" are two sisters whose love for each other and their mother extends out to embrace the world. Their unexpected adventures with a huge bear and a temperamental dwarf form one of the most widely known, best loved of all stories, again from the Brothers Grimm. (4+ yrs.)

The Yellow Star

The Legend of King Christian X of Denmark

by Carmen Agra Deedy
illustrated by Henri Sorensen

What an example this story is for our children about the importance of living your beliefs! World War II is filled with stories of remarkable heroes, including King Christian of Denmark. Greatly loved for his acts of kindness and wisdom, he was a hero in his people's eyes before the war. But when the Nazis occupied Denmark, his heroism became more pronounced. It caused him great anguish to think of his country divided by hate. When the Danish Jews were ordered to wear a yellow star to distinguish them from the other Danes, legend has it that he had his tailor sew the yellow star onto his coat and he rode through the streets silently announcing to his people what they all must do. Soon, all the citizens of Denmark wore a yellow star on their clothes to proclaim their solidarity with their fellow citizens. In this beautiful book, the story of one man's courage is brought to light.

If we teach our children only a handful of lessons in this day and age, let us teach them to stand up for what they believe in. (4–8 yrs.)

Beauty and the Beast

retold by Marianna Mayer
illustrated by Mercer Mayer

Beauty and the Beast is a haunting tale of a young girl learning to love with love's own eyes, the eyes that see the beauty of the true self and not the form that covers it. The Mayers have elegantly retold this timeless story in both words and pictures of stunning beauty. The paintings capture subtle nuances of meaning and symbolism that evoke a deep emotional understanding for young readers. We live Beauty's pain with her. We see it in her eyes as she struggles to understand the meaning of her mysterious dreams.

The rich visual imagery and poignant story will enrich the reader through numerous readings. This amazingly beautiful book clearly is a feast! (5+ yrs.)

Our children need models of courage to have the strength to do what is right in their lives, to avoid the many temptations of our culture. Fairy tales and other archetypal stories are filled with models of ordinary people doing impossible tasks. When children live and breathe stories filled with archetypal heroic figures, somehow the stories become a part of them and they can draw on them in times of need. As the mother of teenagers, I often find myself encouraging my children to remember the courage of heroes we have read about when they are called upon to do something they feel is hard. I can see in their faces a soul recognition of how they too have the skills they need to fight and conquer their dragons and tame their beasts. I am so thankful now for all the hours we spent reading these age-old tales when my children were young.

The Mousehole Cat

by Antonia Barber
illustrated by Nicola Bayley

This is the unforgettable story of a tiny Cornish fishing village where life is good and catches are plentiful. Mousehole, this little settlement, is so named for the smallness of its harbor and the narrowness of its harbor mouth. Old Tom and his cat, Mowzer, take each day as it comes, and bask in each other's loving companionship. It is when one particular winter brings the Great Storm-Cat that life turns worrisome, for no boat can make it through the tiny Mousehole gap and venture out into the wild, crashing waves of the churning ocean.

Old Tom and Mowzer, though, know that they've nothing to lose if they attempt to make it out to the open sea to fish, for their families are all grown, and they no longer have parents to grieve for them. So, locking up their cottage securely against the stormy night, they set out one wild evening for the open sea. What follows is the poignant and action-packed account of how Mowzer sings to the immense and powerful Storm-Cat, calming him, playing with him, disarming him, making him a friend. In the end, enough fish are caught for the village to allow everyone—people and cats—to feast to their hearts' content.

This is a beautiful story of heroes who do what they do out of love and selflessness, and problems that are resolved by a meeting of hearts and minds. The full-page, magically detailed, richly colored illustrations on nearly every spread are breathtaking. (5–8 yrs.)

The Quiltmaker's Gift

by Jeff Brumbeau
illustrated by Gail de Marcken

Here is a fine tale about what lies at the heart of the spirit of giving. It is the story of a kindhearted quiltmaker who magically sewed the most beautiful quilts in the world. On the darkest and coldest of nights, she would journey into town and wander the cobblestoned streets until she found some poor soul sleeping outside. She would then take a newly finished quilt from her bag, wrap it around the person's shoulders and tiptoe away.

Meanwhile, ruling this town was a greedy, self-absorbed king. This guy liked getting gifts so much that he passed a law that his birthday be celebrated twice a year. The more the king heard about the magical quiltmaker, the more he became convinced that one of her quilts could be just the thing that would finally make him happy. But there was a problem. The quiltmaker never sold her quilts. She made them only for the poor and needy—with no exceptions, not even for a king, miserable or not. Since the king was as greedy as the woman was generous, you can imagine his response to the proposal she offered him: "Make presents of everything you own, and then I'll make a quilt for you. With each gift that you give, I'll sew in another piece. When at last all your things are gone, your quilt will be finished."

A word of caution needs to be given at this point of the story. While the quiltmaker is the embodiment of goodness and light, the king's dark side may be a little intense for very young children. The king became so angry with the woman's offer that at one point he ordered her to be taken to an island so tiny that he hoped she would drown during the night. On the very same page, the woman is saved miraculously by a flock of sweet sparrows, but nonetheless, this scenario may be too disturbing for some young children (while for others, it may simply add to the suspense). In the end, though, the story turns out even better than you could ever imagine.

You also might want to share with your child that the author, illustrator and publisher are dedicating one percent of the revenue from *The Quiltmaker's Gift* to worldwide projects that implement the spirit of generosity portrayed by the quiltmaker and the king. (5–8 yrs.)

Grimm's Tales for Young and Old

The Complete Stories

translated by Ralph Manheim

When I first started reading these stories to then five-year-old Becca, some of the blatant gore and violence shocked me, and frankly, I was worried they would give her nightmares or worse. Over time, as I kept reading them to her at her request, I have found that these have been *the* most rewarding stories I have read to her. The power and conflict that worried me seem to be just what satisfies her. It is as if in the resolution of these stories she hears a message that helps her to understand the power struggles and deep emotional conflicts she feels inside herself as a small person with a big soul confronting a confusing and sometimes scary world. I purposely chose to read her mostly pictureless versions of these stories, in their original form, so that the words themselves were not watered down and therefore retained their full symbolic meanings, and the pictures she saw came from her own imagination. I have always felt that a child cannot imagine a dragon scarier than she can process, unless she has seen one somewhere else (on TV or in an illustration). This has certainly held true with my children.

This edition of *Grimm's Tales* is a treasure—a complete and well-translated, undiluted edition of the original stories. It contains stories for a wide variety of ages. You likely won't read it straight through, but instead as a pickup book. We've kept our copy out on the coffee table for years and just read a story whenever the spirit moves us or when we are between books. A true gold mine for any family, for children and adults. (6+ yrs.)

Helping Your Child

Develop a Sense of Gratitude

♥ Make a point to be appreciative yourself. Say "thank you" at every opportunity. "Thank you for hanging up your coat." "Thank you for being gentle with the cat." "Thank you for caring for your toys by being so careful with them." "Thank you for that hug; it felt so good." The more your child hears you saying "thank you" to him (and to others) for the big and little things of life, the more likely it is your child will learn to recognize all the things there are to be grateful for in this life.

♥ Be explicit. Teach your child specifically when it is considered polite to say thank you. Many children these days ignore simple, often basic manners because they have not been adequately taught. Manners require specific, consistent teaching to be instilled. A gentle reminder works the best. When your child is offered a cookie and takes it but doesn't say those magic words of gratitude, discreetly lean down and remind him to say, "Thanks for the cookie. I love chocolate cookies." For best results, model the manners you wish your child to exhibit. He will learn from your good example and kind, reliable teaching.

♥ Practice the "I'm lucky because" game. Sometime when your child is snuggled close on your lap, express how lucky she is. List off the many ways you see that she is lucky—a warm bed, a loving family, a big sister to play with. After a while, ask your child to name a few of her own "I'm lucky's." At first she may only be able to list a few, but over time, her awareness of the many ways she is lucky will grow, as will her words to describe them. Aidan loves to play this game. Even at six, he has little to contribute word-wise, but his eyes shine whenever we play it, so I know the point is well taken.

♡ Teach your child to send thank-you notes, even if those notes are simply one of her drawings embellished by your writing and her dictated thoughts. As she grows, expect more and more thought to be placed in each note. A quick "thank you" alone is not enough. Have her add a sentence or two about herself or what she thinks she will use the gift for, and always send best wishes to the giver. Ensuring your child takes the time to write thank-you notes will be an investment on your part, for it will take time; but the rewards are enormous. These letters teach children to look deeper into their gifts to see the kind thoughts and loving care beneath each present, especially when it is something the child doesn't particularly like or want.

♡ Encourage your child to say "thank you" to her teachers at the end of the day or class. Help your child recognize that by the very act of teaching, a teacher has given the gift of himself and deserves recognition. Your child may not have much to say at first, but as time goes on she will learn to say "thank you" for a special moment in her day. These little comments help teachers to know your child better and teach her to realize the many ways people give to her.

♡ Offer a prayer or song of gratitude before meals. Read a short inspirational passage. Even the simple act of holding hands in silence helps children recognize how fortunate they are to have food and a loving family. In our family, we take turns choosing which grace will be observed. Sometimes we sing, other times we sit in silence. Always, we make a circle of our hands. After years of this simple practice, a meal doesn't feel quite right without some kind of moment of thanksgiving.

♡ As much as your family is able, get involved in holiday gift-giving programs for the needy. Include your child by choosing to give to another child who is the same age and gender. Let your child accompany you when you buy the gift. It may be hard for him to pick what he likes and then offer it to someone he doesn't know, but this act of generosity will help him learn to appreciate the abundance in his own life.

♡ At the end of every day, while you are sitting at your child's bedside, ask her to name one thing she is grateful for. Some people like to offer their children a chance to vent their frustrations, too. A dear friend of mine calls this moment a time for "the gratefuls and the grumblies." One favorite moment and one challenging moment are noted. Acknowledging both helps children learn that life is light and dark and that we can find things to be grateful for even in the midst of darkness.

♥ When your child feels sad or lonely, have him send a letter to someone he loves. Connecting to a bigger world—like a faraway grandparent or auntie—can help his problems seem more manageable. Reaching out to someone they love helps children feel gratitude for the love that surrounds them, even when they are feeling down.

♥ Every day, in some small way, make sure your child knows you are grateful for the gift of being his parent. Thank him for being himself. Acknowledge something specific about him that makes him special and that you appreciate—even if it frustrates you at times. Heidi is a grand foot-stomper when things don't go her way, but I love her tenacity when it comes to getting what she wants or resolving some perceived injustice. By appreciating the very thing that she knows frustrates me (all the while reframing it in slightly different terms), I help her see that this trait is something special about her that will assist her in her endeavors as she grows, even if it is annoying me right now.

♥ Notice and appreciate the small things in life—the smell of the air right before a rain, the warmth of the house on a cold night. Let your child know how glad you are to be alive in this wondrous world of ours, even if at times it doesn't appear so wondrous. There is always something to be grateful for in every situation. Sometimes we just have to look a little bit harder to see it.

♥ Use famous sayings or quotes to punctuate the need for gratitude. One of my favorites comes from Ma in the *Little House on the Prairie* series. After another amazingly awful tragic event would happen to their family, Ma would inevitably say, "There's no great loss without some small gain." And then she set about finding the small gain. Help your children appreciate the small gains when life seems filled with loss.

The Rainbabies

by Laura Krauss Melmed
illustrated by Jim LaMarche

Here is the story of a woman and man who have no children, although they wish with all their hearts that they did. When a rare moonshower occurs one night, they find that it has dropped twelve babies no bigger than a big toe into the dewy wildflowers at their feet! Overjoyed at their blessing, the couple cares for the children, finding that there is easily enough love to go around to divide it twelve ways. Just as life gives all of us challenges to handle, it doesn't forget the man and woman, either, who are called upon to risk their lives for the well-being of their babies. (A near-drowning here, a fire there, etc.) The illustrations feel nearly larger than life. When we see the couple, we find ourselves almost drawn into the picture to be right there with them. Facial expressions speak just as loudly as the text, which makes the story hit so close to home that we feel practically in it ourselves. So, when the rainbabies are loved, it is we who are loving them; when they are being saved from drowning, it might just as well be us getting wet. So it follows that when Mother Moonshower gently replaces the rainbabies with a human baby, as happens at story's end, the sadness and then joy is ours, too. LaMarche's illustrations nearly have a life of their own.

This is an unforgettable book you'll want to hold on to forever and ever. (5–8 yrs.)

The Water of Life

retold from the Grimms by Barbara Rogasky

The Water of Life never fails to enchant. It is the story of the youngest brother of three, a boy pure of heart and a joy to his father's soul. On a mission to find and return with the Water of Life for his dying father, the king, the young man repeatedly must choose his course of action from the pureness of his heart. The tale is brimming with stories-within-the-story, sometimes full of intrigue and suspense, and always with situations that leave no doubt as to how the pure of heart would act.

The finely detailed illustrations are deep, rich and "luxurious," with the added treat of having the princess portrayed as competent and a dark brunette! This is one of those books that will always have a space on our bookshelf, never to be handed down to friends with younger children. (7+ yrs.)

A bedtime reading ritual offers a wonderful opportunity to impart your values to your children. When you read inspiring books that align with your values, your children are comforted by the consistent pictures these books paint, compared with the reality in which they live. What you say and what they read are complementary. Unfortunately, books won't always affirm the worldview we hope to teach our children. When books present alternative perceptions, parents are afforded a fantastic window for discussion. In the end, these kinds of discussions may actually do more to confirm values than the passive reading of books that are in natural alignment with your values. When a character does something you don't believe in, speak up. "Why did the store-keeper treat Julie differently just because she was African American? Do you think this is right?" Letting young children *know* that you question the ideas presented in books helps them learn to question the world around them. The younger they are, the more gentle your words. In the beginning, you are just planting seeds. But these seeds grow when they are nurtured and each gentle step we take to teach our values to our children plants our values deeper into their souls. We begin by being a living example of what we want them to learn, but we continue our teaching by commenting in kind ways upon the injustices we see in the world. Our children are always watching us closely for clues about how to interpret the world and live their lives.

Dear Friends,

On my last birthday, my children (Elizabeth, who's in college, and Evan, who's in high school) gave me the best present I can possibly imagine. What looked at first glance like a glass vase full of tiny rolled-up pieces of paper turned out to be something infinitely more. That evening, after birthday dinner festivities were over and the house was quieter, I put up my feet and emptied the vase's contents onto my lap. What could these be? Coupons, perhaps, like the ones I've been known to give them for their birthdays? A parent version of "Good for one ice cream cone" or "Good for a trip to the movies" maybe? But no. Instead, on each piece of paper they had simply written one of their own memories of something in our lives together.

I suppose that nearly any parent can relate to how such a gift affected me. It was so much more than a "thing." This was nothing for which I'd need to clear off a shelf in order to display, or find room for in my "cool kitchen gadget" drawer. It was nothing that would go out of style or eventually wilt. This gift was simply memories. But there's more to it than that. You see, the memories weren't those I'd have guessed. They weren't memories of the "big" things I'd made happen for my kids during their lives: the birthday trip to Disneyland, the set of drums, the extravagant Halloween party. They were memories of much smaller things I'd almost forgotten, but that are truly the rather mundane happenings of which lives are made.

Evan remembered his three-year-old "mad scientist" days, when I used to allow him to mix past-shelf-life herbs and spices together in order to make "concoctions" while I was busy cooking dinner. He remembered loving my reading to him as he played with his Brio train set. He remembered long and leisurely mornings of gardening with me and eating breakfast out on the deck, in the dark, when our kitchen was being remodeled. Elizabeth's memories included equally unearthshaking events, but obviously ones that had made lasting impressions. She said she used to love being woken up by me in the morning as I stroked her hair. She remembered her passion for preschool Show and Tell—and the freedom I gave her to take just about anything. (We have a photo of her leaving the house for school—holding a saucepan and a skillet.) She wrote that even though she resented it at the time, she was happy now that we'd severely restricted TV watching in our family. On and on went the memories, captured permanently on these tiny scraps of paper.

Yes, I absolutely loved this gift! But what I loved most about it isn't what you might think. Indeed, I was crazy about the creativity that went into the idea in the first place, the fact that it involved more than a simple purchase at the mall, the fact that my kids really thought about what they were creating for me and in the process came to see what is enduring, what it is that matters most to them. What I loved the best, though, was the reminder this collection of memories held for me: that, really and truly, it's the small things that count. It's the small things that make up the tapestry of our lives, that nourish our souls, that make us feel connected. While so much of our culture's mantra is "Bigger, Better, Faster," it is so often those quiet and unpretentious goings-on in our families that show us how much we are deeply cared for. While the world seems to speed up and spin out of control all around us, it is the predictable rhythms and unhurried moments that tell us that we are safe. While everywhere we turn there is the message that the more money we have the happier we will be, it is experiences of intimacy, acceptance, encouragement and trust that are priceless and tell us what we humans most long to know above all else: that we are loved. Amid all of the extravagances in which our culture encourages us to partake, may your family's extravagance be pure, unadulterated and elegant joy—joy that you have each other, joy that every single moment offers the possibility of a simple memory that may last a lifetime.

Throughout the Year

Seasons

The old Lakota was wise. He knew that man's heart away
from nature becomes hard; he knew that lack of respect
for growing things soon led to lack of respect for humans
too. So he kept his youth close to its softening influence.
—T. C. McLuhan

J ust as our planet is meant to be a highly diverse, intercon-
nected web of life, we humans are meant to live a highly in-
terconnected life, too. We join in community to celebrate,
to work, to survive. Long ago, we gathered together to honor the things
that brought us life. After a long, cold winter, people rejoiced in the
coming of spring. They danced and sang and feasted as a community,
exulting in the return of the earth's abundance. They didn't shop in
grocery stores, where food came wrapped in Styrofoam packages or
cardboard boxes that had little to do with the food in its original form.
Nourishment came from the work of their own hands: sowing and
reaping, hunting and gathering the plants and animals that lived in the
wild. Human life was fully sustained by the connection people had
with the earth. Without this connection there was no life, for there
was no food. Today life is not so. Today our country's seasonal celebrations have more to do with shopping patterns (back to school, holiday and summer shopping extravaganzas) than they do with the earth
herself.

The question that remains is: how do we reconnect our lives to the earth, to the seasons, when we live in a highly technological world that dictates by marketing campaigns how we are to conduct our lives? How do we come home at six o'clock, exhausted from our busy jobs, and find the energy to step back into "earth-time" and slow our lives down enough to move with the rhythms of the living world around us? The answers lie in our willingness to take small steps toward grounding ourselves in the beauty of our planet. Luckily for us, the rewards are grand if we take the time and effort. For each time we reach out toward the earth, the earth responds and nourishes us in ways we had no idea were possible.

I remember learning this when Becca was a baby. I didn't quite know what to do with my long days home with an infant—days that often seemed as if they stretched into eternity. Before this time in my life, my days passed quickly, consumed as I was with working and going to school. My time was highly focused and ordered by the demands of the outside world. Suddenly, when Becca was born, the world shifted. Time became my own; well, mine and Becca's, anyway. My husband was entrenched in medical school and gone for long hours every day. Becca and I generally had a solid twelve to fourteen hours to ourselves. I usually felt fairly content in the morning doing this and that, caring for my baby, but by midafternoon I'd become restless. Mainly to keep myself from going batty, I would bundle up Becca in the backpack and head outside. We walked for a couple of hours every day before I would come home to cook dinner. Occasionally I would walk to a store and do an errand, but mostly we just walked around the city, checking out different neighborhoods and parks. With no agenda, we talked to anyone we met, looked at trees and flowers and ultimately watched the seasons change. During these walks, I talked to her virtually the entire time. "Here's an old oak tree, Becca. Look at how it shades the walkway." "The snow is clinging to the branch of the old maple. I wonder when it will fall down." Reaching over my shoulder, I handed her leaves to look at and held up little stones and nuts for her to see. Walking by gardens, I pointed out all kinds of blossoms and animals we happened to observe. We stopped to smell any flowers within reach. It didn't surprise me when her first word was "tree." She was quickly becoming a girl of the natural world.

When she was almost a year old, we moved so my husband could start his internship. This meant much longer hours for him and a lonelier life for me. With few friends to keep us company, I filled our days with even more time outside. Our new city had a wonderful policy of ensuring that a park was within walking distance of every home. These parks made our late-afternoon explorations exciting. One day we would walk to the chestnut park (a shady refuge lined with stately chestnut trees), another day we would walk along the riverfront park, looking and listening for birds. It wasn't long before Becca could identify almost twenty birds by their sight and sound. The simple, everyday explorations we took into the world were teaching her more than I'd ever imagined she could learn while still so young.

As Becca grew, we worked together in the garden—she digging in her own little "garden" and I planting our real garden. Side by side, we spent many happy hours. I grew lots of child-friendly fruits and vegetables (snap peas and cherry tomatoes, strawberries and raspberries) so she could walk the paths and nibble when she was hungry. With careful instruction, she quickly learned which plants were for her to eat and which were better left alone.

The years passed and soon the rhythms of the natural world became an intrinsic part of our life. It didn't seem to matter where we lived—city or rural settings—we found comfort in the changing seasons. We moved a lot in those years as my husband continued his training and found his first couple of positions. Throughout all these many transitions, we relied on the constancy of the earth's rhythms to make us feel at home. We found deep satisfaction in simple seasonal activities (jumping in piles of leaves in the autumn, sledding in winter, splashing about in the mud of spring and lounging in the shade on hot summer days). We didn't have to spend a dime or travel anywhere special. Everything we needed for fun was right before us. And being outside so much helped us make friends wherever we lived. Over time, as more children were born into our family and life became more complicated, our walks became shorter, but our love for the outside world never waned. Each child brought his or her own interests into the mix. Aidan was our bug expert, Laura our collector. Heidi spent hours concocting mixtures of flowers and other natural treasures into potions and brews filled with magical healing powers.

In a world that moves so fast, it can be such a joy to simply slow down and notice the beauty right at our feet. The glories of the natural world wait patiently for our attention. We don't have do anything but open our eyes and our hearts. If you have lost track of these wonders yourself, let your children guide the way. Closer to the ground, children are brilliant observers of the subtle jewels of the seasonal world. It doesn't take long; even a ten-minute walk after dinner or after work can bring the seasons alive in your life. The act of walking settles the soul and makes transitions easy. After a long day of work and with the evening ahead, nothing is more soothing than a short walk with no agenda other than just being together. The relaxed pace helps children talk about their day, sharing their joys and tribulations. Together you can gather leaves, stones and blossoms to decorate the dining table as a tangible reminder of your time together. Although brief, this type of time holds a special potency in young children's hearts.

Connecting to the earth is simple. It doesn't require great amounts of time or energy, but rather an attitude of reverence. When we go outside, do we greet the day with our hearts and eyes or do we rush headlong toward the car and our next event? Simply noticing the sky as we walk does much to reconnect our lives to the seasons. Do we take the time to smell the wind, to feel the sun, to touch a leaf? It is in these simple actions that we begin to rebuild our bond with the earth. It's highly unlikely that we will ever go back to an agrarian society that lives and breathes in relationship to each seasonal event. But we can watch the cycles of the moon; we can feel the days growing longer and shorter as the seasons pass. We need not worry whether we live in the city or the country. The earth surrounds us no matter where we are. Even the cracks of the city sidewalks burst with life as the little weeds make their way to the sun. It is up to us to reclaim our birthright and lovingly reconnect our hearts to the earth that brings us life.

Many joys are to be had if we take the time to connect with the passing seasons. The following is a collection of books and practical tips designed to help us embrace the joys hidden in the natural world around us.

Fall

♥ Roasting chestnuts (with or without the open fire) is just as romantic as it sounds. Some blustery afternoon, when the Italian chestnuts are in season, we sit down with a big pile of nuts before us.
We haven't figured out the open-fire routine yet, but our stove has
always worked nicely to prepare this unusual treat. An adult cau-
tiously cuts an X in the top of the chestnut about half an inch
wide, and then we toast the nuts in a covered cast-iron pan over
low heat. Then we read aloud while we wait for the buttery nuts to
roast. Depending on the stove, it takes about twenty minutes or so.
When the corners of the X start curving outward, the chestnut is
starting to be done; test the nut meat to see if it is tender. Keep
roasting until it is tender through and through. Be careful to turn
the nuts every few minutes to keep them cooking evenly. Once the
nuts cool a bit, our kids love to peel and eat them. Occasionally, a
nut is hard to peel but that just adds to the mystique: why are
some chestnuts so tender and buttery and others such trouble?
(Remember to buy Italian chestnuts at the store; the horse chestnuts so prevalent in American cities are poisonous if eaten.)

♥ If you have access to an apple tree or a farmers' market, gather the
season's bounty and make yourself a pot of fresh applesauce. Small
children love the job of cranking the apple peeler (a small device
you attach to your counter that turns with a crank). We've found
making small, Crock-Pot-size amounts of sauce is perfect to do
with little children. The Crock-Pot automatically watches the sauce
for you, so if you get distracted, you don't accidentally burn the
sauce. With instruction and careful supervision, children as young
as three or four can cut apple quarters into chunks using a butter
knife. We make our applesauce using my grandma's special recipe—
peeled and cored Gravenstein apple chunks, some water to cover
the bottom of the pan, and one lemon sliced and seeded, all cooked
together until the apples lose their shape. Then remove the lemon
slices, add a touch of sugar to cut the tartness and sprinkle in cinnamon to taste. (If you can't find Gravenstein apples, almost any
apple will do. They were just my grandma's favorites.)

♥ Pumpkin patches are always an adventure in the fall. Arm your feet
with waterproof boots (for it's bound to be squishy out there) and

head out into the fields to find your perfect pumpkin. If driving to a patch feels like too much trouble, grocery stores have plenty of pumpkins to pick from. Grab a bunch and invite a few friends over for pumpkin carving and hot apple cider. For an extra treat, roast the washed and dried seeds by tossing them with oil, placing them on a cookie sheet, sprinkling them with salt and baking in a 250-degree oven, stirring now and then, for ten to fifteen minutes or until crunchy.

As the days move toward the equinox, my thoughts move toward creating balance in my life. What is alive for me at this time? What is dying and in need of cutting away? What must I readjust in my life to find better balance? A simple game to help children look at the balance in their own lives involves balancing a board across a log (a log five to six inches in diameter works best with a two-to-two-and-a-half-foot board). Place the board across the log and have them find their equilibrium while standing on it. Children love this game and will play it over and over until they understand this balancing point in their bodies and the game becomes easy. It's a fun game and easy to try, especially as a family, since the adults are not always the ones who are the masters of it! I am always drawn to the hidden symbolism beneath the action of the rolling log. I am reminded that balance is a fluid motion, not a rigid stance that once achieved remains static. This realization helps me to remember in my day-to-day life that balance is a constantly adjusting sense of equilibrium. Balance is achieved over time, not all in one moment.

Pumpkin Pumpkin

by Jeanne Titherington

Eloquent in its simplicity, this lovely book is not only the most basic of stories, it might also be your child's first encounter with science (without even knowing it).

It is about young Jamie, who plants a pumpkin seed. Sprout to plant to flower to pumpkin to big pumpkin—Jamie keeps an eye on it all in the garden throughout the summer. Halloween's arrival brings about one more step in that pumpkin's life: to be carved into a jack-o'-lantern. First, though, Jamie saves six pumpkin seeds for planting in the spring.

The unpretentious text never comes close to overwhelming the purity of the story, and the colored pencil illustrations on every spread are a perfect complement. (1½–4 yrs.)

A Fairy Went A-Marketing

by Rose Fyleman
illustrated by Jamichael Henterly

Quite a few picture books have crossed my desk over the years. Never have I seen illustrations such as these. It is not only their nearly glowing, rich colors, but also the remarkable spirit that shines through as being the work of someone who has observed nature and has a love of it.

Couple this quality with the text, which is singsongy and about a fairy who treats her animal friends with the utmost care and respect, and you have quite a special picture book. Text is minimal:

> *A fairy went a-marketing.*
> *She bought a little fish.*
> *She put it in a crystal bowl*
> *upon a golden dish.*
> *An hour she sat in wonderment*
> *and watched its silver gleam,*
> *and then she gently took it up*
> *and slipped it in a stream.*

That is four pages, and the text talks about another four creatures in addition to the fish. *A Fairy Went A-Marketing* is likely to evoke some *very* wide eyes in children while it gives them one of their first experiences with a book that portrays nature with a whimsical reverence. (2–5 yrs.)

Each Living Thing

by Joanne Ryder
illustrated by Ashley Wolff

This simple book is an uncontrived tribute to the idea of humans living their lives true to the awareness that we aren't the only beings that matter on earth. Lovely and not the least bit preachy, *Each Living Thing* is a big picture book right up most children's alley. As so many parents have realized, youngsters tend to relate to the animal world—if not out of compassion and a feeling of connection with the underdog, then out of sheer intrigue.

Here are rich, warm and inviting illustrations, accompanied by the very simplest of text—text that suggests we watch out for spiders dangling in their webs, for toads lurching and leaping across the road, for wriggling worms and creeping snails. That we be wary of bears lingering in the dark (shown eating fruit high on a hill overlooking a cozy farmhouse in the fall) and of jellyfish floating in the sea. In every cheery and perfectly detailed illustration is a child looking but not touching, enjoying the surroundings while coexisting with the natural world. There's plenty of detail to point to and talk about, too. (2½–5 yrs.)

When Winter Comes

by Nancy Van Laan
illustrated by Susan Gaber

Where oh where do the leaves all go
When winter comes and the cold winds blow?

This lyrical question introduces us to the magic of winter's first snowfall, seen through the eyes of a family and their dog. A small child darts from place to place, asking the grown-ups what happens to the flowers, the field mice, the fish, the caterpillars and the songbirds when snow blankets the ground and the winds blow cold and blustery. The first questions come when the ground is still visible and the sky not yet thick with snow. By the time the family discovers where all of the creatures have gone, snowdrifts cover the ground. The answers to the child's questions come in simple poetic verse, painting lovely word pictures just begging to be read aloud.

What a perfect book to share with little ones when winter arrives. Children are full of questions just like these. Each page is reassuring and comforting, letting the child know that all living creatures find ways to be cozy amid the cold. (3–5 yrs.)

Winter

♥ Few of us make maple syrup anymore, but we can still have the pleasure of fresh maple candy. Some late-winter day, when the snow is getting crusty, heat some maple syrup on the stove. When it's hot, carefully carry it outside to some cold, clean snow. Pour tiny blobs of syrup (a tablespoon or so at a time) onto the snow and watch it congeal. When it's the texture of taffy, it's ready to eat. (Make sure an adult does the heating and pouring; hot syrup can cause a nasty burn.)

♥ Winter is a great time for old-fashioned family fun. We love to make a hearty winter soup and invite friends over for an evening of games and singing. Silly games, board games, cooperative games, charades; it makes no difference to us. Having fun together is the important part.

♥ Ice candles are one of winter's magic delights. For each candle, you will need a plastic tub (a large-size cottage cheese or yogurt container will do). Fill each tub almost to the top with water and either place it in your freezer or outside, but only if it is below freezing. Keep an eye on their progress and remove from the cold when a thick layer of ice has formed around the edges of the tubs. Pour off the unfrozen water from the center. Pop the ice out of the molds. Replace the water that you have poured off with votive or tea lights. Light the candle and place outside, near your front door or lining your sidewalk. As long as the weather stays below freezing, they will be usable (and reusable with a new votive). As with all fire, do use caution around children.

When I lived in Maine years ago, a dear friend of mine used to have a solstice potluck to celebrate the return of the sun. Late in the day of the solstice, Penny would take a candle and a magnifying glass outside in the freezing cold and light a candle from the dying rays of the day's sunshine. (It always seemed like magic to me, that she could really do this!) Then she would take this carefully kindled flame into the house and turn off all the other lights in her home— pure darkness illuminated by one bright light. She and her family would then gather around the candle and consider the significance of the day. (Her husband was a solar-home builder, so their lives were very much entwined with the journey of the sun.) Soon friends would begin arriving at her home, appearing out of the darkness, their arms laden with food, and a candle for each member of their group. As each person arrived, he lit his candle from the flame of Penny's solar-lit candle and placed it somewhere around Penny's home. Gradually, the house was ablaze with light. I tried to arrive early to be there to absorb the full glory of the magnificent transformation of darkness into light. Years later, these simple solstice celebrations still kindle the spirit of the season in my heart.

Annie and the Wild Animals

by Jan Brett

This is the story of a young girl, Annie, whose cat, Taffy, is acting strangely and who eventually wanders off. In a futile attempt to replace her feline friend with wild animals, Annie tries to lure them with corn cakes on the edge of the forest. But for one reason or another, this doesn't bring the intended result: the moose is too big, the bear too grumpy, the wildcat too mean, etc. Annie despairs that she will never have another friend, when lo and behold! Taffy struts out of the forest, followed by three kittens.

This story is sure to appeal to a child who likes animals or loves kittens. But the really special aspect of this book is the double-page spreads whose intricate borders foreshadow Taffy's final return. (As Annie feeds corn cakes daily to various potential friends, we see Taffy finding a place to give birth, licking her newborn kittens, nursing them and romping with them.)

This is one of those magical and incredibly detailed books that consumes you for longer than you ever dreamed possible. (2–5 ½ yrs.)

Fireflies

by Julie Brinckloe

Fireflies! Is there anything quite like them? I'll always remember hot summer nights, a game of hide-and-seek with the neighborhood kids that went on a little later than our parents would have liked and sighting the first firefly of the evening. It sent something like an electrical shock of excitement through us. Then, before long, we had raided our respective kitchens, found empty mayonnaise jars and were tearing through the night, collecting our very own fireflies. The only problem was that their lights, just the thing that made them so very special, almost immediately started to fade in the confines of the near-airless jars.

This is a book about the very same experience. Neighborhood kids scarf down their suppers and race outside with their jars. Darting and running through the twilight, they each catch a jarful of fireflies for their very own and disperse to their homes for the night. What makes this a wonderful book is that the boy in the story catches on to the fireflies' plight a little sooner than we ever did as kids. And in a gigantic stretch of selflessness and, yes, heroism, he makes the decision to release them, as they twinkle ever more weakly in the jar by his bed in the middle of the night.

Colored-pencil illustrations and sparse text do a fine job of conveying both the thrill of the hunt as well as the deeply felt realization that with the simple act of release comes a joyful sense of relief at having done the right thing. (4–7 yrs.)

A House Is a House

by Mary Ann Hoberman
illustrated by Betty Fraser

This delightful, rhyming narrative of homes and the shapes and sizes they come in is one of a kind. Just as a read-aloud it is wonderful, but throw into the mix the fact that it is a lovely lesson in how there are all kinds of homes all around us, and you have a book that will open your child's eyes.

> *A web is a house for a spider.*
> *A bird builds its nest in a tree.*
> *There is nothing so snug as a bug in a rug,*
> *and a house is a house for me!*

The rhyming goes on and on, and the colored illustrations are soft, detailed and enchanting. The book finishes with this:

> *A flower's at home in a garden.*
> *A donkey's at home in a stall.*
> *Each creature that's known has a house of its own*
> *And the earth is a house for us all.*

A fine reminder that we are all sharing space on this beautiful planet. (3–5 yrs.)

Spring

♥ Do the unexpected . . . offer your children the wild taste of spring. Gather (or buy) a stalk of rhubarb for each of you (though it is highly unlikely your children will eat a whole stalk) and sit down at the table with a small bowl of white sugar. Ask them to gingerly dip the rhubarb in the sugar and bite. And then, remember to watch as they taste that first very sweet bite. It will be followed by a very sour expression spreading across their faces. This has become a yearly tradition with my children. They hardly eat any of the rhubarb/sugar, but we wouldn't miss that exhilarating first taste of spring for all the chocolate in the world. (P.S. Do remember to explain that we only eat the stalk of the rhubarb plant and that the leaves are poisonous. I always make a big deal of hand washing after we gather our rhubarb from the garden and before we eat.)

- Become mud puppies. Put on those rubber boots and old clothes and go out in search of puddles to splash in. The bigger the person, the bigger the splash, so be prepared. It's amazing how much tension a good splashing in a mud puddle can release.

- Grow wheat-grass Easter baskets. Plant an even layer of wheat seeds, available at any natural food store, under a light covering of dirt in a basket-size pan; keep slightly moist and watch the amazing green burst of spring emerge. With a bit of warmth, the wheat will likely be four inches high in seven to ten days!

- Find some baby animals and watch them frolic. Drive to the country, go to the zoo, check out the feed store. There is nothing like the sight of a baby chick in spring, or a lamb frolicking in a pasture, not to mention the sweet, sweet smell of a tiny bundle of fur otherwise known as a kitten.

- Make a splatter painting on a rainy day—sprinkle dry tempera paint on a piece of paper and let the rain do the painting. It's an adventure to see what the rain will design.

Mud

by Mary Lyn Ray
illustrated by Lauren Stringer

Imagine a whole book about mud. "Squishy, soppy, splatty, slurpy mud." Lauren Stringer's illustrations are big and bold and remarkable. As the pages turn, hard, frozen winter ground thaws and flows into fluid mud and returning green. One experiences the pictures from a small child's perspective (mostly legs and feet!), so every image is oversize and embracing. It is as if you are tiny and standing close to the ground, so the world is very big and the earth is the most intimate friend you have.

The words are poetic and beautiful, a song soaring out of the earth to welcome spring.

"One night it happens . . . A cold, sweet smell rises in the ground, like sap in the snow . . . The hills will remember their colors . . . Winter will . . . melt in mud . . . Happy mud . . . Gooey, gloppy, mucky, magnificent mud . . . Come spring . . . Come grass . . . Come green."

The total acceptance of mud and its many delights will make this book very appealing to the young ones who know mud magic already, and are simply waiting for slow grown-ups to catch on. (3–7 yrs.)

Owl Moon

by Jane Yolen
illustrated by John Schoenherr

No matter what time of year you find yourself reading this book, you will discover that Jane Yolen has written this story in such a way as to convey perfectly and magically the very special aura of a winter's evening. Indeed, a May morning of reading can magically become a January night!

In *Owl Moon* a father and a child venture from the light and warmth of their rural home in the dead of winter to go owling in the snow-covered forest. As the father calls, "Whoo-whoo-who-who-who-whoooo," and waits hopefully for that owl (who's out there *somewhere*) to answer, we feel the same anticipation, the same need to be ever so still. Narrated from the child's point of view, the descriptions of the scenery, the visual and tactile sensations and what is going on in that young mind make this story simply come alive.

The soft watercolor illustrations are breathtaking and the text, too, is superb. It would be difficult to imagine a children's book doing a more convincing job of putting the reader right in the middle of a quiet yet somehow thrilling adventure. (4–7 yrs.)

Once There Was a Tree

by Natalia Romanova
illustrated by Gennady Spirin

Originally published in the Soviet Union, this edition is breathtakingly beautiful. It follows a tree that has been struck by lightning as it sits as a stump for many years afterward and offers shelter and food to creatures: beetles, ants, bird, bear, man. The illustrations sometimes give us a microscopic view of the activity on or in the stump, and sometimes a panoramic view of the surrounding forest. Throughout, the reader is asked, rhetorically, who owns the tree stump: the beetle that gnaws tunnels inside, the earwig that sleeps under its bark, the bear that sharpens her claws or the man who believes he owns the forest? It is suggested that the tree stump and the young tree that has grown now in its place belong to us all, because they grow from the earth that is home for all.

The incredibly detailed and deeply rich illustrations are sumptuous and realistic at the same time. This book is a real keepsake; it is undeniably lovely and its message, too, is priceless. (4+ yrs.)

Making Friends with a Tree

I don't necessarily think kids really need ideas about what to do once they're outside, but this is something worth sharing. Perhaps you and your family will find it as remarkable as we have. Next time you find yourself among a cluster of tall trees (they have to have accessible trunks), grab something that can work as a blindfold and try this. Blindfold a willing person. (This is as much fun for an adult as for a child, but from here on, I will refer to the willing person as a child.) Carefully guide the child to one of the trees—any tree—in the immediate area. (Slowly! Remember, she's blindfolded!) "Introduce" the child to the tree, suggesting that she touch it all over, feeling for identifying bumps or knots and such. Let her know that in a few minutes she will be led back to the starting point, the blindfold will be removed and then she will attempt to find "her" tree. But first, leave her alone with the tree for a few minutes. Soon the two of you go back to the starting point. (A zigzaggy route on the return helps to make finding the tree a bit more challenging.) With the blindfold removed, the child is now free to check out all the trees in the area until she finds "hers." It will look as if she's hugging them in searching for the identifying marks she discovered when she was blindfolded. In the end, it is remarkable how often the child finds her tree. Try it.

The Story of the Root Children

by Sibylle von Offers

Originally published in 1906, *The Story of the Root Children* is a gentle, sweet story of the earth mother and her children. Early each spring, when the land is still bare and just a hint of green is coming to the earth, Mother Earth comes and awakens her children. One by one they wake up from their slumbers and take the materials she gives them to make their new suits of clothes. They sit together in a cozy circle sewing their new outfits and singing spring songs. Finally, when their work is done, they bring their suits to Mother Earth for her to see, then busy themselves washing and painting all the little bugs and insects to get them ready for spring.

Von Offers' tender illustrations tell her story completely. They show the gentle waking of the earth as the children are busy with their tasks below the ground. Each picture shows just a bit more life above the ground until finally the earth is awake and the children come out of their subterranean home. Though simple, this is a special story. It tells of the process we all know in our bodies if we listen closely enough to hear each spring. Von Offers captures the wonder and awe of the changing seasons. By creating little people to live the lives of the seasons, she tells the story in a concrete way that children can understand in their hearts. They experience the rebirth of the earth through the reawakening of the Root Children. (2½–6 yrs.)

The Salamander Room

by Anne Mazer
illustrated by Steve Johnson

There is something utterly magical about this book, for it captures that delightful childlike sense of imagination and wonder. Young Brian finds a salamander in the nearby woods. Bringing him home, he makes a small bed for him in a bedside drawer. Brian's ever-practical yet gently loving mother leads Brian's imagination along by asking relevant, practical questions like "Where will he sleep?" or "And when he wakes up, where will he play?" With each question, Brian imagines in more and more detail his life with his salamander friend. As he answers each question, Brian must bring more and more of the forest environment into his room. The illustrations lovingly depict Brian's magical imaginings as his room gradually turns into a forest. The gentle love and wonder on Brian's face as he watches his salamander friend is a truly beautiful sight. By the end of the book, Brian's room no longer exists and he and the salamander are peacefully sleeping under the canopy of the forest.

The Salamander Room teaches many things. The complexity of what a living being needs to survive (and be happy) and the web of interrelationships in an environment are just a couple of ideas that are masterfully expressed. What is perhaps most magical about this book, though, is how it shows the beauty of where an imagination, when well honored and respected, can lead. This is a tender and truly special book. (2½–6 yrs.)

Small Cloud

by Ariane
illustrated by Annie Gusman

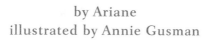

This book's subject matter alone will spark questions and end in some conversations about what makes rain. For that, it is worth several readings. But the manner in which the story is woven, the illustrations, clear as a summer day and soft as the dawn, and earth's endless ability to provide for her creatures are what make this book remarkable.

"In the beginning, there was Small Cloud's mother, Singing River, and her father, Big Sun. One day Singing River called to Big Sun. Big Sun smiled and warmed the heart of Singing River. One drop at a time, Small Cloud was born." And soon, Small Cloud ventures, with the help of Whistling Wind, across the earth, eventually joining with other clouds to become one great cloud and giving of themselves to a particularly parched area of land. The dry earth is replenished and in the process, Small Cloud returns "home" to the river in the form of rain. And before long, the remarkable continuity that resides in the natural world begins the cycle again: "Big Sun smiled and warmed the heart of Singing River—who danced in the warmth, and a mist rose slowly into the air. One drop at a time, Small Cloud was born again."

There is something reassuring for all of us about this subtle, yet powerful predictability of nature. This gentle story brings the wondrous process of how rain is made to a place where children can get their arms around it. In the end, knowing how wilted plants and thirsty bugs get their water is not only enlightening, it is comforting. (3–7 yrs.)

Summer

♥ When the summer temperatures soar and just about everything is too much effort, don't forget the simple joy of an ice-cold Popsicle. My kids especially like the yummy taste of homemade juice Popsicles. I stock up on frozen fruit juice concentrate (the kind with no added sugars) when the prices are low and keep a stash hidden in the freezer. Then with reusable plastic Popsicle containers, we make our own healthful Popsicles all summer long. That way, when my kids ask if they can have yet another one, I can say, "Go ahead and have a fourth Popsicle!" without a hint of remorse. And chances are, if it's really hot, I'll be joining them, sitting side by side in the shade somewhere.

♥ Remember the contagious fun of a good water fight? With hoses, water balloons or just plain glasses of water, nothing cools you off like a good dousing on the head. And toddlers love nothing more than watching their parents get silly and wet. Do be careful of the little ones, though. (What seems like fun to you might feel scary to them.) Start with their toes and see how they react. The wetter you let them get you, the more likely they are to join in the fun.

♥ Stargazing is one of my favorite parts of summer. I love lying on my back, silently looking up at the sky on a moonless night. The air is so warm as the soft evening breeze blows across my face. The sky, illuminated with millions upon millions of stars, shines with a gentle radiance emanating from these tiny sparkles of light, speckles that texture the absolute blackness of the universe.

♥ If there is a farm near you with public picking areas, go berry picking, even if it means making a day of it. Pack a picnic, put on that sunscreen and go forth to pick the summer's abundance. Pick until you can pick no more and then drive home and feast. And what you can't eat, store in the freezer as a topping for your winter's breakfast. You don't have to make jam to enjoy the season's bounty. Just freeze your berries on cookie sheets and then pour them into freezer bags.

♥ If you have the space and inclination to grow a garden, a fun way to engage your children is to plant pumpkins. When the pumpkins are small (three to four inches in diameter), lightly scratch your child's name into the pumpkin skin—enough to scar the pumpkin but not kill it. Then, as the summer progresses, watch your child's name grow bigger and bigger as the pumpkin grows. If you've planted the big jack-o'-lantern kind of pumpkin, the results can be quite impressive.

The Snail's Spell

by Joanne Ryder
illustrated by Lynne Cherry

This book is a one-of-a-kind treasure of artistic detail and imagination stretching. Set in a lush garden, the story is of a young boy who imagines himself into feeling smaller and smaller—until he is able to picture and feel what it would be like to be as small as a snail as it glides along. As the process of shrinking takes place, the illustrations zoom in, closer and closer, to show a vegetable garden teeming with wildlife, all of which you will probably not spot until the one hundredth reading. Text is in the second person, succinctly describing what it might feel like to assume the characteristics of a snail and immerse yourself in its world—where lettuce leaves are gargantuan, and it takes an hour to travel a couple of feet. There is really no story here. Instead, it is a quiet, imaginative and visually stimulating walk through something that many of us have in our own backyards, but of which we are not aware.

The detail is astounding, and the illustrations are done in both earthy and vibrant colors. You and your child will be glued to this book until you know all the creatures in the illustrations by heart. (3–6 yrs.)

 ## The Lady and the Spider

by Faith McNulty
illustrated by Bob Marstall

In the green hills and cool valleys, amid the jeweled pools of dew on a head of lettuce, a spider has made her home. She has no idea that her home is in a woman's garden, and that soon the lettuce head will be pulled from the ground.

It happened like this. While the spider lives a typical garden spider's existence, the footsteps that tread near the lettuce every day seem to the small creature to cause an earthquake. The woman's thumb crushes the spider's den (a "cave" created by the fold of a leaf), and when at last all is still (on the kitchen counter), the spider attempts to see with her eight eyes and to feel with the tips of her legs and to think with her tiny brain. How was she to know that she had made her home in a head of lettuce in a lady's garden and that the lady intended to eat that lettuce for lunch?

Thank goodness the woman notices the spider. (We feel quite an affinity by now!) She sees that the spider's color matches the leaves, and notices the tiny dots that are her eyes. With a new realization and respect for the creature, the woman stops herself from throwing the spider and leaf into the garbage, and instead treks back to the garden and deposits the spider onto another plant, a new home, thinking,

"Isn't it wonderful that a creature so small can live and love life, find food, and make a home just like me!"

Need I say that it will be a rare human who reads this book and then doesn't think twice about the oneness of us all? (3–8 yrs.)

The Year at Maple Hill Farm

by Alice and Martin Provensen

You know, this is more—much more—than a book about the seasons. It is about how the year changes oh so gradually and magically through the months, and how the animals at Maple Hill Farm somehow know how to live within the flow of those changes.

January is a winter month; the ground is covered with snow; it is a cold, gray time of year when night falls early. In a detailed watercolor barnyard scene with bundled-up people hauling hay over to the horses, the sheep huddled nearby and deer grazing off in the distance, the text goes on to tell us some of the other things that do—or don't— go on in January. The cows stay in the barnyard; the chickens don't lay as many eggs because the days are so short; the horses and sheep don't mind the cold and are fine eating grain and hay. And so on, through the year.

It's not easy to do this deservedly well-loved book justice in a description because it is so deceptively simple. Before the year is out, we feel somehow connected to all of the life at Maple Hill Farm. Our eyes are opened to a part of our world that still operates in step with nature, and in our fast-paced lives that make it such a challenge to stay connected to earth's cycles, this is a true gift. While we think we're simply reading the text and enjoying the friendly and colorful illustrations throughout its pages, we are really embraced by the stories of the rhythm of the seasons on what must be the best farm in the world! (2½–6 yrs.)

Scarecrow

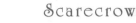

by Cynthia Rylant
illustrated by Lauren Stringer

"It takes a certain peace, hanging around a garden all day. It takes love of silence and air. A liking for long, slow thoughts. A friendliness toward birds." A scarecrow possesses such wisdom, and can teach us humans a thing or two. His life is quiet and unassuming; most of all, wondrous. Crows, grackles and jays think he's a lovely, gentle chap (so much for scaring crows!). Seeds drop, sprout and grow into ten-foot-tall sunflowers, pumpkins and beans all around him. The owls come in the evening, the rabbits at dawn. He is a witness to all parts of life—blossoming, wilting, yellowing, greening, vining. The scarecrow knows we may not really need much else in life, and there is one small person who seems to know as well.

A child comes to dig the earth, plant the seeds and hoe the rows—working quietly and steadily 'round the seasons to create a lovely home for the scarecrow. Though it is never explicitly said, we know they are the best of friends, guardians of one another. I guess such companionship is a natural gift of living so closely to the earth and the cycles of life.

The book's words are simple but hold layers of meaning, and the bold, beautiful paintings fit so seamlessly with the words. *Scarecrow* is a reminder to be a simple witness to life, learning to love and be thankful for each day's tiny happenings and beauty. What better lesson could our children learn? (4–8 yrs.)

The Brambly Hedge Books

by Jill Barklem

There are four specific Brambly Hedge books that stand out as simply wonderful: *Winter Story, Spring Story, Summer Story* and *Autumn Story*. I have many a fond memory of sitting on the couch, wrapped in my grandma's blanket, reading these dear sweet books with my children. Peering into the incredibly intricate pictures, we found ourselves in a world far away, a world where there is enough of everything—enough warmth, food, love and security. And perhaps a little bit of adventure, too! The stories revolve around an almost-hidden area on the other side of a stream, across a field, amid tangled roots and stems, which a community of mice call home: Brambly Hedge. All of the plots have to do with this group of mice, who have human characteristics and spend a great deal of their time interacting as a community, in the best sense of the word. The illustrations are incredibly detailed and imaginative, portraying the cozy and dreamy lives of mice who have set up housekeeping in the trunks of trees—replete with stairs, chimneys and well-stocked larders.

These books exude the warm, happy feelings that abound when everyone is getting along and life is good. (3–6 yrs.)

The Raft

by Jim LaMarche

The Raft teems with life, perhaps because the author creates the book directly from his own experience. His illustrations are exquisite, warm and luminous, gentle and endearing. They glow with summer light and the joys of creation. This is the story of a young boy's first close encounter with a river, but yet it is so much more than that, for he is surprised to discover abundance, mystery and his own imagination during his adventure. There are creatures to look for in each picture, and watching Nicky's face soften and transform from that of a lonely, sullen boy to that of an ecstatic participant in life and the natural world is worth the price of the book. The quiet, unobtrusive wisdom of his grandmother permeates each page. It is as if Grandma is the spirit of the river, and the land itself, offering a young, growing boy the vital gifts of art, solitude and true communion. What better gifts can we give our children in today's frantic world? Go seek out a river and a raft when you can, but meanwhile, place this book in your children's hands, for reading it will surely take them halfway there! (4–8 yrs.)

Bringing the Seasons Alive

in Busy Families

♥ Designate a small space for nature in your home. Whether it be a small table or a spot on a shelf, have a place where anyone can put a treasure from the natural world that they consider beautiful. (Children will often have quite different definitions of beauty and add "interesting" contributions.) Accept all offerings with grace; an understanding of beauty grows with time and exposure. If you live in an urban environment, you may want to enhance your nature spot with the occasional purchased flower.

♥ When you are driving around town, comment on the beauty you see. Be it a cloud in the sky, a beautiful sunset or the color of a leaf, make your observations known.

♥ Decorate your dining table with small seasonal offerings—colorful leaves and Indian corn in the fall, paper snowflakes on the window in winter, flowers in the spring and summer. Look for seed pods or grass flowers in empty fields or along roadsides. Once you open your eyes to the natural world, it's amazing what you'll find. And your children will love accompanying you as you search for seasonal treasures. It doesn't take long to collect some fine objects. I have found the most amazing seed pods growing along the edges of inner-city parking lots! Simplicity is the key—a small beautiful rock can be all it takes to bring the outside world in.

♥ If you live in an apartment or other home without a garden, force bulbs in pots to experience the glories of spring inside. In fall, when the bulbs go on sale, stock up on those for the flowers you love. Daffodils, paper whites, crocus and hyacinths are particularly easy to force. Put the bulbs in the crisper section of your fridge (tape the bag shut to keep curious toddlers out, as some bulbs are poisonous) and leave for six to eight weeks. After this necessary cooling period, remove from the fridge and plant in a shallow pot and leave in a cool basement or cold closet (preferably below fifty-five degrees Fahrenheit), checking occasionally to make sure the soil is slightly damp but not wet. When the bulbs break through the soil, move the pot to a sunny window in the coolest room of your home, paying close attention to the soil for moisture—always seeking damp but not wet. (Bulbs can rot if overwatered.) Once the buds set, keep the flowers away from a heat register to lengthen their lives. With minimal supervision a five- to six-year-old can manage the whole process quite nicely. (Forced bulb gardens make marvelous homemade presents for teachers and in-town grandparents and take relatively little time to create for the amount of joy they beget!)

♥ When buzzing about your day, try to slow down enough so you have the five extra minutes it takes to meander a bit when walking to and from your car. Look at a tree, watch a cloud, smell the air. If you are with a toddler, get down on her level and look for bugs hiding under bushes, even if the bushes are only planted in the median strips of your grocery store parking lot. Surprising things are hiding almost everywhere, if you have the eyes to see. But if you are always hurrying from one place to another, it's hard to take the time to savor the beauty that exists around us every day.

♥ Keep an eye out for birds. Birds live everywhere and are great fun to watch. Keep a small bag of birdseed in your purse or your child's backpack for impromptu feedings. Stopping for just a few minutes to feed the birds can change the whole tenor of your day.

♥ Allow time in your day for a short walk. Try to plan ahead and pack a small snack in the morning so that you and your child can take a ten-minute walk after you get home from work. As your child eats her crackers, you both can readjust to life at home, and the transition to your busy evening. Or after dinner and before bed, head out to look at the stars or the city lights. Slow down, breathe together. Enjoy the feel of your child's small hand in yours. If your evening is too hectic, try getting up ten minutes early and taking a short walk before you leave for work. Pile all those backpacks and briefcases in the car, and then set out for a short walk together. Hold hands or carry the baby. You don't need any extra equipment, just open eyes and open hearts. Look for the morning dewdrops as you spend a few treasured moments together. Feel the winter wind on your face, eat a falling snowflake, soak up the summer sun. Savoring the earth for just a moment can sustain you through a long day of meetings and hours of missing your child. Small rituals like these do much to bridge the long hours of separation that working life brings.

♥ And don't forget picnics. My family enjoys picnics all year long; not the elaborate kind you see in magazines, but simple picnics. Fish and chips grabbed on the way to watch the sunset at a lookout point in winter. (All of us cram into the car, eat like pigs and watch the beautiful sun as it sets into the sky. No dishes, no fuss and a whole lot of fun.) In the summer, we eat any meal we can outside. Peanut butter sandwiches, fruit and a bottle of lemonade become a banquet when we eat at the riverfront park. Fifteen minutes to pack the food, another ten to gather the family and we are on our way. Occasionally, we make our food more elaborate—good bread and cheese bought at the store on our way to the park, but mostly we just grab what we have. The point is eating outside together. Simplicity is the key. If it becomes too much work to get it all together, it's no longer fun and the temptation is there to simply not do it. Keep fussing with the food to a minimum (and shop with picnics in mind, so there are easy things to grab at the last minute) to make picnics happen with ease. And any picnic (no matter the cuisine) makes the moment memorable.

Winter Lullaby

by Barbara Seuling
illustrated by Greg Newbold

I don't think you can read this book and not feel winter enveloping you. From the quiet text to the gradually more wintry illustrations, and finally to its climax showing a father and two children reading by the fire, it moves over you surely, just like the season.

Beginning with a gorgeous double-page spread of a late-summer landscape of rolling farmland, the text asks: "When the breeze blows the petals off the flowers, where do the bees go?" Turn the page and there's another detailed, vibrant illustration of the same landscape, but from a slightly different perspective, this time including a gnarled old tree toward which hundreds of bees are flying—"Inside their hives till spring arrives." Along the way toward scenes of winter at its whitest and coldest, we visit a snake in the desert, slithering into its den till it's warm again; we see mice snuggling up in the loft, see bats leave the tall forest to sleep in a cavern; and so on. By book's end, snow is on the ground and two children are returning home after a moonlight sledding to a radiant fire warming the entire cozy room with the heat of its orange glow.

This is a lovely book that somehow brings winter to your family's favorite reading chair, but keeps you cozy the whole way through it. (2–4 yrs.)

Dear Friends,

Spring finds me out in my garden every chance I get. Nothing is as nourishing to me as working the warm soil, seeing new growth on trees and stumbling across new shoots of plants that looked all but dead in the torrid days of August. Few other things are as much of a delight as receiving my order of seeds from my favorite seed catalog, sketching the vegetable garden layout and then preparing the soil. My son, Evan (a.k.a. Mr. Dirt), loves to help me. He's the self-appointed organizer of the earthworms, and as we move along digging in the soil, he picks up every one, says something admiring to it, then places it exactly where he thinks life will be good to it. The cats drop by to visit us, mourning doves touch down a safe distance away to check us out and if I hear our phone ringing, too bad. When I'm in the garden, I'm immersed in another world.

When it comes time to plant the seeds, the dirt is so fine and smooth that all we need do is run our fingers through it, making a shallow line. Evan's the expert at distributing the seeds, and does so one by one, no matter how tiny they are. (Last year, he admonished me for shaking the seeds directly from their package into the soil, explaining that each seed needs to be touched by the person planting it. "That makes sense," I think to myself.) So the seeds go in, the rows are reasonably straight, I note in my gardening journal exactly what went where, and finally we lightly mist the soil, wishing the seeds a healthy life. Few times during a year do I feel as alive, as accomplished, as good as I do when I've planted my garden with care. Then, about two weeks later, the sprouts appear, and soon it's time to thin the seedlings according to package directions.

Now, as anyone who gardens knows, "thinning" means to pluck from the soil sometimes about three quarters of the baby plants so that the ones left will have enough room to grow. It's my least favorite part of gardening. In fact, most of the time I can't bring myself to do it. I can't simply discard what turns out to be most of the seedlings—healthy seedlings—that have sprouted, at my beckoning, in the soil I've so carefully prepared. Nope. I can't do it. I won't do it. "Somehow, they'll all manage to survive," I tell myself. But, of course, what always happens is that as the plants grow, they eventually crowd each other out. Not having the space or nutrients they need, all of them become less pest and disease resistant. Gnarly and mottled, they die an early death, and even though I know from experience that this will happen, I still can't bring myself to thin the rows of seedlings.

Yesterday afternoon, as I scrutinized the dense new strips of one-inch-tall sprouts, I was struck by the similarity between those crowded rows and a pitfall of modern family life. In an effort to expose our children to the "right" things, we expose them to too much, in hopes that a few of their encounters will "take." But what really happens is that life gets too crowded and nothing really flourishes. It just seems to be made up of a bunch of experiences, all of which turn out to be shallow, because there is no time in between them. There is no time to daydream; no time to be with one experience (or toy or whatever) before the next experience is plopped in front of them; no time to dig deeply enough into anything and realize that it could grow to be a passion if it were well-tended. It is so easy to lose focus of the fact that just as seedlings simply need good soil, the right environment and room to grow, children's true needs are just as simple: love, respect, space to be themselves. Life can get so cluttered, and then it's hard to thin it out— just like my rows of seedlings.

Then early this morning, before it was light, I heard the unmistakable sounds of one of our neighborhood skunks rooting through the garden. I sneaked out our bedroom door and sat for a long time on the steps in the warm night air, straining to see him (her?) in the darkness. I didn't want to scare him away, for I knew he was up to something very important, indeed. In dawn's first light, he finally left, and I made my way over to the garden, knowing what I would find. Sure enough, he'd been feasting on grubs and things, and in doing so, had uprooted most of my seedlings. Granted, the job wasn't quite as orderly as I'd have done it (had I ever done it), but my rows were now thinned, and each plant would have enough space, soil, sun and fresh air in which to thrive. I chuckled, and wondered if some giant skunk would ever lumber into my life and thin it out!

Growing Pains

Handling Life's Challenges

O Lord, remember not only the men and women of
goodwill but also those of ill will. But do not remember
the suffering they have inflicted upon us; remember the
fruits we brought thanks to this suffering, our comrade-
ship, our loyalty, our humility, the courage, the generos-
ity, the greatness of heart which has grown out of this;
and when they have come to judgment, let all the fruits
of that we have borne be their forgiveness.

—PRAYER OF AN UNKNOWN WOMAN, FOUND ON A PIECE OF
WRAPPING PAPER IN RAVENSBRÜCK CONCENTRATION CAMP

Life is filled with challenges. Some make us stronger and some can damage our spirits. As parents, we must somehow discern which challenges our children face are the ones that strengthen their characters and which are the ones that will injure their sense of self. We must learn when to step in to offer our wisdom and when to let them struggle on their own. During these times we must take care to open our hearts with compassion for their struggles so they can feel our love and support as they battle their demons.

How do we teach our children to see obstacles as opportunities for growth, rather than as brick walls? I think the answer lies within ourselves and how we deal with the obstacles life throws our way. Our ever-observant children will watch us closely for clues about how we deal with life. With what attitude do we approach the troubles we encounter? Do we rail and fight against them or do we befriend them, drawing them inside for reflection, seeking to understand what the crisis has to teach us? If we find ourselves facing the same battles over and over again, do we stop and listen to the message this confrontation has for us? How we approach our troubles will make all the difference in how our children will approach theirs. One thing is certain: we all come to life with lessons to learn. And unfortunately, these lessons are not doled out fairly or at an even pace. Life is more intense at some times than it is at others. If our child is in the midst of one of these particularly intense periods, how do we help him rise above his struggles and not feel like a victim? In my opinion, the first response comes in the way we view our child. Do we feel sorry for him because life is hard or do we see how intrinsically capable he is of handling what life has to offer? A strong vision builds a strong child.

My daughter Laura is a highly spirited being. On the scale that rates children's temperaments, she was off the chart as a young child—highly persistent, highly sensitive, highly spirited, exceptionally strong-willed. She was highly whatever-it-was they were testing. Her vivacious quest for life was, and is now, basically insatiable. She is extremely sensitive to the world around her, so she feels everything, absorbing it into her beautifully loving heart. As a baby, she was both extremely physically precocious (i.e., walking at eight months, climbing stairs without aid at ten), and exceptionally empathic. That's a hard combination. An hour spent in a room with unprocessed emotions (i.e., someone was angry but not talking about it) left her filled with pent-up physical energy and crying inconsolably for hours afterward. She picked up on the undercurrent of feelings in the room and didn't know what on earth to do with those feelings, so she would cry. Nothing could soothe her. It would upset her sleep patterns, her behavior patterns, her eating habits. It made it difficult to take her anywhere for fear of what would follow in the aftermath. As a young child, this was a tremendous challenge for her, one that made for long days for everyone in the family. Her sensitivity made it difficult for her to understand which feelings belonged to her (and therefore were hers to process) and which ones belonged to someone else. She had much to learn about personal boundaries. I remember Laura getting hurt over and over again when other people's feelings overwhelmed her. No matter how closely I watched her, by the time she was two she had experienced a bad burn, a broken leg and severely hurt her finger, all a result of her own actions when someone else was angry or upset. When I realized this pattern, I saw how important it was for me, as her parent, to be perfectly clear about my feelings and learn to teach her about boundaries. And what work that was! Day in and day out, we labored together to begin to understand the place where Laura ended and where the world began. We worked to help her learn to manage her tremendous will with kindness so it became her servant and not her master. The first six years of her life were a daily challenge for us all. And yet these same traits (i.e., her sensitivity, her strong will, her perseverance, her emotional intelligence) that caused us so much heartache are what make her the remarkable young woman she is today.

Throughout her years in school, Laura's teachers have remarked to me about her unique sensitivity and how she has learned to use it to help others. Children often choose her to be the mediator in their conflicts because she so accurately assesses both sides of an issue. My favorite story along these lines came from Laura's special-ed teacher. (Laura also had challenging learning differences—a.k.a. disabilities— that made school learning a severe challenge for her.) Luckily, through her high intelligence and incredibly persistent, creative personality, she developed strong coping skills that have allowed her to succeed in school. Yet, for many years, school was a highly frustrating and difficult experience for her. While her friends were whizzing through books and multiplication tables, Laura labored to gain every ounce of book knowledge. Eventually she began to spend part of her day in special education, receiving the personalized help she needed to succeed. There, Laura had many classmates who were literally shunned by the other kids in school. Many of them looked or talked differently. Often, they had trouble making friends and even finding people to sit with at lunch. Laura knew these children as people *beneath* their obvious differences, saw the beauty inside them. She, who always had plenty of friends herself, empathized with these other children's social struggles. Her teacher told me that Laura made a special effort every day to greet these kids in the hallway, to invite them to lunch with her friends and to include them in the larger school social structure. Her teacher told me that this small effort changed these children's lives. I don't tell you this story to boast about my child, but rather to show that, as parents, we have great power to teach our children to use their special strength (which may also seem like weakness at times) for the greater good of all.

Our children come with such precious gifts and yet, until they master these gifts, these traits will generally challenge them. As parents, our job is to recognize the beauty in our children and encourage that beauty to blossom. We seek to teach them to use their power within, rather than trying to exert power over each other. Children who tend to be bossy can make great leaders once they learn that leaders know to listen and guide rather than authoritatively command the masses. Children who tend to be reserved often make great friends, for they tend to be quite observant and offer a gentle ear in times of trouble; their observations about the world make them wise counsel. Our job is to help our young ones feel safe expressing themselves, which means allowing them to open up to new situations at their own pace and in their own way without fear of judgment or labeling. For example, if we introduce our child as shy (as if this feeling were a permanent label or state), our child is quite likely to live up to our expectations and become more and more shy in social situations. By labeling him, we don't give him the opportunity to adjust to new situations at his own pace. Saying, "Yes, Jimmy, it takes you a few minutes to observe your surroundings and get comfortable in a new situation. That's okay. I can stand here by your side until you are ready. I trust *you* to know when you are ready to play with the other children" is quite a different message from announcing to the world (and Jimmy) that he is shy, and then cajoling him into what he perceives to be an uncomfortable situation before he feels prepared. One response empowers a child to face his demons and master them; the other encourages the child to feel limited by his fears.

Throughout our lives, we each face painful situations that cause us to grow and stretch. People get sick, families change through death and divorce, friends hurt our feelings, we move away from our home and loved ones. There is no end to the possible situations that can cause us pain. It is our job as parents to help our children see beyond these difficulties and find compassionate responses to their pain. Sometimes children need lots of physical comfort; sometimes they need to have a heart-to-heart talk and then encouragement to do the right thing even when it feels hard. Each situation and each child require an individual response. By looking into our own hearts, we can find the response that best suits our child's particular temperament. If we see ourselves being overly reactive emotionally to certain situations, chances are *we* have something to look at, too. Does this situation remind us of a hurt from our childhood that remains unresolved? If so, it's our responsibility to address this issue in ourselves so we don't cloud our child's experience with our own. Learning to deal with our own pain helps our children see that it is possible to move beyond that pain into a more loving space.

We can't keep our children from suffering. Yet, by recognizing their pain, acknowledging it and teaching them to compassionately process it in their hearts, we give them the lifelong skills they need to deal with misfortune. For most children, the misfortunes of life start out small—a lost friend, a hurt feeling. But the process is the same regardless of the intensity of the experience. We begin by identifying the pain, accepting it and then making room for it in our hearts. Once we contain our hurts there, we can give them the time and care they need to heal. By showing compassion for our children's pains—large or small—we teach them to show compassion for themselves and others. When we teach our children how to deal with pain, rather than avoid or run from it, we give them the skills they need to be healthy adults in a complicated world full of hurt and confusion. What better gift do we have to offer?

Life is often a challenge. The following books and ideas help to guide our children through difficult times.

Go Away, Big Green Monster!

by Ed Emberley

Personally, I'm not that big on books that are meant to teach young children things. I would much rather see children learning from real-life experiences; but, every once in a while, one of these concept books comes along and it grabs me. *Go Away, Big Green Monster!* is one such book.

Technically, it teaches about color. In reality, it is an exceptionally fun book that allows very young children a chance to feel powerful, and, in my view of the world, this is a pretty welcome feeling for a preschooler when everything in the world seems bigger and more knowledgeable than she is.

Using die-cut holes and the addition of various outrageously colored body parts with each turn of the page, the book sets the stage for great fun. Eventually, we are faced with a funny, trying-to-be-scary-but-not-really-scary monster face. At this point the words read: "You don't scare me! So go away, scraggly purple hair!" From here on, each page is subtracting a scary monster feature by telling it to "Go away!" By the end of the book, you've gone through each color twice and there is no more monster; and, in fact, the monster is admonished to "Go away and don't come back! Until I say so."

If you have a preschooler who is grappling with the powerful forces of his or her world, this is the book for you. The die-cut holes are as fun as a pop-up book and aren't nearly as likely to break, *and* I can't imagine anything more fun to a power-hungry two- or four-year-old than telling a monster to disappear and having it listen. (2–4 yrs.)

I'm sitting here remembering Evan's memorial service for Frisky the mouse. The little fellow died one night, not unexpectedly. He'd been looking and acting rather ill. The night before, as Evan and I checked up on him as our last gesture of the day before settling in to read for bedtime, I heard myself saying things that I hoped were bracing Evan for the worst. Then the morning came, and Evan uncharacteristically asked *me* to check up on Frisky as he uncharacteristically tidied up his room.

Frisky was indeed dead. We hugged and cried for a few minutes, and I reminded Evan that he had been especially attentive and caring toward his mouse over the last few days, and that Frisky surely must have felt that love in some way. Evan wished the burial site to be next to that of Sparky, Frisky's mate, who had died in mousebirth several months ago, so out we headed to that particularly pretty part of the yard. As Evan dug, I collected flowers to sprinkle over the top of the little corpse before dirt covered him up. It was Sunday morning, so there was nothing to hurry us. Evan dug a deep hole and I found pink, purple, red and even some blue flowers. When he was ready, I tipped them from my palm into his so that he could do the honors.

As I watched Evan scatter flowers into Frisky's grave, it struck me that each day parents have something to learn from their children—perhaps how to slow down, how to be curious, how to be silly, how to be honest. In this case, I learned how to ritually honor the death of someone we loved, even if that someone was a mouse. Evan, from the bottom of his wise young self, knew how to lay a life to rest with honor. These lessons, or what I see now as gifts from our children, will come as surely as the dawn will arrive and whether or not we want them.

As Evan was burying his mouse, I think I was crying more than he was. But I wasn't crying for Frisky, or even for Evan in his sadness. Perhaps I was crying because at that moment I felt how immense this "commission" of parenting really is—that it isn't just for us to teach, it is for us to learn, too. I can't articulate what I discovered in that period of Frisky's final hours with us, his death and his burial, but whatever it was, it brought me closer to Evan and made me love and appreciate him even more. And maybe that is what all our pains and struggles have to offer us in life—a chance to grow and to love more fully.

Badger's Parting Gifts

by Susan Varley

The essence of this book was a blessing to me in dealing with the death of my mother years ago. It was instrumental in showing me and my children that we have not "lost" her; she has simply taken another form, and the things she taught us and the memories she's left with us are part of that new form.

This is the story of the life and death of someone very special. Badger was a friend and almost everyone knew him and had warm, loving memories of him. Initially, his friends felt a loss after his death, but in time they were able to appreciate their recollections of Badger. They were eventually able to smile again. Each remembered something different: Mole remembered how Badger had taught him to use scissors; Frog remembered his skating lessons, etc. Because of these "gifts," they recognized that Badger was still part of their lives.

This book's essence is very special. It's good for the heart, even if you don't, at this moment, have a loved one who is getting ready to take, or has already taken, leave of this earth. (4+ yrs.)

Alfie Gets in First

by Shirley Hughes

Alfie (about three or four) is returning home from a walking trip to the market with Mom and baby sister, Annie Rose. He races ahead of them down the last leg of their trip, to their house. Amid juggling the groceries, the baby and the keys, Mom ends up outside the door and Alfie inside. You see, Alfie, in his excitement at being the first to make it to the front steps, slammed the door shut. And it is one of those that automatically locks.

Uh oh! He is just too short to carry out some of the door-unlocking suggestions that Mom is cheering through the mail slot, and when the neighbors, milkman and window washer from across the street converge on the porch to see what the problem is, they've got quite a crowd! Anyway, Alfie comes through—and the door ends up wide open. The crisis officially ends with the celebration in Alfie's kitchen—with tea and cookies.

Facial expressions in the illustrations are simply priceless. There is just something so *real* about Alfie and this predicament! Reminds me of my friend who locked her keys inside the car by mistake—along with her baby, secured snugly into her car seat. (2–5 yrs.)

To Be of Comfort

In acknowledging our children's true spiritual nature, we know that they are "in" this world and not "of" this world. Life can and will bring each of us a variety of experiences, some pleasurable and some quite painful. Learning to be of comfort to our children as they experience life helps them learn the skill of comforting themselves as they grow older. The more we pay attention, the more we learn to comfort our children by being truly present in the moments of their lives. We attend to their needs while they are needy, not twenty minutes later when it is convenient for us. To be of comfort, we strive to reach out to our children in tender ways, offering them rituals of pleasure at predictable times to help them feel secure. The consistency of ritual holds them and makes them feel safe in a fast-moving world that is not always focused on the needs of a small child. Two stories and a backrub at bedtime; meeting your child at the same corner every day after school; a special cup of tea to talk about the day in the late afternoon: each of these actions brings solace to the soul. Even silly family jokes are a source of comfort. A story after nap or simply a long cuddle on the couch holds a child securely as she transitions from sleep to wakefulness. One of my favorite ways of bringing comfort to my children is putting clean sheets on their beds and a vase of flowers nearby. Often it is the little things that bring the greatest comfort. My mother frequently baked cookies on Thursdays. On those days, it brought me great joy to know that a warm cookie and a glass of milk were waiting for me when I opened the door. My friend's mother made chicken soup from scratch. The smell alone was enough to make any day better. Today, a favorite comfort around our house is the hot water bottle. My children love using it to soothe their bodily aches and pains, but I also know it is wonderful to use when their hearts are hurting, too. Wrapped snug in a blanket, cuddling the hot water bottle and listening to a favorite piece of music or story tape feels mighty good when you are low. It is amazing how quickly our pains pass when we give them the attention and care they deserve. I fully believe that children who are taught to care for their pains, to nurture themselves in times of woe, are far less likely to turn to drugs or alcohol as teenagers, for they will have learned compassion for their pain instead of fear of it.

When my children are fighting, I love to sit them both near me and simply stroke their hands or foreheads while they try to work out their problems. Such a gentle touch can help facilitate their communication, since they both feel held and safe instead of defensive and in trouble. If the fighting continues or my children are just generally grouchy (you know, like on those windy days when nothing goes right), I like to light a beeswax candle. Scientists have shown that the lighting of a beeswax candle releases negative ions, which help change the energy of the room in a positive way. Giving a surprise bath, especially with sweet-smelling bath oils or bubbles or even sprays of fresh lemon balm or lavender from the garden, can also turn cranky children into peaceful souls in a matter of minutes. So can a backrub with soothing oil—my favorite is one we make at home out of almond or apricot oil (any good health food store will carry these unusual oils) and a few drops of lavender or chamomile essential oil.

Periods of illness are another time when all of us need comfort. Sickness can be very stressful for the whole family. Taking the time to slow down when a small child is ill can be an amazing blessing. Sitting by the child's bed and doing a quiet task such as mending or folding great heaps of laundry can bring peace to the child and to the parent. Often, in the presence of this quiet form of attention, a feverish child will drop right off to sleep. Rubbing a sick child's back or belly with warm oils infused with essential oils can ease the fears and anxieties that often accompany illness. Taking the time to simply hold a child while he is hurting surrounds him with the knowledge that he is loved. And communicating our love is the whole purpose behind the comforting aspects of being a parent. Giving our children the comfort they deserve is a gift we give them for life, for through these efforts we will teach our children that they are strong and capable, that they can withstand life's misfortunes and find peace once again. Our compassion for their pain will teach them compassion for themselves and others. Comfort is a blessing that multiplies.

Mommies Don't Get Sick

by Marilyn Hafner

It feels so horrible to be so sick that you know—you absolutely *know*—you can't do what your family counts on you to do. In a way, though, feeling that wretched is somehow reassuring: you simply have to surrender and take care of yourself in hopes that tomorrow the situation will be better. This is a book about what happens downstairs when mommies get sick. Obviously, the author had to have been in this situation to have created a book so right-on.

We may be out of it and feel as though we're on our deathbed, but there is a part of us mothers that is aware of what is indeed going on as the family attempts to cope with our absence and our illness. Young

Abby wakes up on Saturday thinking of pancakes and no school to rush off to. On the other hand, she senses that things seem different. Soon the word is out: Mommy's not feeling well and breakfast will have to wait. A quick visit by Abby to her mom in bed verifies the news: Mom looks horrible and is living proof that mommies *do* get sick. Abby, though, turns out to be quite a help with her baby brother as Dad nurses Mom and goes to the grocery store. Not only that, Abby attempts to tidy up the disaster-area quality that the kitchen has taken on, picks some flowers for the tray she takes to Mom and puts in a load of laundry. But before long, the baby is desperately itching for attention, the washing machine goes bonkers and—you get the picture. Eventually, everything gets back on track, as it always does. When all is finally in order, the family ventures upstairs to see how Mom's doing. Abby combs her hair, Dad finds her robe and the baby crawls up onto the bed. She feels better, thank goodness! So it's downstairs to a lunch of comfort food and a lovingly set table.

I love this book and its expressive detail in the watercolors on every page. (Be sure to take your time and really look at the pictures.) I love the humorous pet dramas that are going on in the background, involving the dog and the cat (and usually the baby), and I love how true this story is. Don't wait for someone to get sick to have this in the house. It's a fine and heartwarming portrait about real life in the warm jumble of a loving household. (3–5 yrs.)

Dinosaur's Divorce

A Guide for Changing Families

**by Laurene Krasny Brown
and Marc Brown**

After talking to many, many children of divorced parents, to Marc Brown's own children, to social workers, psychiatrists, attorneys and pediatricians, the author designed this book to assist families in dealing with divorce in a sane, insightful, emotionally nonjudgmental way. Its reassuring manner helps families deal with the confusion, misconceptions and anxieties apt to arise when divorce occurs. In picture-book format (the characters are rather lovable dinosaurs), the book addresses the following: why parents divorce, dealing with two homes, celebrating holidays and special occasions, telling your friends, meeting parents' new friends, living with stepparents, having stepsisters and stepbrothers, and divorce words and what they mean (this is a glossary of words like "separation agreement," "half-brother," "child support," etc.). It compassionately covers many issues you would probably not have dreamed could have arisen during a divorce unless you've already been through it once before.

Having this information in picture-book form makes dealing with the divorce issue more comfortable, and makes everyone involved know that they aren't the only ones in this situation. The colorful, detailed illustrations are funny, or touching, or both. (4–8 yrs.)

 ## Something from Nothing

by Phoebe Gilman

This is the loving story of a baby boy whose grandfather, a tailor, makes him a blanket. By the time Joseph is a toddler, the blanket is frazzled and worn and, as far as his mother is concerned, isn't fit to be used for much of anything. But Joseph knows that Grandpa can fix it, and indeed he does—not into a repaired blanket but into a coat, using the fabric, which is still in good shape. Time marches on, and before long Joseph's coat is too small, so Grandpa works his sewing magic to transform it into a vest. And so on.

But here's part of what makes the book so wonderful. Each double-page spread has a lot going on in it, inviting marathon perusals. Joseph and his family live in a two-story house right above the grandfather and grandmother (the story looks as if it takes place in an Eastern European country of not too long ago) and in the illustrations there is a mini-story going on about the mice under the house's floorboards. As Grandfather snip-snip-snips, and his needle flies in and out of the fabric each time that Joseph requires an alteration, little remnants of the blanket filter down between the floor slats, where the mice let nothing go to waste. As Joseph's blanket evolves over the years into a fabric-covered button, we see that the mice in the house have decorated their living quarters and attired themselves completely in that ever familiar blue and white blanket material.

Something from Nothing is a sweet and lively story about how things change. About loss and about what can be created from loss. It is both poignant and lighthearted at the same time. (3–7 yrs.)

Comfort Food

"Comfort Food." Say those two words aloud and some level of your being responds. Perhaps something sort of melts in your gut, giving you a warm, fuzzy feeling. Perhaps the response takes place more on a cerebral level, conjuring up memories of being taken care of when you were a young child. The concept of comfort food is about nourishment, not nutrition. It's about food, but not for the sake of satisfying hunger.

Now, I'm not talking about eating disorders or food addictions. I'm talking about food that feeds us down to our souls. I'm talking about food that touches more than our taste buds and whose raison d'etre is to do more than fill the belly. Comfort Food comes in almost as many different forms as there are people. What is just a bowl of soup to one person can be a spiritual experience to another. What is a simple lunch to me can remind someone else of one of the ways her mother took care of her, one of the ways her mother showed her love for her when she was a child under the weather. The concept of Comfort Food is bigger and rounder and softer than the concept of food. My humble opinion is that everyone should have one. It is a wonderful thing to prepare and give to someone you love who is having a hard time, or to yourself when the world is feeling harsh. It's not a frequent thing; it's special and rare.

Some would say that chocolate is their Comfort Food. Really, really good chocolate. Some would say that it's cinnamon toast. Then there's roasted garlic mashed potatoes. (Roast a couple of heads of garlic, drizzled with olive oil, in the oven for about an hour at 350 degrees until the cloves are the consistency of butter. The garlic is now ever so mild. Squeeze some cloves into your favorite recipe for mashed potatoes and stir them in. Keep at it until the garlic flavor is just right to your taste buds and to your soul. (If you don't care about the "roasted" taste in your mashed potatoes, simply boil a few cloves of garlic with your potatoes, then mash as usual.)

My Comfort Food? It's a toss-up between garlic mashed potatoes and risotto. Risotto is a creamy, big-flavored dish made from short-grain Italian rice. The most common type is called Arborio rice, but you may also find Superfino Roma at your grocery store. Both produce the same comforting concoction. Risotto is quite simply nothing more than this rice constantly stirred in a simmering broth until all the flavors of the cooking liquid have been absorbed. It is this constant attention that helps to make this Comfort Food especially comfy. It almost becomes part of the family during the half hour or so it takes to make. To Italians, it is "the porridge of the gods." To me, it is the ultimate in Comfort Food.

Here's how to make risotto:

Bring six or seven cups of chicken broth to a simmer in a pot separate from the one in which you'll be cooking the rice. Canned broth will do, but homemade is better. You may use beef broth or vegetable broth, if you wish. At our house the type of broth depends on what additions we will be adding to the risotto as it cooks (e.g., shrimp or zucchini or mushrooms or . . .). Because the rice absorbs the flavors of the broth and its additions, let your imagination guide you.

In a large and heavier pot than the broth pot, heat on medium high two to three tablespoons of extra-virgin olive oil. To that add one small onion, diced, and, if you wish, a few cloves of finely chopped garlic.

After the onion and garlic turn light golden in color, add two cups of unrinsed rice. Start stirring, coating all of the rice with the olive oil. After about a minute, the grains of rice will no longer be white, but will be translucent, with a white speck—the "eye"—in the middle of them. When this phenomenon occurs, continue stirring the sautéing rice for two more minutes.

Then lower the heat to medium, add some salt to taste and add two thirds of a cup of the simmering broth. Continue stirring until almost all of the liquid has been absorbed by the rice. (Important! Never stop stirring the rice or let it sit or swim in the broth!) Then add one third of a cup of the broth, and stir until it, too, has almost been completely absorbed. Continue this one-third-cup-at-a-time-stirring/absorbing process until the rice is al dente, soft yet firm to the tooth. This process usually uses almost all of the broth, and takes about twenty minutes.

When the last one third of a cup of broth is added, stir in one half cup of freshly grated Parmesan cheese. Pepper to taste. Serve while it is piping hot, preferably in warmed bowls.

Dogger

by Shirley Hughes

There is just so much about this book to love: how *real,* how down-to-earth it is, how the love in a family lightens the darkest hours, how hard times can bring out the best in us. Customers used to buy it in multiple copies, knowing that it would be read to shreds by their own children and loved by parents who would receive it as a gift. It is one of those really special books.

Little Dave loves his stuffed animal, Dogger, so much. When he loses Dogger, the whole family pitches in to help find him because they know how miserable life can be without that special friend. Yet, they are unsuccessful. In a heartwarming turn of events, the school fair ends up being the place where a small miracle of love takes place. When Dave's older sister wins a stuffed bear there, and has the chance to strike a handsome deal with the child who has somehow acquired Dogger, she comes through as the best big sister ever. This is an engaging story standing wonderfully on its own, but add in the feel-good factor and the detailed and rich watercolors, and you have a book that will likely stay in your family for years! (3–5 yrs.)

I'll Always Love You

by Hans Wilhelm

Our dog, Phreddy, was our "baby" long before my husband and I had children. He went everywhere with us. We cut vacations short and came home early because we couldn't stand knowing he was pining away for us. Basically, he was a huge part of our lives. Those with beloved pets don't need any elaboration.

Ol' Phreddy took a back seat when our children hit the scene. About the only thing he can be sure of is that he'll get food and water and an occasional pat on his bony little head. Reading this book, though, I've gotten an inkling of what life without Phreddy will be like and how important it will seem to me ten years from now to know that I told him every day that I'll always love him.

This is the story of a little boy who was a baby while his dog was a puppy. They grew up together, had great times and watched each other mature—the dog more quickly than his master. The boy sees his dog becoming less active, less agile, sleeping more—but always remembers to tell her he'll always love her. When she dies in her sleep and is mourned by the family, the boy is consoled by the fact that he had told her every day of his love for her. And he knows that if he ever has another pet—even a goldfish—he'll do the same.

I recommend this for *anyone* with a pet. The love of the boy for his dog just shines through. The watercolor illustrations are sometimes funny, sometimes touching. (3+ yrs.)

Now One Foot, Now the Other

 by Tomie dePaola

This is the very special story of a grandfather and grandson over a five-year period. As the book begins, young Bobby is an infant with a doting grandpa. When Bobby takes his first steps (*Now one foot, now the other!*), his grandpa is there to help. Before long, the grandfather and grandson are spending hours building blocks together and telling stories. As the story (and life) progresses, they both grow older—Bobby becoming more capable, and Bob (the grandpa) eventually having a stroke. It is at this point that the roles become reversed—with Bobby nursing an unable-to-communicate Bob back to life, using the same patience and love that were used with him five years earlier. He teaches Bob to walk and talk, experiences the sweetness of being able to *tell* Bob their favorite story, instead of having it told to him, and they build blocks together.

Now One Foot, Now the Other is a lovely book about so much more than a grandpa and a grandson. It is about life and the loving, giving and taking that sharing can be. (4–8 yrs.)

Knots on a Counting Rope

by Bill Martin, Jr., and John Archambault
illustrated by Ted Rand

It is a dark, cool night. Sitting by the fire under a canopy of stars, a young Native American boy says to his grandfather, "Tell the story again. Tell me who I am." And as Grandfather recounts once again the story of the night the boy was born, of how a fierce storm raged through the darkness, of how the boy was very weak and almost died, the child *and* the reader of the story feel strength and hope and courage and love welling inside their hearts. We see the ceremony that occurred after he smiled his first smile, when he was given the name Boy-Strength-of-Blue-Horses. We are with him as he is present with Circles as she is ready to foal the colt that will be his. We watch as the boy and horse race on tribal day. You see, the boy was born blind, and it is through the telling and retelling of his story, the counting rope being a metaphor for the passage of time, that he finds the emerging confidence to face his greatest challenge: the dark curtain in front of his eyes. And when we watch the boy discover what the color blue smells, feels and sounds like, we rejoice with him.

Perhaps what makes this book so special is that the boy's blindness is not the main issue. Yes, it happens to be *his* challenge, but somehow we come to find in the story that we all have challenges we must face. And just as the boy swells with excitement and joy at the story of how his grandfather views his growth from a weak newborn to a strong boy capable of anything he attempts, we find hope and assurance that we, too, will never be alone. While on a technical level, this book is not accurate (clothing, intergenerational interactions, etc.), its worth lies in its spirit, not in any claim to correctly portray Native American culture.

Bright and rich watercolors not only enrich the story, each page is a work of art in itself. (4–8 yrs.)

Children suffer all kinds of growing pains throughout the years of their childhood: losing friends, having a harsh teacher, experiencing nasty interactions with an unfriendly neighbor. All kinds of things can happen that are just a part of normal everyday life. By attending to our child's feelings, listening carefully to her story and occasionally stepping in to advocate for her needs, we can generally navigate the little things with ease.

But what happens when something really horrible happens? The kind of growing pain that changes a child's life forever—a death, a divorce, a tragic illness? What do we do then? I believe we must somehow open our hearts really wide, as wide as possible to help our child face this unbearable pain. Find your deepest connection to compassion and love and then sit with your child, holding that space. You, as a parent, may be filled with emotion, too, for likely this experience is happening to both you and your child at the same time—such as a death in your immediate family or a divorce. It is okay (within reason) for your child to see you cry and see the depth of your real emotions. It isn't okay for her to hear you speak badly of someone she loves, as in the case of a divorce. Tell your child exactly what you are feeling so she knows that your emotions aren't about her and then make room in your heart to really listen to what your child has to say. Small children react in different ways; sometimes they ask odd questions over and over as if trying to understand, especially when a death is involved. The more compassion you can hold for everyone, the easier (and in the end, emotionally cleaner) this transition will be. Make sure you allow yourself plenty of opportunity to grieve, be angry or feel whatever it is you need to feel *away* from your child, so when you are *with* your child you can be of more comfort to her.

Old Jake's Skirts

by C. Anne Scott
illustrated by David Slonim

Some of our very favorite books are about folks softening and about hearts being opened up, and this book is, simply and beautifully, one of those.

Jake's the old codger living out in the middle of nowhere. He is perfectly self-reliant, watching the seasons turn, whittling and going about his days in an honest, upstanding way. The story begins on the day he finds a trunk in the middle of the road. He hoists it up onto the bed of his old truck, stops at the general store and posts a note saying he's found the trunk and that it will be at his house out at Stillwater's farm should the owner be looking for it.

Jake doesn't bother looking inside the trunk. In fact, it soon gets scooted off into the corner and ends up a catch-all for dirty clothes and things. Spring eventually comes, and his dog uncharacteristically begins to insist on sleeping inside the house, next to the trunk, rather than outside, where he's been sleeping all his life. Now curious as all get-out, Jake opens the trunk. Somewhat amazingly, he does not find the gold that we're kind of hoping for. (Jake's place is pretty run-down and could use some spiffing up.) Nope. Just a bunch of soft and wildly colorful calico skirts.

Saying too much more will make the story lose its punch. But I will tell you that in the end a young girl is comforted, and Jake is softened, by what these skirts bring to his life.

All together, everything about this book—text and illustrations—adds up to it being one that will fill your heart and your eyes with richness. It is one of those special gems you don't run across often. (4–7 yrs.)

 ## The Red Woolen Blanket

by Bob Graham

Our children all have that special object or toy they bond to, a beloved companion through the ups and downs of growing up. Julia is wrapped in her blanket the moment she is born, and from that day on, they are inseparable. As Julia gets bigger, her blanket gets smaller, until, on the first day of school, her blanket is no bigger than a postage stamp. And when that last little bit of blanket slips quietly away, Julia "hardly misses it at all."

Graham gives children the reassuring message that their attachment to and love of blanket, doll or bear are right and good, and, when they are ready, they will be able to let it go with ease. And he does this in such a simple, homey way. I marvel at his choice of words, and the hilarious, endearing pictures of Julia's family and life with the red woolen blanket. Remember when a favorite bear was left somewhere, or you spilled indelible ink on Baby's cloth face? Graham's book is a comforting, healing antidote for such times. Or for any time, for that matter! (3–6 yrs.)

St. George and the Dragon

retold by Margaret Hodges
illustrated by Trina Schart Hyman

The perfect symbolism of this story speaks of our journey here on earth, the hardships and joys we face on our paths. *St. George and the Dragon* is the tale of one person's challenges to find his courage, to persevere despite unspeakable odds. Every one of us, our children in particular, need to see humans rising to the occasion in impossible situations. This book is a remarkable gift to us for what it shows.

George is raised by the Queen of the Fairies. At the end of his childhood he is a brave and able knight who has sworn his service to the Fairy Queen and rides through the countryside, on his way to vanquish dragons and other worthy foes. In the course of his duties he meets a fair and beautiful maiden who is searching for a knight to come free her kingdom from the clutches of a fierce and horrible dragon. St. George accepts the challenge and follows the lovely Una back to her lands. Once there, he fights and kills the dragon in a series of three battles. As you might guess, in the end, the dragon is slain and St. George and Una are wed.

The illustrations in this book are absolutely stunning and the retelling of this ancient English legend is enchanting. It speaks volumes about the courage we need to live in times such as our own. In big and little ways, all of us face challenge in our lives. Children are strengthened by hearing archetypal stories in which a hero faces unbeatable odds and rises to meet the occasion, anyway. Such is the story of St. George and the Dragon. (4+ yrs.)

The Tenth Good Thing About Barney

by Judith Viorst
illustrated by Erik Blegvad

Barney, the cat, dies and leaves his little master feeling like never before: not even in the mood to eat his chocolate pudding or to watch TV. While tucking him in that night, Mom says they'll have a funeral for Barney the next day, and that he should think of ten good things about Barney to say at the ceremony. Nine qualities come easily, but the little boy falls asleep before he can think of a tenth. (By this time, good luck if you're attempting to read this aloud without hearing more sobs than words.) Throughout the story, we see unfolding some of the stages that people go through in the grieving process. The little boy is numb, then angry, then sad, then curious, then accepting. Supportive parents are by his side the whole time. In the end, he has come to terms with Barney's passing, and has been able to find a silver lining to the experience (the tenth good thing).

Don't wait until a pet is terminally ill to get this book. It is a priceless book about love and acceptance; the fact that it happens to be about a cat is almost secondary. (4+ yrs.)

When hard things happen to children (and adults), formal or informal rituals help to ease the pain. Excluding children from funerals or other important events denies them the chance for closure and emotional processing that these rituals were designed to facilitate. Small children need not spend hours at a wake, yet they need to know that, yes, the grandma they love is really dead, not just gone away. There is no question in anyone's mind, after seeing a dead person, that Grandma isn't in there anymore. Attending the funeral allows children a model of what to do with the sadness they feel. And it opens the door to the questions that they need to ask to find completion with their feelings.

When my grandma died, Laura was four. She was very close to her and took her death hard. Because she was an Irish Catholic, my grandmother's funeral involved an open casket ceremony. Seeing the dead body fully clarified to Laura that Grandma's spirit had left her body. But she wasn't gone from Laura's heart. Laura felt that connection deeply. For years, whenever she was sad she slept with Grandma's picture in her hand. She kept this picture on her bedside table until she was well into her teens. For a couple of years after my grandma's death, Laura would occasionally wander downstairs at night crying, saying she was missing Grandma (and I am sure she was), but I think, too, she was missing the comfort and connection that Grandma represented to her. So when she was sad or troubled about other things in her life, she longed for Grandma's touch. Allowing Laura to deal with grief in her own way and in her own time taught me much about myself. I realized that in always wanting to hurry through my own painful experiences, I tended to deny myself as much compassion as I needed to fully process something.

Laura's slow but steady grief process strengthened her in ways I marvel to see. When her best friend's mom was dying of cancer last year, Laura was able to be so present for herself and her friend because, I am convinced, she knew the power of grief. She had fully grieved the loss of someone she loved and on some level knew what her friend was experiencing. She could hold that grief in her heart, feel it and make room for her friend's pain, too. It was a powerful dynamic to witness. It seems that only when we can hold our own hearts with tenderness can we offer true compassion to another.

The Worry Stone

by Marianna Dengler
illustrated by Sibyl Graber Gerig

Seldom does a book this beautiful cross my desk. The story begins with an old woman who comes to watch the children play in the park and to forget how lonely her life has become. Each day she notices one boy who is left on the outskirts of the other children's world. She sees his sadness and longs for a way to help. One day she brings him a small stone that she found as a child and then tells him the story about this stone. The story is an old one told to her by her grandfather. It is a folktale from the native people of that land, the Chumash Indians. And just as her grandfather's stone did for her, the old woman's stories gradually heal the little boy's pain. Soon they are friends, each giving the other the love they need.

This is a remarkably tender story. Both the luminous pictures and the compassionate words leave such a hopeful feeling in our hearts. (4–9 yrs.)

Dear Friends,

Oh, to have been the person I am now when I first became a mother! Over the years, my children have taken me to places I never dreamed I'd go—places that changed me forever. I'm able now to see some of the things I've done right and some of the things I've done wrong. The less than stellar moments in parenting are (of course!) often crystal clear in my memory. In my cases I'm convinced that had I acted in a manner I now know would have been a better way, my children would have had at least a slightly greater chance of growing up more emotionally healthy and balanced people.

The instance that keeps popping up for me lately is the time when Eliz-abeth was about four or five. She'd been playing a few houses away with a couple of her friends who were a year older than she was. As I later learned from the other mother, what had happened is what often happens with chil-dren: in a matter of minutes, cooperative play had turned bad, two kids had ganged up on one, toys all of a sudden were not being shared, hurtful words were said, and a tearful, rejected Elizabeth came running home. I'd been gardening in the front yard and heard her coming. I dropped what I was doing, ran over to hug her and escort her home—and while doing so (this is where I blew it, I believe) lectured her about how she should remember how awful she feels right now so that if she were ever tempted to be cruel to somebody, she'd know better and take the high road, so to speak. The whole incident took no more than a few minutes. Before long, Elizabeth was off doing something else and I consoled my mother hen self by thinking that this "lesson" I'd preached to her about how others might feel had kept her distracted from her own pain.

There. I said it. I tried to protect her from pain. That's noble enough and what parents are there for, right? I don't think it's as simple as that.

Now, there are certain pains and uglinesses and struggles and horrors that don't seem right for any parent or child to go through. We all know that far too many lives are filled with nightmarish situations that are hard for us to even read about in the newspaper, much less live through. I am talking here about protection from the emotional bumps and scratches of life—protection that we as parents can certainly orchestrate much of the time, and which may not be in our children's best interest. In devising this protection, though, we are likely creating an unsustainable utopia that will, in the end, mold our child into someone who doesn't understand that life's pain and uncomfortable challenges can be transformed into something valuable. Who doesn't understand that life isn't fair. Who doesn't understand that without expansion and contraction, ebb and flow, light and dark there would be nothing to soften our sharp edges as human beings. And we need to know as parents that when the sharp edges have been smoothed down a bit, there is a lesser chance that our children will snag themselves later on in life, when pain might come in a much bigger package than having some words with your five-year-old friend.

What I am talking about is knowing that pain, anger, disappointment and those emotions that aren't considered very pretty are okay. Not fun, certainly, but okay. It is about knowing as parents that when we let them see and try to make them feel only sweetness and light, we are doing them a disservice. And worse than that, we are raising children who aren't real and true and who won't know how to be when they are adults.

So if I had to do that long-ago afternoon all over again, I'd have done what I now know would have been better for Elizabeth: I'd have grimaced inwardly at the anguish she was experiencing, taken a deep breath and held her and her suffering in a long embrace—an embrace big enough and wise enough to accept that pain is a part of life and that all we can do is hold it—and then let it go.

Surrendering the Day

Bedtime

If a baby is busy, restless, struggling at bedtime, and yet you know he yearns to rest, see if you are not busy, too—with ten thousand thoughts. The thoughts can be any-thing—he's got to sleep, he needs it; he's got to sleep, I need it; I have to get some time to myself; maybe if I do this; maybe he wants that; why won't he sleep? Is it so? Then try to acknowledge that, at least for the moment, neither you nor the child has any needs beyond the awareness of love. Corny? Try it.

—POLLY BERRIEN BERENDS

Bedtime is, in many ways, a moment of opportunity, a time of release and transition. We may anxiously await the moment our children go to bed, for once the little ones are sleeping, the day takes on a different tone. An air of peace descends upon the house and the frustrations of the day melt away. You can almost hear the gentle sigh as we tired parents bestow that last kiss and silently close our child's bedroom door, gratefully stepping away into adult time. And while it is crucially important for adults to have this time alone, time to reintegrate and renew themselves for the next day, the atmosphere of bedtime is also vitally important to the well-being of the child. When we parents create a serene bedtime experience, we help our children move into a calm and restful sleep.

With our help, our children learn to approach sleep with a sense of gentleness and rhythmic security that will aid their sleep habits for the rest of their lives. If we address our children's fears as they sit on the threshold of the dark, unknown night, we help them gain courage to master the future difficulties of their lives. If, on the other hand, we send our children off to bed rather carelessly, with a rushed and harried air, we lose an opportunity to help them learn the art of peaceful transition. Sleep can easily become a war between two opposing forces—parents who desperately want their children in bed, and children who will do anything to delay the inevitable. It takes time and conscious attention to create a peaceful bedtime. A story, a simple song, a gentle backrub, all take effort; but it is effort well spent.

We parents will end up spending our time and energy one way or another. The choice of how is up to us—either we can put our efforts into making bedtime a treasured part of the day, or we can spend the same amount of time and will policing children back to bed again and again, as they repeatedly seek our attention by asking for one more glass of water or one more kiss.

When our children are young, we have the chance to establish the bedtime routine that will carry parents and children through the first years of family life. Will you sing a song, light a candle, say a prayer or read a story? Will you take a bath or pick up toys? It is for each family to decide which activities constitute the bedtime rituals. The habits we cultivate with our toddlers become the habits our school-age children will expect. If a tidy bedroom is important, a short, happy pickup at the end of the day will soon become a habit that pleases everyone, bringing order where there once was chaos.

It is important, then, to consider each action deeply before we adopt it as part of our bedtime ritual. A simple choice soon becomes routine—a routine that may endure for years to come. All the more reason to make sure we create habits that bring us joy, not tedium. A complicated bedtime routine might not feel burdensome to the parents of one toddler, but as their family grows this same routine, carried out for three children, might become oppressive. Bedtime is an occasion to remember that less is more. An attentive, loving heart is all our children really ask of us. What we choose to do is less important than how we do it; the connection between the parent and child is what really matters. We can make choices that encourage our emotional presence instead of choices that leave us rushing to finish, just to be done. The peace we leave with our children at the end of the day is the peace we bring to them in our hearts. And the peace we bring to bedtime is the peace that stays with them throughout the night.

If the day has been difficult or full of frustration, a ritual of transition may be necessary for us parents, too. Before I go to my child's room, I try to take a moment to find my center. I see in my mind's eye the children I love. I see them shining in their wholeness. And I try to leave all the mischievous or annoying behaviors of the day outside their bedroom door. That way, I can enter the room with a feeling of love in my heart. I often find myself washing my hands with warm water and soap right before I begin our bedtime routine. This small ritual helps me to let go of my frustrations and find my center once more. The physical act of washing away impurities becomes a potent symbol of my washing away the accumulated annoyances and weariness that keep me from greeting my children with love. For, certainly, this is the sense that I wish to leave them with at the end of each day. On hard days, I need to remember that things have been a struggle for both of us and we are both in need of love and nurturing. A loving bedtime can offer sustenance to both the parent and the child. That is why it is so crucial to have a bedtime routine that nourishes us both. If you love to sing, include a song as part of your bedtime ritual. If, on the other hand, singing brings back visions of your third-grade teacher ridiculing the timid quaverings of your small voice, choose something else, something that brings you joy. Tell a story. Read a book. Give a foot massage or lie quietly by your child's side. If it comforts you, chances are it will comfort your child, too, for young children are so acutely sensitive to our emotional experiences. And the lovely thing about young children is that they are seldom harsh critics. Any act performed with love will be accepted. No matter how out of tune our song may be or how disjointed our made-up stories are, a child receives our gifts in the loving spirit in which they are given. Soon they come to treasure whatever it is we choose to give.

Bedtime is the perfect chance for parents and children to reflect upon the passing day and make peace with whatever has happened. A quiet chat can transform an unsettled incident into a powerful lesson. I am constantly amazed at how much children will open up and confide their deepest pains and secrets in the quiet moments right before sleep. It is almost as if they need to let go of their struggles before they can relax into sleep. I often find myself sharing my thoughts on how the world works with my children as they are lying in their beds before sleep. They may bring up a problem or a question and, after listening carefully to their concerns, I reframe it so they can see the issue with bigger eyes. "Yes, Josh hits and we know hitting is a mistake, but maybe he hasn't learned that yet. How can we help him learn to use his words instead of his body to tell us his feelings?" By reframing their questions, we can empower our children to be helpers—and they often exhibit the most surprising depths of understanding of their friends and enemies. These tender times on the threshold before sleep are especially teachable moments.

Children learn another valuable lesson when we have the wisdom to take responsibility for our bad behavior. Often at bedtime, when we are looking back over the day, we see how we contributed to the day's hardships. When we, as parents, apologize sincerely for our cranky words, our children learn to see their day through a new lens. It is astonishing, and comforting, for them to realize the simple truth: "Mom was just in a bad mood, it wasn't me that was bad." The extra bit of warmth and nurturance we provide at bedtime gives our children's hearts the extra strength to open and grow.

However you choose to approach bedtime, it is helpful to remember that bedtime is a transition from one state of consciousness to another. Our children are most open and, in some ways, most fragile at these times. As they pass from a wakeful consciousness to one of sleep, their hearts and psyches are exquisitely receptive to every influence around them. And so we must choose our words and actions with care now. Bedtime is a time for reverence and gentle hearts.

Bedtime stories often become the focus of a family bedtime ritual. Here are some books and suggestions for crafting soothing bedtime traditions that you'll be happy to share night after night.

Many parents find it helpful to ritualize bedtime. Each aspect of bedtime becomes a routine done in the same order, over and over again. Young children respond to such rhythms and tend to settle down more reliably when bedtime is treated with such formality. They come to expect each aspect of this time in the evening and love how settled the trusted rhythm makes them feel. Lighting a candle is a powerful way to signify the beginning of bedtime, lending a bit of magic to the moment. The soft candlelight helps children gently adjust to the idea of darkness, and the act of lighting the candle itself says "We are ready to begin. This time belongs to you and no one else." Gently blowing (or snuffing) out the flame tells the child "Now, bedtime is over and it is time for you to sleep."

Tell Me Something Happy

Before I Go to Sleep

by Joyce Dunbar
illustrated by Debi Gliori

Willa can't sleep. She's turning this way and that, that way and this, but she just can't sleep. She tells her big brother in the upper bunk that she's a bit afraid that she's going to have a bad dream. "Think of something happy," he advises. And so begins a bedtime book like no other.

Anyway, Willa can't sleep and her big brother, Willoughby, puts down the book he's reading to patiently do a little sleep therapy, advising her to think of something happy. And what might that be? Willa wonders. Well, her favorite chicken slippers are there, under her bed. Those slippers, Willoughby tells her, are "waiting, just waiting, for nobody's feet but yours." And her jumpsuit on the bed, that's waiting for Willa to jump into it in the morning. And, carrying Willa downstairs, he points out the bread, honey, oats, milk and apples on the shelf—you guessed it—just waiting to be made into breakfast. All of these are happy things that Willa can think of, you see. And before long, she herself spots things around the house that are waiting, dreaming of tomorrow, when they will be part of her day. Even the night, Willoughby explains, is waiting, waiting for the morning, which is on its way around the world, and the morning is waiting to do all of the things that mornings do with flowers growing and leaves blowing and clouds floating. The morning, though, is waiting, too, to wake Willa up, but it can't unless she goes to sleep.

Tell Me Something Happy Before I Go to Sleep is brilliant. The sibling love and patience and admiration are tangible. The illustrations make you feel warm and fuzzy from the first page on. The text is lively and gentle. The story is a story for every child. And Willoughby, as a big brother, is destined to do great things in his life, whether it's being the world's best big brother or whether it's being the most creative and patient sleep inducer around. And not only that, he's inspiring. Before long, you and your child will be thinking of your own happy things on the nights when sleep comes reluctantly. (2½–5 yrs.)

A special storytime/cuddling chair in your child's room helps to create a predictable, soothing experience right before naptime and bedtime. Just make sure it's comfy. Perhaps use a dim light in the room. Maybe calming music, too. Using that chair when my children were little made sleep come easier, the effects of scary dreams fade faster, and feverish nights somehow more manageable. Our "story chair"—no matter how many times it ends up being reupholstered through the years—will always be special, for it was the place of that last sweet connection before sleep.

All the Pretty Little Horses

illustrated by Susan Jeffers

I remember one night when newborn Evan was so colicky that he simply would *not* be put down. He had to be held in an upright position, against my chest (for two hours, then his dad's chest for two hours, then mine for two hours, etc.), while his tiny little feet were massaged—of all things! As the night moved from simply being "late" to "in the middle of . . ." to "early morning," I must have sung "All the Pretty Little Horses" hundreds of times. I'll always have a soft spot in my heart for this lullaby.

Susan Jeffers certainly has the knack for hitting the nail on the head when it comes to illustrating gentle, soothing books such as this. It's dreamy, comfortably predictable and lovely. The text is minimal (just the words to the lullaby), and traces a young girl who drifts off to find herself among horses, horses and more horses (blacks, bays, dapples and grays). A quiet sort of book, perfect for winding down and relaxing, its uncluttered pen-and-ink and watercolor illustrations inviting the reader to point to each horse, perhaps counting them, perhaps even giving them names. (Don't be surprised if your young one adores naming the horses; it's as if they're old friends returning each time you open the book.) (1–3 yrs.)

Don't be afraid to sing to your children. Our culture has become such a culture of experts; we often forget the simple pleasures of just sharing ourselves. We don't have to know the perfect songs or have the perfect voice. It is the act of singing that our children will come to love. My husband and I often sing lullabies at our children's bedtime. Our children are equally accepting of my husband's renditions of '60s rock tunes as they are of my obscure lullabies. Just pick a song you love and sing. Your children will love you for it. Three of my four children have adored "I've Been Working on the Railroad," a song we resorted to one time on a long, unhappy car ride. Ever since then, that song has meant comfort to my children. On the worst of days, we can sing this song and be assured it will bring a smile to our children's faces. Find your own family's trademark song. These are moments that become treasured memories long after your child is grown.

Goodnight Moon

by Margaret Wise Brown
illustrated by Clement Hurd

Absolutely, positively no home with children should be without this magical, tender bedtime book. Volumes have undoubtedly been written about why *Goodnight Moon* has become a classic since its 1947 debut, but still, there is just something about it that words will never be able to describe and that just can't be analyzed and dissected. Trust me. This book goes straight to someplace deep within children that wants to feel secure and comforted. Over and over again, it works its sweet wonder and offers that security and comfort.

The singsongy text is relaxing. The color illustrations of a marvelous green bedroom gradually darkening as the moon comes up, and the bunny who just can't seem to keep his eyes closed, are things we always watch for when reading it. Be sure to keep your eyes open for the little mouse that, with a little perseverance, can be found on each page. What children might like best, though, is pointing to each object the text mentions. Would that every child had this book! (6 mos.–3 yrs.)

At night when I tuck Heidi in, we have a little ritual. The very last second before I turn off her light and close the door, together we perform a three-step hand movement in which we say to each other, "I love you, sweet dreams, good night." She made up this little personal form of sign language when she was two or three, and insisted that we do it every night. Now, good night is not good night until we have said our "I love yous," as she calls it. I am sure, for as long as we live, this will always be our code of love. All of us find our special way of saying "I love you." When we allow it to become a formalized part of our bedtime ritual, it embeds our message of love in our children's hearts.

Goodnight Hattie, My Dearie, My Dove

by Alice Schertle
illustrated by Linda Strauss Edwards

A good "bedtime" book is really a good "anytime" book, you know. It has a story or rhythm that is pleasant to hear at all hours of the day. It has illustrations that make one feel cozy and safe, no matter what the hour. It doesn't obsess about "getting sleepy" and/or "going to bed," but rather just happens to be about that quiet time of day: evening.

This is one of those books. It happens to be a bit of a counting book, though that is not its main thrust. It's a new rendition of the well-known tendency of children to insist that all of their favorite toys go to bed with them. Hattie parades through the living room while her mom plays the piano. Accompanying her are Lumpy (who was white when he was new, but now is gray), Tom (who used to sing "Yankee Doodle" until something inside him went *snap!*), Clam Chowder (named thusly since he fell into Hattie's soup) and six other friends. It is when Hattie is all tucked in that night, and her mom has said, "Goodnight Hattie, My Dearie, My Dove," that she realizes that her toys, one by one, simply must sleep with her (for various and outrageous reasons!). It's not hard to guess how many of Hattie's friends are crammed into her bed at story's end, with Hattie sound asleep. (2½–5 yrs.)

Good Night, Good Morning

by Helen Oxenbury

Nobody catches the nuances of the relationship between toddlerhood and parenthood better than Helen Oxenbury. Without so much as one word, she conveys such toddler phenomena as the boundless energy that is followed by sleep's abrupt arrival; wide-eyed curiosity at 6 A.M.; the one-track love of a favorite book; the propensity to lie *across* Mom and Dad's bed (effectively pushing them out); etc. We promise: you will be chatting about this wordless book to your little one and inside you'll be chuckling, marveling how Oxenbury so accurately hits the nail on the head when it comes to toddlers.

This is a favorite of a number of toddlers we know. It is a wordless masterpiece! (1–2½ yrs.)

Teach your child a bit of responsibility and allow him a chance to exercise his autonomy by providing a light and a clock near his bed. Giving him a few minutes to quietly wind down in bed (looking at books or playing with small toys) lets him feel a bit more in control and can remove some of the power struggles common to bedtime. As you leave, let him know when "lights out" is and then allow him the chance to take charge.

Grandfather Twilight

by Barbara Berger

No home should be without its own copy of *Grandfather Twilight*. This is a wondrously illustrated and superbly executed book for bedtime, one of our all-time favorites. A calming text tells how Grandfather Twilight lives among the trees, and how, when day is done, he opens a wooden chest filled with an endless strand of pearls and takes one pearl from it. It is this pearl that is destined to become the moon that evening. The rest of the story follows Grandfather Twilight as he walks along with that pearl in his hand. Leaves begin to whisper. Little birds hush. The pearl, all this while, is getting bigger and bigger as he walks. When it is too large to hold in the palm of his hand, he gently gives the pearl to the silence above the sea, and there it becomes the moon. He then heads for home and his bed.

The brightly yet softly colored illustrations are practically luminescent. This is simply a magical, serene book about something that elicits more wide-eyed wonder from children than just about any other thing: the moon. Go for a moon walk (it's especially fun when your child is all ready for bed), then read this book. (2½–6 yrs.)

Every parent knows that some days are incredibly difficult. Kids are tired. Parents are tired. Moods are swinging and life feels out of kilter. No matter how conscientious we are about our parenting, we are all going to experience days like this when nothing feels right. And by the end of one of these days, what could be more daunting—yet more desperately yearned for—than bedtime? How do we transform our out-of-control, tantrumming toddler into a peacefully sleeping child? At moments like this no technique offers a surefire guarantee, but here are a few suggestions that have worked for us.

- Go for a walk, no matter the weather. A spontaneous ten-minute walk can work wonders on cranky parents and children.
- Draw a warm bath and add a few drops of lavender essential oil to the water. Water has the magical ability to soothe inflamed emotions and calm the psyche. (Lavender has been used for centuries to calm the weary soul.)

- ♥ Massage your child's feet, back or tummy. Gentle touch is almost always calming.

- ♥ Breathe together. Slow, deep and easy breaths. Imagine your breath floating away on a cloud. If you slow your breathing down, your child will naturally be calmed.

- ♥ Lie down on your child's bed and whisper her favorite story. In order for her to hear you, she will have to quiet herself inside and out.

- ♥ Put on a soothing piece of music and sit quietly with your child in a candlelit room. The soft candlelight helps the child calm down and the music gives her something to focus on besides her distress.

- ♥ Avoid giving your child too many choices. When children have lost their center and are acting completely out of control, choices tend to overwhelm them emotionally and make things worse.

- ♥ Above all, don't worry. Everyone has days like this. Sometimes children just need to release stored emotion and frustration. That's okay. Another day you can help your child learn to express her feelings more appropriately. Know that your child (and you) will be okay and that tomorrow is another day. Take a moment to feel in your heart how much you love her and imagine that love surrounding your child.

The Midnight Farm

by Reeve Lindbergh
illustrated by Susan Jeffers

How often do you find a book that treats the wee hours of the night as a time of sharing and warmth? How many of us have attempted to quell our children's nighttime fears by taking them outside? I suppose that if we lived on a farm such as this family's, that is where we'd frequently end up, effortlessly connecting with the serenity we were after. In this story, a wise mother takes her child for a walk outside, offering him a chance to meet up with familiar animal friends in the sweet, dark summer air. They see three raccoons, six cows, eight chicks, etc.—you get the point. Each encounter brings about a verse such as this:

Here is the dark of the orchard pond,
where nine deer gather from all around,
to drink at night without any sound,
in the dark of the orchard pond.

Gradually the little fellow falls asleep in his mother's arms after seeing ten field mice, and is tucked safely in bed:

Here is the dark of the midnight farm,
safe and still and full and warm,
deep in the dark and free from harm
in the dark of the midnight farm.

Susan Jeffers' delicately colored, realistic art is perfectly compatible with this lovely story. (2–5 yrs.)

When you are working hard to help your child move toward bed, nothing can be more distracting than the phone. An innocent phone call from a friend can ruin the entire atmosphere of bedtime. By the time you return from a two-minute conversation, twenty minutes of your moving toward a calm bedtime is lost. Your children are revved back up and running around the house. Let your children know how important they are to you by putting them first at bedtime. If possible, turn off your phone or let the answering machine take your calls. There are very few calls more important than your child's bedtime. Focus on the moment and take the call later. (And don't feel bad about letting your close friends and family know when bedtime is.)

The Sun's Asleep Behind the Hill

by Mirra Ginsburg
illustrated by Paul O. Zelinsky

There is something so wonderfully soothing about this book. Just the simplest of end-of-the-day stories, it gives us a glimpse of a child and mother spending the last few minutes of daylight in a park. As hints of dusk take over, and the child is carried home, sleeping on his mother's shoulder, we are witness to the breeze becoming quiet, the bird resting, the squirrel sleeping and, of course, the sun's descent and the moon's rising.

The text is uncluttered and calming, while the deeply colored illustrations have just enough detail to pause over and talk about, if desired. A soothing bedtime book with an intriguing and comforting concept: that the sun is going to sleep, just like we all are. (1½–4 yrs.)

Plagued by the "I need a drink" syndrome? Let your children meet their own needs by setting up a bedtime station right by their beds with a light that they can control, tissues for blowing noses and a small water bottle for getting drinks.

The Random House Book of

Bedtime Stories

illustrated by Jane Dyer

We think every child deserves a beautifully illustrated book of classically told bedtime tales. You know the ones I mean: "Goldilocks and the Three Bears," "The Billy Goats Gruff," "The Little Red Hen," etc. Unfortunately, it is not as easy to find such a book as one would suppose. Certainly there are plenty of collections out there, but seldom do you find well-told tales and gorgeous pictures in one spot. Often, in an attempt to modernize the stories, the words have been changed enough to lose some of the deeper meanings these stories hold for young children. Or the illustrations are scarier than are appropriate for a young child's mind. I was, therefore, delighted to find this Random House edition so lovingly illustrated by Jane Dyer. Bright, cheerful watercolors capture the happy innocence of a young child's life. The animals have a very human quality about them, which makes even the scary ones agreeable (e.g., the bears in the Goldilocks story look perplexed and a bit mournful, but not a bit scary). Dyer has done a masterful job of enhancing, rather than dominating, the stories with her illustrations. There is still plenty of room for children to imagine the story in their own minds!

In addition, I especially like that the editors have chosen to mix the old classic stories with a few modern tales. All the stories share a common thread of warmth and gentleness that nurture a young child's soul. This book would make an especially fine gift. It is the kind of book you will return to over and over again. It is hard to imagine it ever getting tiring. It is so very lovely. (2½–5 yrs.)

Sleepytime Rhyme

by Remy Charlip

This sweet ode to the love between mother and child is so resplendent with love intoxication that it's reminiscent of the first months with a newborn—when parents are passionately hooked on their baby and everything about him. His toes are the best toes in the whole world; and, oh!, that wise, clear gaze!; and, of course, no one thinks that changing the diaper of this amazing baby is a chore! No matter what else might be going on, it's always uplifting to see parents adoring their baby.

And a book that eloquently and cheerfully puts all of this down on paper? *Sleepytime Rhyme.* Here's a taste (try reading it aloud):

I love you.
I think
You're grand.
There's none
Like you
In all the land.

I love your hair,
Your head,
Your chin,
Your neck,
Each ear,
Both cheeks, your skin.

And so on. All the while there is a mother and baby on each spread, facing this ultrasimple text, and outside their window one can always find another loving pair of *something*: cat and kitten, big hill and small hill, big cloud and little cloud, etc. The lively and subtly bright colors of the uncluttered illustrations might be perfectly described as serenely joyous.

This is a simple, fast read. Although the duo—and all of the pairs we've been seeing outside the window—are cuddled up asleep by book's end, the book has much more to do with sweet, nonsensical love than with sleep. Thus, it's just as appropriate to read at 7 A.M. (for that early morning book wake-up call!) as it is at 7 P.M. (18 mos.–3 yrs.)

Children's bedtime fears are a very real experience for them. What appears ridiculous or insignificant to an adult can be extremely frightening to a young child. Somehow as parents, we must honor our children's feelings without overly dramatizing their fears. Therefore, it is important to give our children the tools to handle their fears and help them learn to distinguish between things they really ought to be concerned about and things that are just imagined. However, because young children's imaginations are so vividly alive, this distinction may be very hard for them to comprehend. At these times, parents can actually use the children's imaginations to creatively conquer their fears. One of my daughters was deeply afraid of monsters in the dark. She imagined scary people scaling the sides of our two-story home specifically to crawl through her window and hurt her. For months when she was four she would wander down the stairs crying, long after bedtime, deathly afraid of her nighttime monsters. Nothing we could say would alleviate her fears. Then suddenly, on one of these nights, when I was downstairs sewing, I had the inspiration to hand her a zipper so she could zip away her monsters. I showed her how it worked and instantly she was soothed. For months after this she would sleep with her zipper clenched in her hand, always ready to zip away any monsters that might appear. This cure was so effective, her older sister (who wasn't at all afraid of the dark) had to have one, too. Now, a zipper might not be the right tool for your child, but with a little creative thinking, you might be able to find a similar "magical" cure to your child's fears.

Time for Bed

by Mem Fox
illustrated by Jane Dyer

This book + your child + you at bedtime will make memories you'll cherish forever. Gentle, reassuring books like this are few and far between. The illustrations will soften you with their beauty and their own feeling of gentleness, sweetness and reassurance.

Each spread depicts a stunning painting of a parent animal and one of its young. In each case, it's time for bed. The goose, the cat, the cow, the horse—they're all softly encouraging their babes to call it a day. With two lines of text such as

> *It's time for bed, little calf, little calf,*
> *What happened today that made you laugh?*

we see how each of them closes the day. Twelve animals in all nuzzle their young. Even if children didn't inherently love animals to begin with, they certainly would after spending time with this book. So realistic that fingers can practically feel the feathers and the fur, *Time for Bed* is magical because of its spirit. At book's end, we see a human mother telling her sleepy darling to sleep tight and have sweet dreams. (2–5 yrs.)

Summertime can make bedtime a challenge. Long evenings and hot temperatures can make bed less than inviting. I tend to relax my strict bedtime routines in the summer. My kids appreciate the extra few minutes to play and we all benefit from a release from the "schedule." If your lifestyle allows for some flexibility, you may wish to move the hour of bedtime until a little later in the evening, hoping your children will sleep in a little later in the morning. Use that extra time for family time. Take walks in the beautiful evening air; breathe in the wonderful smells of summer; take an extra little while to explore the natural world; pick berries; listen to the evensong of the birds. Our family often transports our bedtime reading out under the trees in our yard. The kids rest on their backs soaking in the beauty of the fluttering leaves and feeling the warm breezes on their skin. We read longer and completely unwind. By the time I suggest it is time for bed, the children have already released the excitement of the day and are ready to settle into sleep. Relaxing our expectations of bedtime encourages our children to experience the glorious expansiveness of summer, which, in this busy workaday world, can be a feeling that, sadly, eludes many children.

When Sheep Cannot Sleep

by Satoshi Kitamura

Don't be fooled into thinking that a great bedtime book has to be soothing and dreamy. Here is one that is neither, but reading it certainly winds things down just enough so that sleep can invite itself in. And all the while, there's a little counting fun to be had.

When Sheep Cannot Sleep is so refreshing, seeming to hypnotize the unsleepiest into a wound-down-enough mood to nod right off. But not before you both have a chance to count everything from seven rungs on a ladder to ten spaceships to twenty-two "z's"—which, of course, will be found on the last page, after our friend, the sheep, has finally fallen asleep. It's charmingly illustrated in rich colors and a fun style. Its slightly outrageous storyline is of Woolly, a sheep who is just not sleepy and finds himself in some odd places during his quest for slumber. Don't save this one just for bedtime, though. Any time of day is fine. (3–5 yrs.)

Where Did You Put Your Sleep?

by Marcia Newfield
illustrated by Andrea Da Rif

I already *knew* my children loved this book. But then a steady stream of friends and their kids came and went through our house over the period of a few weeks and when all was said and done, *Where Did You*

Put Your Sleep? had been picked up, read and enjoyed so many times by so many different people that I knew it was a winner.

It's about a six- or seven-ish-year-old girl who can't get to sleep and so is trying every trick in the book to get herself there (or, actually, *avoid* getting herself there!): glass of water, trip to the bathroom, etc. Her mother's patience is wearing thin but, thank goodness, there's her good-natured, innovative dad around to lighten things up and ask her where she put her sleep. After all, she had it *last* night! Is it in her closet? Her sneakers? Etc. (The two reach their silliest when she opines that it may be in his noseholes!) Then she begins to calm down as he speaks soothingly and warmly about letting the sleep come find *her.* The text becomes rather hypnotic, and soon, of course, the girl's asleep, as her dad quietly closes the door. (3–7 yrs.)

Lavender Fairy Sleeping Spray

To make your own lavender misting spray, add ten to twenty drops of lavender essential oil to a cup of water. Pour into a clean misting bottle (we use a beautiful, cobalt blue one) and spray on your child's pillow-case or favorite stuffed animal. The soothing smell of lavender will help him unwind and he will come to associate that smell with sleep.

Who Is the World For?

by Tom Pow
illustrated by Robert Ingpen

"Who is the world for?" asks a baby bear as she snuggles into her mother's furry tummy. And her mother tells her to look around and see: "The world, with all its deep dark caves for you to shelter in, with all its spring rivers, shining in sunlight, shimmering with fish, and with all its forests you'll never be lost in, no matter how far they stretch—the world is for you!"

As the pages turn, other tiny ones ask the same question: "Who is the world for?" Ingpen's absolutely stunning pictures introduce us to a lion cub on a dry, hot plain; a baby hippo in cool water; a little whale swimming beside her mother, etc., and finally, a small boy kneeling beside his father in "a rumpled nest of blankets," looking out a city window at the stars. The young ones are nestled cozily beside their mother or father as they gaze out on the vast worlds beyond their homes. They each learn something about the place they inhabit; they each are told, "The world is for you!" The human father tells his son that the world is a place made for everyone, people and animals alike. He speaks of those other parents and children way, way out there on "cold mountainsides and hot, dusty plains," who are different, yet just the same. On the last page, we see the boy tucked in, dreaming of all the other kinds of children with whom he shares his world.

Tom Pow is a renowned Scottish poet who wrote this book for his own children when he was traveling through Africa and missing them desperately. His words bring the message that our world is for us, surely, but we must remember that all living creatures feel the same way, and we share our world together. What a lovely picture to paint for little ones (in words and art). (3–8 yrs.)

When I'm Sleepy

 by Jane R. Howard
illustrated by Lynne Cherry

You may find that your child picks this book for you to read even when bedtime is the last thing on your mind.

Richly illustrated in warm, subtly glowing colors, with an abundance of detail, this book is about a little girl who wonders what it would be like to sleep with lots of different animals wherever *they* sleep. Sometimes, she wishes she could curl up in a basket (with a couple of dozing cats), or sleep in a swamp (on a log with two turtles) or crawl into a cozy cave and sleep all winter (with a bear to cozy up to). All in all, she wonders what it would be like to cuddle up with twelve different animals—but she decides that she's glad she "can go to sleep in my very own bed under my own warm blanket with my head on my own soft pillow."

Any animal-loving child will enjoy, if not love, this book. It is serene, reassuring and tender. And I don't want to harp on it, but the illustrations are truly memorable. (1–4 yrs.)

Asleep, Asleep

by Mirra Ginsburg
illustrated by Nancy Tafuri

Whenever this author-artist duo team up, we can hardly wait to see the results. Filled with stunning artwork in Tafuri's typical style of soft yet vibrant watercolors, *Asleep, Asleep* is a book whose art could enhance the walls of any house—it is that beautiful. The words are soft and gentle, asking

> *Are the wolves asleep?*
> *Asleep.*
> *And the bees?*
> *Asleep.*
> *Are the birds asleep?*
> *Asleep, asleep.*
> *Are the foxes asleep?*
> *Fast asleep.*

Ginsburg gently follows the animals and the earth around until the reader is inside the baby's house with the baby wide awake in the mother's arms and then cuddled in the mother's lap with the wind singing her to sleep. (1½–3 yrs.)

My kids are lucky. They have craftsy relatives who, over the years, have made or given them many wonderful blankets and quilts. Other blankets have been handed down through time and come from the distant past. I like to connect my children to this heritage of love as I tuck them in at night. Pulling their covers up one by one, I affirm all that love by chanting "Here is Grammy's love" as I pull up the baby quilt that Grammy made and "Here is Grandma Hall's love" as I pull up the hand-knit blan-

kie my husband's mother made; "Here's Santa's love" as I pull up the
blanket Santa gave one year and "Here is Great-great-Grandma Rose's
love" as I pull up an ancient, somewhat ratty, wool blanket of my great-
grandmother's. Finally, I end with "Here is your mommy's love" as I gently
place the quilt I made on top. By the end, each of their blankets has told
a story that connects them to their past and they are buried in warmth.

    If your family isn't craftsy, perhaps you can modify this idea by
tucking in your child with all of the stuffed animals that loved ones have
given him.

Good Night

Enchanting Story Visualizations

with Sleepytime Music

Audiorecording by Jim Weiss

Unlike most of even the best "guided visualization" bedtime record-
ings, this one doesn't last so long that it becomes a big deal to fit it into
your bedtime routine. It is the perfect answer for the family who ekes
every minute out of the evening and just needs something short and
sweet to relax that tired little cowboy/girl.

    Jim's voice is perfect for this sort of thing: guiding someone to a re-
laxing place by means of visualizations that won't overstimulate. Each
of the six short stories draws the listener in and evokes images that
conjure up the feelings of being safe and being loved. In each case, the
visualization progresses to the listener imagining him/herself asleep in
the setting where the story took place (a farm, a treehouse in the forest, a tropical island, etc.). A minute of soothing music follows, then
we are given a substantial pause before the next story in order to turn
the tape player off before a new visualization begins.

    Your child will get a lot of mileage out of this recording due to its six
different "vignettes." Go ahead and crawl into bed with your little one,
listen to a story together, and be the one to turn off the tape or CD
player as you tiptoe out of the room. (We even know of some adults
who use this recording on a regular basis for themselves.) (2½+ yrs.)

Hot Vanilla

Every once in a while, a child may have more trouble than usual falling asleep. Offering her a warm drink often gives her that extra little bit of relaxation she needs to drift off. A moderately warm cup of chamomile tea is an age-old remedy for sleeplessness. Another favorite idea around my home is hot vanilla. Simply add half a teaspoon of real vanilla extract to a cup of warm milk and *voilà!*—hot vanilla. It's a simple yet soothing taste that my children have loved for years; and, unlike hot chocolate, it has no added sugar or stimulating cocoa to keep them awake. Studies show that warm milk releases a chemical that gently induces sleep.

How Many Kisses Good Night

by Jean Monrad Thomas
illustrated by Eloise Wilken

I don't know how many bedtime books are in your collection, but as far as I'm concerned you should get prepared to add one more: *How Many Kisses Good Night*.

Aimed at the child who's still at the age of appreciating simple bedtime stories like *Goodnight Moon*, it has been printed on heavy stock and illustrated in soft yet bright watercolors. It is the brief story of the bedtime ritual of a mother and toddler daughter. Its text is lilting and simple:

> *How many eyes?*
> *How many noses?*
> *How many fingers?*
> *How many toeses?*
> *How many ears,*
> *like roses curled?*

That is the entire text for eight pages. The illustrations on those pages are of the mother helping the daughter get her tights off (that's the toeses part), and of bathtub scenes. As the simple story progresses, the little girl can be seen in her P.J.'s brushing her teeth, looking at a book while her mother braids her hair, crawling into bed and getting tucked in. The mother-daughter duo obviously adore each other and the scenes in the house make you feel, well, warm and cozy inside. (15 mos.–3 yrs.)

Heart to Heart

Dear Friends,

While giving one of our bookshelves a thorough cleaning not long ago, I happened upon our tattered and well-loved copy of Goodnight Moon. *Putting the cleaning operation on hold for the time being, I got comfortable on the floor, opened the book and read aloud, my echoing voice searching the empty house for some small ears to fill. I wondered at that moment when the last time was I'd read it to Evan, my youngest. Was he perhaps three, then? Had it been at bedtime or in the middle of some afternoon that he'd last asked me to read it to him? Whenever it was, I now sat on the floor a little sad that I hadn't been aware that it was the last time I'd be reading it, that no angel had tapped me on the shoulder, so to speak, to let me know that it was the end of . . . well . . . an era.*

Often when I dig into the ragbag nowadays and come up with an old diaper, I feel the same way. How many times did I put on and take off and wash this very diaper that now serves us so well for washing the car and dusting the furniture? Was it in the wee hours of some morning or during a trip to the playground that I last pinned it securely onto a little bum? I wish I'd have been aware at that very moment that this was it: my last diaper job. Instead, it was just business as usual, and the moment was gone. The same goes for that toy boat Elizabeth had to have in the tub with her for every single bath she took when she was a toddler. I placed it on the side of the tub one night after her bath, like I always did, but it had already been played with the last time, and I didn't know it then. It was only a few months later, while preparing a pickup for the Salvation Army, that I realized that yet another milestone had come and gone.

I don't know why I've been struck so many times lately by how easy it is to miss important moments, but I feel fortunate to have had these small encounters, for they quietly urge me to live in the now. That frayed diaper and dusty Goodnight Moon are reminders that nearly every day holds a "last" just as it likely holds a "first." Quite simply, nothing will ever be quite the same as it is today. It is only by living each moment as if it is the most important moment of my life that I can sense both the magic and the immensity of my job as a parent.

We spend so much time looking forward—anticipating the birth of our baby, awaiting the first step, counting down the days until soccer season, saving for that college education—that it is easy to miss the now. It seems like a paradox that it took running across things from the past to make me better able to savor the present, but that's just how it worked out for me. And even though I felt no angel tapping me on the shoulder to tell me I was indeed reading Goodnight Moon to Evan for the very last time, I believe one was there as I cleaned the bookshelf, sorted through rags and packed that Salvation Army bag. Those quiet, seemingly uneventful pauses in our day when we glimpse the vastness of life and understand that it is made up of simple moments in time are true gifts.

Afterword

I f you choose to look at it this way, parenting is nothing short of a pilgrimage, a pilgrimage to the very depths of your soul. As much as any other form of spiritual pilgrimage will take you into the wilderness, so will parenting take you to the deepest, hardest, darkest parts of yourself. Situations will compel you to look at what you have hidden in the recesses of your life. The anger you repressed as a child and never looked at will show itself in your anger toward your child. The joy you felt at being alive will be rekindled in the joy you feel seeing the simple miracle of your child's life. Without a doubt, you will encounter peak (ecstatic) moments in which you know you are face-to-face with the Divine, perhaps while you are looking at the face of your child. These are the moments that feed you, the nectar that allows you to continue on your journey inward. As with any journey, the rewards are great, yet you will not always know them until the journey is complete.

You may choose to begin this journey by deciding to become a parent, or the journey may choose you, but once your pilgrimage begins, you will never be the same. Even if you never acknowledge that transformation is at work, your life and the changes in your essential being will show that transformation is inevitable. Parenting, if you choose to accept its innate spiritual nature, will compel you to look at what you don't like about yourself in order to be more loving—both to your child and to yourself. You can resist, but the lesson will remain. Learning to love is the lesson *all* children offer their parents.

In my mind, parenting is a gift from the Divine to allow us the chance to grow as humans; to see more clearly, feel more deeply, to open what remains closed in our hearts. We can refuse the call, but the possibility for transformation exists in every interaction we have with our child. Each moment of our life as parents we can choose to love or not. And to experience love to its fullest dimension is what we come to earth to do. There is no greater work than learning how to love well. Our children are such wonderful teachers. Again and again, they will forgive us our transgressions, always with the hope that we will love them as they are, for who they are, in this moment. Each time we can love in this way, we touch the Divine and everyone blossoms.

Acknowledgments

L ife has a habit of blooming in the loving care of relationships and so has the life of this book. For so many years, our lives have been enriched by what we like to call the Chinaberry family—our customers and coworkers who, every day, make what we do worthwhile. We would especially like to express our appreciation for Robin, Janet, Lucinda, Shannon, Laura and Mary. What would our lives be like without your wise words, warm hearts and listening ears? Thank you, Anita West, for your part in Chinaberry's conception and for your huge and contagious love of children and their books. We'd also like to thank Tanya McKinnon, who patiently nudged us to believe in our own possibilities; Tricia Medved, our editor, who trusted in us from the very beginning; and Katrina Kenison, who held our hands and hearts as we tried to transfer over twenty years of our life's work onto the pages of this book. And, of course, no thanks would be complete without acknowledging our families—our children, who, each day of their lives, have challenged us to express our love with clear, true hearts. Opening to their love has transformed our very beings. We offer heartfelt gratitude to our husbands and true loves, the men who have walked this parenting path with us, day in and day out. Your loving care of our children and ourselves has enabled us to be the mothers we are. And, last, our deepest gratitude goes to those who guide our way from the spiritual realms—those we call the Chinaberry Angels—for your constant guidance and support. Who would we be without you?

Index of Titles

Index of Authors
and Illustrators

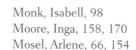

K

Kaye, Buddy, 32
Kellogg, Steven, 157
Kennedy, Dorothy M., 74
Kennedy, X. J., 74
Kindersley, Anabel, 100, 101
Kindersley, Barnabas, 100, 101
Kitamura, Satoshi, 281
Kleven, Elisa, 86, 94
Krensky, Stephen, 196
Kudrna, C. Imbior, 20

L

LaMarche, Jim, 209, 235
Large, Judy, 135
Lasker, Joe, 44
Lavallee, Barbara, 42
Lent, Blair, 66, 154
Lindbergh, Reeve, 86, 275
Lindgren, Astrid, 132
Lippman, Sidney, 32
Lobel, Arnold, 19, 20
Loh, Morag, 43
Lynch, P. J., 126, 183, 185

M

McBratney, Sam, 36
MacCarthy, Patricia, 9, 63
McCloskey, Robert, 14–15
MacLachlan, Patricia, 178
McNulty, Faith, 232
Mahy, Margaret, 9, 63
Manheim, Ralph, 205
Marshall, James, 152
Marstall, Bob, 232
Martin, Bill, Jr., 68, 257
Mayer, Marianna, 202
Mayer, Mercer, 147, 202
Mazer, Anne, 229
Melmed, Laura Krauss, 209
Menzel, Peter, 103
Minarik, Else, 13

Monk, Isabell, 98
Moore, Inga, 158, 170
Mosel, Arlene, 66, 154

N

Newbold, Greg, 238
Newfield, Marcia, 281
Numeroff, Laura Joffe, 151

O

Oxenbury, Helen, 114, 273

P

Patz, Nancy, 124
Polacco, Patricia, 120, 183
Pomerantz, Charlotte, 152
Porter, Janice Lee, 96
Pow, Tom, 282
Prelutsky, Jack, 72
Provensen, Alice, 233
Provensen, Martin, 233

R

Rand, Ted, 129, 257
Rawlins, Donna, 43
Ray, Mary Lyn, 225
Robinson, Aminah Brenda Lynn, 123
Rogasky, Barbara, 209
Romanova, Natalia, 227
Rosen, Michael J., 123
Ryder, Joanne, 220, 231
Rylant, Cynthia, 88, 177, 234

S

Saul, Carol P., 173
Sayles, Elizabeth, 18
Schertle, Alice, 272
Schlein, Miriam, 44
Schoenherr, John, 226
Schuett, Stacey, 96

CLAY CHAPMAN

About the Authors

ANN RUETHLING, founder of Chinaberry, and PATTI PITCHER
came to know each other when Patti was one of Chinaberry's first
customers over twenty years ago. Her frequent orders always included a chatty letter and the omnipresent book suggestion. It
wasn't long before they were the best of friends, even though
they'd never met. One thing led to another and soon Patti's voice
was added to the Chinaberry catalog. Today, the two of them
offer their readers over ninety-nine years (but who's counting?) of
combined parenting experience. Ann is the mother of Elizabeth
and Evan, and lives in La Jolla, California. In her spare time she
enjoys yoga, digging in the garden, and folding laundry. Patti lives
in Snoqualmie, Washington, with her husband, four children, and
too many pets to mention. She has way too much laundry to have
any spare time.